CONFERENCES FOR BOYS

BY

REV. REYNOLD KUEHNEL

ADAPTED BY DEBRA ANN BOOTON

Lanternarius Press

Nihil Obstat
Remigius Lafort, D.D.
Censor

Imprimatur
John Cardinal Farley
Archbishop of New York

New York, September 7, 1914

Cover by C. Alexander Moore

978-09839758-4-7

PREFACE

IF, as is generally claimed, the welfare of holy Mother Church depends largely upon well-instructed, loyal and pious men of the laity, sodalities for boys and young men should hold an important place among the organizations of every parish. One cannot gather figs from thistles; nor can one expect that the men of tomorrow will rally around the standard of Christ, if the boys of today are permitted to shift for themselves in religious matters.

Even though a small parish contain but twenty boys and young men, these twenty deserve as much attention and supervision as the hundreds of a larger parish. If these twenty boys are neglected it will soon mean twenty men sadly lacking in filial devotion and loyalty to holy Mother Church. Nor is this all. These twenty, whether they stay at home or scatter abroad, will exert an influence for the worse. They will help to tear down where we try to build up.

There is no parish so small but it should have well-conducted sodalities, not only for girls and married women, but for boys and men as well. Pious girls and women are of great help to the parish; but if there be a dearth of religious-minded and dutiful boys and men, the parish must soon lose ground. Where boys have no sodality to regulate the performance of their religious duties, they will receive the Sacraments when "they feel like it," which will, at best, mean once or twice a year. Such boys will not supply the well-instructed and pious men that are needed in our day. A well-conducted sodality will, in its promotion of frequent Holy Communion among men, be a powerful means of "restoring all things in Christ."

In the following Conferences, it is hoped, spiritual directors of boys' sodalities will find practical thought, and suggestion, which, applied with their own ripened experience and judgment, may help in making their talks to boys interesting, instructive and productive of a healthy spiritual condition in the young fellows.

The Author

Feast of St. Ignatius Loyola, 1914

CONTENTS

WHY READ THIS BOOK?

In the one hundred years since Fr. Kuehnel wrote his series of talks for sodality members, the world and the Church have changed dramatically. No one has spoken to the majority of young Catholic men about their psychological and spiritual development in almost 50 years.

Gone is the large family, graduation from 8th grade, factory work and families talking around the dinner table every evening. Gone, too, are church sodalities, lines for confession and, pretty soon, if something doesn't happen, Mass within a short distance drive on Sunday

This book is a one hundred year old explanation of the most Catholic behavior expected of a young man in the world, not in a monastery or other closed group. The writings are directed to those aged about 14-20, those starting to make decisions on their own and planning their own futures. Modes of gaining Heaven have not changed.

Some of the chapters have been adapted because of their references to sodalities which no longer exist. Comments on current society have also been amended to give today's young men a better perspective by giving them situations they are familiar with. For example, a boy with a few quarters in his pocket had much spending money one hundred years ago. The same boy today would be considered a pauper.

The phrasing which Fr. Kuehnel used is kept the same throughout the book as much as possible. This is his book, after all. He speaks to the boys in a familiar tone and he sees what their objections to sanctity could be.

The goal of the editor is to expose boys and young men to the holy value of virtue, a sadly missing element in today's culture. This book is full of explanations of thought patterns and behavior reflecting the various virtues.

It is hoped that the young men who read the book will heed the words and develop the goal of reaching for Heaven.

CHAPTER I: THE BADGE

My dear boys: Every society has a badge or emblem by which we can recognize its members. So, too, a church has its badge that distinguishes you from those who are not members of it. You wear this badge at every public function, like Masses, parades, funerals of fellow-members and the like. Before you leave the church or hall, this badge is not carefully laid aside. Now, since we are told to let our light shine, you can scarcely be content with wearing this badge only for an hour once a week. You certainly should wear some badge by which you can be distinguished from the rest.

You might feel ill at ease were I to ask you to wear always the medal of the Church. The badge to which I have reference is.....your conduct. Your conduct should be such that people may be able to say of you: "This boy belongs to the Church. His example is edifying."

No one can convince me that a boy outside of the Church can be as good as one who is in it. The main reason a boy will have for staying away from the Church--if he has the redeeming feature of being candid--will be Confession and Holy Communion. And what can be expected of a boy who has grown careless about the receiving of the holy Sacraments? Let his manners be ever so polished, like beauty they are only skin deep. Your conduct should be such that, at first sight, you can be distinguished from such others.

Unfortunately, even members of the Church are not always what they might or should be. If, with all the helps and graces of the frequent reception of the holy Sacraments, they fail to meet the expectations God and His holy angels have placed in them, how they would fail if these favors were denied to them! From this you can readily understand how the boy, who misses his monthly Confession and Holy Communion from time to time, cannot be as good and pure at heart as the boy who never breaks this all-important rule. Hence, too, you will see that Christian conduct does not adorn each one of you like a badge of honor.

God expects much of you. Your guardian angel looks to your welfare like an older brother; your parents place in you all their hopes, their consolation and their pride. The parish looks up to you as the future supporters. The world, knowing you are Catholic boys, expects you to be cleaner, purer, more pious and more honorable than others. The whole world, God and His angels are interested in your daily conduct. Is it a wonder this conduct of yours should be a badge whereby all can distinguish you from such who are a disgrace to God, Church and Country?

Since the best are not without faults it will not be out of place to consider in detail the requirements of conduct.

What is your conduct like at home?

Are you ever ready and willing to do little favors even though they are inconvenient? How many boys there are who expect any amount of favors from others at home; but, if it is a question of returning a favor, the very smallest is considered an imposition! You expect every favor from your parents. They feed you and clothe you and board you because they love you more than themselves. Many a night they watched at your bedside when you were sick. Gladly

2

would they die for you if by that sacrifice they could promote your welfare. Let them ask a favor of you and you grumble! Some boys even venture to ask a bribe of money to go to the grocery for a tired mother! If we could read the meaning of some of the wrinkles care and worry have carved upon the brows of parents we would discover the secret of many a broken heart.

How do you treat your brothers and sisters? Are you fault finding, spoiling every pleasure or play unless you can be the self-constituted head? A certain class of boys are constantly on the alert to play tricks upon others, always ready to tease, ever prepared for any joke or prank at the expense of others. The moment, however, a trick is played at their own expense they are insulted. Do you treat your brothers and sisters with the consideration they deserve on account of being of your own flesh and blood? Toward your older brothers and sisters you should at all times show deference and good will; toward your younger, patience, kindness and prudence. The older brother must never forget that, to some extent, he shares the responsibilities of his parents. He must, by his own example, teach his younger brothers and sisters the virtue of obedience. For the present, you will not be able to understand how much more pleasant and easy you render the burdens of your parents by exercising the virtue of obedience, nor can you realize how sad and distressing parental duties grow when, by your own example, you teach your younger brothers and sisters to rebel against the authority of parents.

How do you conduct yourself away from home?

Boys, as a rule, are fair judges of one another. When a boy cannot find a chum or friend in the wide world, the fault is, usually, his own. There is something about his conduct that is repelling instead of attracting. His disposition, his bearing and temper prevent the growth of true friendship. And so we find boys who are shunned by all, they keep to themselves--not of choice but of necessity.

Still another class of boys are models everywhere but at home. One would hardly think, knowing the conduct of some at home and elsewhere, that they can be the same ones. At home they will be rough and overbearing; away from home they will fall all over themselves in trying to show all their good points to the best advantage!

Can you say candidly and sincerely that by your conduct people can point to you with pride and say: "You boys are a credit to the Church to which you belong?" If not, you know what is expected of you! Conduct and good manners will, I admit, be at times misunderstood. To show good manners it will not be necessary to have a crease in your trousers sharp enough to cut a two-inch plank; it will not be necessary to use the longest words of the dictionary; it will not be necessary to keep up with the latest styles of handshakes and sneakers; it will not be necessary to study the thousand and one rules of etiquette of the "upper circles." That may be well and good for people who have nothing else to do.

It is by no means a sign of good manners to give your seat in a bus to a handsome young lady while a poor woman with a child on her arms or carrying a bundle of groceries is left standing; it is not good manners to creep and crawl before the rich and mighty of this earth to gain some favor; it is not good manners to act like a king toward those beneath us. True politeness does not consist in any of these actions.

The key to good manners and politeness is nothing else than Christian charity.

It would be uncharitable to talk of the faults of others. It would be uncharitable to laugh at the whims and

4

ideas of old people, it would be uncharitable to expose the faults and shortcomings of those at home. It would be uncharitable to be domineering, gruff and insolent. Hence, it would be impolite. Practice charity in thought, word and deed and no one with an ounce of common sense in his system will doubt your genuine politeness. Your conduct will open every heart to you. You will find good will where others may be like strangers in a strange land.

The badge, then, I want you to wear at all times is conduct based upon Christian charity. Wear the badge at all times and all places. Your opportunities for good will be countless.

An older brother may be struck with the force of your good example; a companion of your shop or school may be moved by your own good example; you may pave the way for some others to the true Church!

And, even though no one apparently takes note of your good example, it will never escape the all-seeing eye of God. Your guardian angel will treasure up for you each one of your efforts to add to your reward and happiness in the world to come.

CHAPTER II. MONTHLY CONFESSION

Very often the question is asked: "Why belong to a church? All there is to it is frequent Confession and Communion and tithes and sermons. That is all!" What is worse, careless members of the church ask the very same question. They say: "What is there to it; it is only a money scheme." Solomon, in his age, so they think, was no wiser man than they. Ever since they have thrown their schoolbooks aside, they think they are lords and masters of the entire world. You were told at the time you were instructed for receiving your first Holy Communion how the world would try to poison your minds with ideas of free thought, so-called liberty, independence of action and a number of similar phrases the meaning of which, though they may sound ever so sweet to the ear, are poison to the mind. In some cases the warnings were prophecies that, alas, have been fulfilled.

In this, as well as the following conferences, we shall consider some of the many reasons why the church is a necessity. I only hope they may be strong enough to encourage you to persevere and to suggest arguments to you against any possibility of backsliding.

It is true that the church has not been intended to give you a picnic every week; nor is it intended to make you finished actors, singers, debaters, ball-players, entertainers or athletes. The Church, may endeavor to promote social benefits. But, the Church can have but one purpose overshadowing all other objects. And that object is the saving of your soul. Considering temporal benefits only, you derive very few advantages from the Church. Its benefits are of a higher, of the spiritual order, far surpassing any worldly or temporal consideration.

The aim, then, of the Church, is to make good Catholic men of you, to teach you to be faithful to God, home and country.

There is no time in your life, boys, when you are tempted more and experienced less than the present time. It is true that you know your catechism, let us hope from cover to cover; you can "read, write and figure." But this is not all you should know. Since you have reached the period of your life in which you begin to earn your daily bread, you meet with difficulties and temptations that, during your time of childhood, were unknown to you. Now you need more strength and judgment than during the days of elementary school. Temptations becoming greater, you likewise stand in need of more grace.

And how, let me ask you, can you expect this additional grace of God when, for months and months, you live in a state of mortal sin!

Here, then, we come to the necessity of monthly Confession. And how many or, rather, how few would think of going to Confession even once a month unless the Church gave them its moral force and help by means of the indulgence with which it is endowed, live the good example one gives to another.

That you may realize what importance the Church attaches to the rule of monthly Confession, I will give you a few reasons each one of which ought to influence you to never break this important rule.

7

The first reason for monthly Confession is to train your mind to a constant submission to the holy Will of God. It is certainly a pity to see how eagerly some boys will strive for complete independence long before they begin to wear long trousers. No sooner have they left school than they do "as they please." It is of no use to exhort them to go to Confession! They do "as they please." They can never go as often or at the time the pastor wishes them to go. They simply "don't have to." And, then, they would lack devotion; nor, so they claim, should they be driven like machines or cattle,-for they are so brilliant and have a mind of their own. They will go to Confession whenever it pleases them and not sooner. Bright and cunning as they are, their zeal for their soul will only bring them to Confession once or twice a year. Poor boys! They may think themselves above you. They are not! In the meantime, the devil has poured the first drop of poison into their hearts and the poison has begun to work upon them. Like Lucifer, they say: "I will not obey God. I will do exactly as I please!"

Now....when are we obliged to go to Confession? We are obliged to go to Confession as soon as we have committed a mortal sin. Pay special attention to the words "As soon as we have committed a mortal sin." That does not mean a month or a year after the sin has been committed, but as soon as it is possible for us to go to church. Be sure to make a perfect act of contrition after you have had the misfortune of committing a mortal sin and do not delay Confession after that. Do not even wait until your next monthly Confession.

Some time ago a young man came to the rectory. It was nearly nine o'clock in the evening. "Father," he said, "I want to go to Confession to you. I had the misfortune of committing a mortal sin, and I dare not think of going to rest with that sin upon my conscience." Which one, do you think, will be the better Catholic in later years: this young man who would not remain in mortal sin for even a day-or the young man who goes to Confession when he feels like it; which means, perhaps, once a year? Which one, do you think will be happier in life and in death?

A second reason in favor of monthly Confession is found in the fact that God made us according to His image and likeness. If our only aim and purpose of life would be to eat and drink and work and sleep, God might have made us cattle or hogs. God, however, wished to raise us to a higher level. He made us to resemble Him. He raised us to a higher dignity than the very angels. We are the adopted children of God, a higher title than which we could ever presume to maintain for ourselves.

As children resemble their parents, and we, being the children of God, bear within us a resemblance of our heavenly Father, let us ask ourselves wherein this likeness consists by means of which God can recognize us as His own! St. John, the beloved disciple, gives us this answer: "For this is your vocation, your sanctification." With the grace of God we are to make ourselves holy. In the proportion of our growth in holiness we resemble our heavenly Father more and more! The very first step towards this aim of holiness is to overcome the prejudice against frequent Confession.

Have you ever observed how easily you have examined your conscience when, for instance, you observed the six Sundays in honor of St Aloysius? You discovered sins the very existence of which would have completely escaped you had you delayed confession for some months. And now, let me ask you, how can we try to resemble God more closely if we fail to know ourselves? How can we try to be free from sin and become more just and holy from day to day if we are not even aware of our many faults that prevent holiness? Unless we know all our weaknesses, our

9

predominant sins, our most frequent temptations and shortcomings, we can never think of overcoming our faults. If you were to work in a garden, you would be very foolish if you were to pull out the weeds only once or twice a year. A poor sight of a garden you would have, indeed. The garden must be gone over every few days. After every rain, the weeds will crop out again.

To drive this example home to you, place "heart" for "garden" and "sins" for "weeds." Then you will understand the necessity of frequent Confession. Then you will understand its relation to holiness. But, some of you may say, Father, you don't want all of us to be saints! Indeed, I mean nothing else. Holiness is not for a chosen few but for all. To be holy it is not necessary to perform miracles nor to enter a convent, nor to die for your holy Faith.   I do not know how better to explain holiness to you than by calling it spiritual cleanliness.

When you rise in the morning, do you run over to the mirror to see whether you should wash your face? You reach for soap and water and wash yourself. If, by some accident, you should get a black mark upon your face will you walk around the rest of the day and simply say: "Oh, never mind, I am going to wash myself tomorrow?" You certainly will not if you have any regard for yourself. You understand only too well that people judge you by just such signs. If you go about dirty-looking, people will size you up to be equally careless and slouchy in every other regard.

If it is so necessary to keep our body clean, even though in a few years it will become the food of worms, how much more attention ought we give to the soul! If we wish to appear clean before people that they may not form a bad opinion of us, how much more cleanly ought we to keep our soul lest God, who sees our hearts, form a bad opinion of us! Just as impossible as it is to have day and night at the same time, so it is impossible to possess spiritual cleanliness or holiness together with mortal sin. Is it any wonder the priest mentions the necessity of frequent Confession as often as he does?

A third reason speaking in favor of frequent or at least monthly Confession is found in the forming of a good habit. We will, in later years, be what we make of ourselves in our youth. "A young man, according to his way, even when he is old, will not depart from it." Such, indeed, is the strength of the habits we form in youth that even though we depart from them for a time, we will never feel like ourselves until we return to them.

One of these ironbound habits you should form is punctuality. A man who is not punctual, who cannot do a certain work in a given time, will have only himself to blame for the failure of his life. If we are shifty and careless about time, if we do a day's work in three days' time, we will never be able to claim that our work is a howling success!

Now, boys, reason for a moment! If punctuality is so necessary for our temporal welfare can we expect to promote our eternal welfare in a shifty sort of way?

The boy who is punctual in going to Confession, will be successful in the most important work of his life, the saving of his immortal soul. Owing to his frequent Confessions, God will give more graces; his understanding being enlightened, he will see to his faults and temptations; his power of will being strengthened, he will more readily overcome evil and so work onward and upward to a greater holiness.

There are boys for whom the Church has neither charm nor inducements. And, if you judge a tree by its fruit--a boy by his works--the reason is not hard to find. They may prefer to remain in mortal sin for months and

11

years; they may prefer bad company to good; the way of the world rather than the holy Will of God. They are often slaves of Satan rather than children of God.

The boy of the Church, however, who makes it a practice to go to Confession once a month at least, will, in later years, be a pious Catholic, an honor to the Church and a joy to God and His angels because in the days of his youth he has not forgotten his God.

CHAPTER III. MONTHLY COMMUNION

My dear boys: It has often seemed strange to me to think of the earnestness of boys during the instructions preceding their first Holy Communion, to think of how they were impressed with the solemn and consoling truths concerning the most holy Eucharist, and to compare this zeal and good-will with their conduct of a few months later on.

Indeed, does it not seem strange to you that, in spite of all the instructions you have received a few years ago, you are to receive another instruction upon the very same sacred subject!

To refresh your memory, I will, with the aid of examples and comparisons, try to recall to your mind the pious sentiments and the earnest resolutions you had formed when, for the first time in your life, you received the Bread of angels.

At times you may have remarked how much more you eat than grown people. A healthy boy will eat more than many a grown-up man. Many a man does not eat as much-- and he is older, taller, stronger and more able to work than you. Still your intense hunger is no mystery. Everybody knows you are growing. Indeed, your growth would receive a setback, you might even get sick if your food were not as good and plentiful.

Now, what food is for the body, Holy Communion is for the soul.

As the well-being, strength and growth of the body depends upon the quality and quantity of food you take, so the soul depends for her growth and strength of grace upon her food, Holy Communion. Everyone of us desires to gain and maintain strength and health of body. Should we think less of our soul? Should we permit our soul to hunger and thirst for Holy Communion while we spare no efforts to keep our bodies well fed? In their development, body and soul should keep step. There is but one difference. In course of time our bodies will cease to grow; a few years more and our strength will leave us; our senses of sight or hearing will grow poorer, sickness will weaken the frame--until death lays his bony finger upon our hearts. The soul, however, being immortal, knows no old age. Therefore, the soul goes on growing in grace and virtue before God and man. Therefore, too, the soul must ever be nourished with at least the same care and diligence you exercise in promoting the growth and strength of your youthful bodies.

From what has been said you will readily understand how natural it is for a pious boy to grow in grace, whilst another boy who goes to receive Holy Communion "when he feels like it"-which means once or twice a year - may live in sin for months and months without the least remorse. The one boy obeys his conscience, the other does not.

To emphasize the necessity of monthly Communion we will now look into some of the effects resulting from it.

Taking for granted that the boy prepares himself properly for Holy Communion and that he does not neglect to make a fitting thanksgiving, the first effect will be an increase of sanctifying grace. This means that, every time the just boy approaches the holy table, he becomes more precious, more lovable and holy in the sight of the heavenly Father. God will much sooner hear the prayers of such a saintly boy than those of another boy who cares little whether he pleases or offends God. To the saintly boy God will grant more blessings, more favors, more graces, because He loves him more. Even, if in an unguarded moment, this zealous boy should have the misfortune of committing a mortal sin, it is not he who will remain in it for months and months. He will return to the heavenly Father long before the prodigal son can make up his mind to ask pardon. He will go to Confession as soon as possible. And only the angels now know how God will reward that one Confession and Holy Communion. Only God knows the zeal, humility and sorrow of that boy. And be sure, He will not forget to reward it.

There is one certain story the priest hears in the confessional more than any other. It is this: "Father, I got into a bad habit and I don't know how to quit it. I try and try, but I cannot let go." If this same boy would say: "I don't want to quit this bad habit," he would not be telling a lie. There is one remedy for every bad habit. It is the only remedy we have, frequent Holy Communion. In virtue of it, the very inclination to evil will be lessened. A boy who receives Holy Communion frequently will not snap at every sinful thought the devil baits for him. The saintly boy will weigh his thoughts, words and deeds, think them over seriously and, usually, see them in their true light. Frequent Holy Communion will make him "walk with God." The saintly boy will recall the presence of God for each good work he should perform and each sinful act he should avoid.

No sooner does the snow melt away than you see the first green blade of grass. A few days more, and you see the first little flowers of spring stretching their little heads over the dead leaves of a bygone year. As soon as frequent Holy Communion begins to melt the snow of evil inclination the first little flowers of virtue begin to blossom. At first, these virtues, like the flowers of early spring, are small and delicate. But, as the sun of grace shines more and more abundantly into our hearts, there grow up loftier virtues just as the summer sun produces the grandest flowers.

Besides promoting in us a growth of virtues, Holy Communion produces still another effect upon our bodies, unworthy though we are. Our divine Savior has promised that He will awaken from their last sleep those who receive Him in Holy Communion. They will arise gloriously from death even as He arose gloriously from the grave that first memorable Easter morning. Through Holy Communion our divine Savior plants in our body the germ of immortality. It is true, we will die. Our body will have to pay the penalty of sin by returning to earth from which it was made. Nevertheless, this body of ours will arise better, stronger and more beautiful than it ever was, never to die again, if we have passed from this life in the love and grace of God.

All these wonderful benefits ought really to make us go and receive Holy Communion every day. And yet some must be admonished and coaxed and encouraged and even scolded to approach the altar railing more than once a year!

Something must be wrong with our minds when we can deliberately think of all these reasons for frequent Holy Communion without acting upon them.

Unfortunately, there are boys thinking that all these instructions coming from the pulpit are, to say the least, overdrawn. Just because God does not punish every sinner at the moment of sin some people think sin is not so bad after all. God would be perfectly within His rights were He to send fire and brimstone upon every wicked city as He did upon Sodom and Gomorrah. He would be perfectly within

16

His rights were He to punish the sinful world as He did at the time of the deluge. He would be perfectly within His rights were He to punish us after our first mortal sin, even as He punished the fallen angels. But how unfortunate would we, poor sinners, be unless He tempered justice with mercy? What time of chance would we have for repentance or conversion unless God showed patience and mercy? Is it not mean and small of us not to make use of this very mercy and patience of God to add sins upon sins? To live in mortal sins for months and months means nothing else than daring God to do His worst.

There are other boys, not quite as reckless as those we have spoken of, who, for a time, continue in the practices of the Church with no other purpose in view than of placing their parents and priest under some kind of obligation for being so tremendously good. In course of time, getting older and bolder, and apparently more independent, they drift with the rest and it becomes a most distressing problem to induce them to receive the Sacraments at all.

If you reason a little, you will discover that such conduct is utterly wrong. Your parents as well as your priest only comply with their duty in telling you what is right and wrong. Here their duty stops and your duty begins. Of course, it will be a source of joy and consolation to your good parents and myself, your priest, when we see that our words of advice have taken root, and brought forth fruit a hundred-fold. But, remember, neither your parents nor your priest will suffer for your folly so long as they have discharged their duty of instructing you. You know the holy will of God. It is a question of life and death for you; heaven or hell depends upon the choice you make. The advantage and favor, then, is all on your side.

Will these reasons be strong enough to confirm you in the resolution of receiving Holy Communion every month? There is another reason! Have you ever thought of death? As we live, so we die! I have seen many die, but I never saw one die unhappily who had received Holy Communion frequently.

Of the number of boys that you know today, it is safe to say that fully a third, if not more, will die suddenly. Do you know what that means? There will be many of us who will pass from this world without a sign of warning; not a touch of sickness will give us a hint that the end is near. Many of us will die without, perhaps, enough time to make an act of contrition. Ask yourself: "Would I want to die this very moment?" If for some reason or other you have to say "No," take this as a warning. You might not want to die when die you must. You may want to go to Confession. Do that now! Who knows! It may be too late even tomorrow! Would you like to die suddenly after having stayed away from the Sacraments for ten or twelve months? Certainly not! But, for all you or I know, you may be one of the many who will die without a moment of warning. Therefore, be prepared.

Imagine an accident in your shop or factory. Several men are killed on the spot. Two men you know lie side by side, dead. You knew them both. One of them had not gone to Confession for a year. You saw him in church very seldom. The other dead man had received Holy Communion only the Sunday before and, apart from the failings and frailties to which each one of us is subject, you could hardly point to a single serious fault in his life. In whose place would you wish to be, if it had been your turn to die?

It will not take you long to decide. You would desire to be in the place of him who had received Holy Communion only a few days before.

18

Because God has hidden from us the time and place of death it is necessary for us to be prepared at all times to meet Him. With this constant danger of death before our eyes, is it asking too much to ask you to receive Holy Communion at least once a month? Think this over!

CHAPTER IV. CONDUCT BEFORE AND AFTER HOLY COMMUNION

A hundred of you, a thousand of you, may receive Holy Communion at the same time and no two of you receive the same amount of graces. It is true, every one of you receives the same Lord and Savior, Jesus Christ, but the graces vary according to the disposition with which we receive Him. The one may receive hardly any grace; the other may be a saint.

Why?

The graces stand in exact proportion to our disposition of heart. They depend upon the manner in which we prepare ourselves and the way in which we act after Holy Communion. In order, then, that you may receive the choicest graces from our Lord, we will devote this chapter to a better understanding of our obligations towards our Savior in Holy Communion.

As a rule, you will make your preparation for Holy Communion as indicated in your prayer books. You will recite a certain set of prayers as given there. But even these will often be prayers merely of the lips, of which the heart knows and feels nothing. And that sort of a preparation will not count for many graces. God may send down the nicest rain, but unless the fields and gardens are kept in a good condition beforehand, the rain will do very little else than give the weeds a fair show of growing all the more plentifully, The most sublime, the most holy act of our life is the receiving of our Lord in Holy Communion. His coming

20

into our hearts is at once the loftiest and most humble sign of His infinite love. From this it will be evident that a worthy preparation and thanksgiving is necessary to show the appreciation of our dignity and the condescension of our blessed Redeemer.

I will not remind you of the necessity of making a good confession if you are in state of mortal sin: That is understood. Nor need I say that you should be dressed becomingly. This does not mean that if you are poor you are to stay at home. If a patched coat is all you have, wear it; but let it be clean. Wear a collar and tie, if you can afford it. Whatever you do wear, be it ever so poor, by all means let it be clean! Let the neatness and cleanliness of your outward appearance be a sign of the purity of your heart. By the way, I might remark that you should be more careful about your appearance in church than if you are in going to a party, or picnic, or theater. The most of us may be poor, but, so long as soap and water are cheap, we should at least look and conduct ourselves becomingly in the presence of God and his holy angels.

Some boys complain about the many thoughts of distraction during preparation for Holy Communion. Those thoughts can be avoided very easily if you try to keep silent in coming to church. How can you help being distracted in your prayers when in coming to church you talk of everything under the sun, from gossips to jokes! When you wish to receive Holy Communion, keep silent from the time you say your morning prayers till after you have completed your thanksgiving. For the first few times it may seem strange to you to come to church without saying a word on the way. After a short while, however, you will wonder how you could ever get along without this silence before Holy Communion. To make your silence appear more easy, go alone! In the meantime busy your thoughts with thinking about our Savior waiting for you in the Tabernacle. Picture to yourself how our dear Lord intercedes for you in the Tabernacle. Think of how impatiently Jesus is waiting for the time to again enter your heart, the gifts He will bring along, the favors you will ask of Him, and your very silence will be a pleasing prayer.

Silence may seem too hard to try. Do try! Our dear Savior is worth this sacrifice and, what is more, He will appreciate how hard it is and reward it.

After your very first attempt of silence, you will notice a remarkable change in your prayers. Your acts of faith, hope, charity, desire, humility, and sorrow will have meanings for you that you never found before. You pray earnestly and fervently, because you have prepared yourself by silence. You have gathered your thoughts before coming to church, and as your whole mind is turned towards God, prayer becomes easy. In such frame of mind it is a pleasure to speak with God. And so the most holy and important moment of your life draws nearer and nearer. The time arrives when you go up to the altar railing with folded hands and downcast eyes. It is the very moment which is desired still more fervently by your divine Visitor. Be sure that the more pleasant and agreeable you render His reception, the more plentiful will be the tokens of His love.

The moments following Holy Communion are the most solemn and sacred of our lives. Jesus rests in our hearts as our guest. If it were possible for the angels to entertain an unkind or envious thought, they would have all reason for looking at us with a feeling of envy. We share a happiness the like of which has been denied to them. For this reason we should make the best possible use of these precious moments. And that means nothing else than a fitting thanksgiving.

Is it enough to simply recite the few prayers indicated in your prayer books? By no means! It is time to say those or similar prayers after holy Mass. You see the priest coming back to the sanctuary after he has taken off the sacred vestments of Mass. He returns to make his thanksgiving. Hence, do not fail to make a proper thanksgiving after your Holy Communion. Do not fail to thank Jesus from the bottom of your heart for the great honor He has conferred upon you.

When you have received our dear Lord, return to your seat with folded hands and downcast eyes. Do not look around, but as soon as you have returned to your seat, kneel down, keep your eyes closed and speak to your Lord and God as you would if you could see Him face to face.

If a friend of whom you thought a great deal should come to visit you, would you let him stand and not say as much as one word of greeting? Would you talk to someone else in the meantime, or leave the house for some reason or other and let your friend do as he pleased, stay or leave? No, indeed not! You would go up to him, tell him how glad you are because of his coming to see you. You would tell him to make himself perfectly at home. You would ask him ever so many questions about himself, his work, his plans, and all his likes and dislikes. You would tell him all about your own plans for the future, and, if you knew that he was ever ready to help, you would ask him his advice and help in the work you have in mind. You would try to entertain him as best you could by sparing no efforts to make his stay with you one of the memories he will cherish for years to come. In a similar manner we should try to entertain our divine Visitor.

The very first moment we may be at a loss to know what to say. We may, for the time being, be dazed, hardly realizing that it is God who has come to our sinful hearts. Our Lord will be pleased even with this, our humble embarrassment. Then, with a sudden burst of joy, we will

23

find words to greet Him, to bid Him welcome, to thank Him for His condescension in coming to our cold, sinful hearts, and to ask Him for all the graces and favors we need for body and soul.

In speaking with our Savior, it is not necessary to look for the choicest expressions and the longest words. Little does he care for well-turned phrases and beautiful sentences. If our plain and humble words have the ring of sincerity, our Lord is satisfied. For He has come to us not for His sake, but for our own. He has come to be asked; come to listen; come to grant. Our dear Lord is actually loaded down with gifts and graces. We have the choice. He is more anxious to give than we can possibly be to receive them.

Where is the boy who has no favors to ask of his divine Guest? What about your temptations, your principal weakness? Your trials or difficulties? Have you no favors to ask? You stand at the threshold of life, beginning to follow a vocation, or at the point of making a choice. Have you no favor to ask? You may have some little sorrow, some trouble. God may want you to make some sacrifice. And do you not need the help of God? After Holy Communion you experience a feeling of rest and safety you feel at no other time. Jesus is with you. You have nothing to fear when He is at your side. Would you like to feel as safe and happy at death? Certainly! Well, ask our Lord to grant you a happy death. How can our blessed Redeemer refuse you this wish since He wishes you nothing more sincerely than this very favor? In His infinite wisdom He may deem it necessary to refuse some temporal favor, knowing that it would harm you more than benefit you. But how could He have the heart to deny you this favor of a happy death if you make it one of the many favors you have to ask of Him? Never receive a Holy Communion without reminding your divine Guest of the grace of a happy death.

You can never repay your parents for all they have done for you. Ought you not ask Jesus to bless them for you? He will like it if you remind Him of the tender love He had for His blessed Mother and His foster-father, St. Joseph, and tell Him how you would like to imitate Him in His love and obedience.

You have brothers and sisters, relatives, benefactors, friends and perhaps, enemies. You have your teachers, your priest. Jesus would like you to say a short prayer for all of them. Ask Him to bless and protect them.

Finally, there are the poor souls asking you to remember them. For some of them you are bound to pray: as, for instance, the souls of your departed relatives, friends, and such others that might be there on your account. In your charity you should likewise remember the rest. There is one dead benefactor whom you should never forget. Pray for the priest who baptized you. People are forgotten soon after death. But the grass does not begin to grow above the grave of a priest before he is forgotten. For your sake he has taken upon himself the gravest responsibilities. All his life he prays for you. Should you not say a little prayer for him after he has passed away? By all means remember your late pastor in your prayers.

Speaking to our Savior in your own humble words, the time passes all too soon. You will rise for the last Gospel and scarcely be half through talking with your heavenly Visitor. After you have completed your appeals to the love and mercy of Jesus, you may open your prayer books to recite the prayers set apart for thanksgiving. If you still find words to speak to our Savior in your own way, leave the prayer book aside. Your own words, plain and humble though they be, will be more pleasing to God.

From this remark you will understand that prayer books are not absolutely necessary to pray with devotion.

Since praying means speaking to God, we are by no means bound to use a set or certain form of prayers contained on a printed page. If we can speak to God in our own words--and with a little practice we can do it--the prayer will be said with much more devotion, or rather, distractions will not be as frequent. Prayer books are like life-preservers. A good swimmer will be able to swim far better without the cumbersome weight around his shoulders. When we cannot keep above water without such help a life-preserver is necessary. The most effective prayer, then, especially after Holy Communion, is a personal prayer--one formed in our own words. Such a personal prayer was at all times the most favorite prayer of the saints. It is nothing else than meditation, or mental prayer.

The only time we must confine ourselves to the prayer book is when we wish to gain some indulgence by reciting some definite prayer. Then we must recite the prayer word for word, carrying out the conditions contained in it. And, by the way, never end your thanksgiving without gaining one or more of such indulgences for yourself and the poor souls of Purgatory.

By following out these few hints regarding your preparation and thanksgiving, your Holy Communions will bear fruit for time and eternity. In the course of time, it will be easier to keep the rule of silence before Holy Communion, and the prayer following will be said more earnestly and more devoutly. Gradually, too, it will become easier for us to speak with Jesus in our own humble way, and as by your prayers and disposition you show that you appreciate the visits of Christ more and more, the graces resulting from Holy Communion will become greater and more far-reaching each time. In some way, all your Holy Communions are a preparation for your last Holy Communion. What emotions and thoughts will cross your mind when Jesus enters your suffering heart to console and strengthen you for your last battle and your journey to eternity. God grant that your last thanksgiving may not be confined to a few moments, but that it may last forever in heaven.

CHAPTER V.   FREQUENT HOLY COMMUNION

My dear boys: A number of you will, no doubt, be surprised when I tell you that monthly Holy Communion is not the very tip and height of perfection. Some boys may think that, since they receive Holy Communion every month, they are as perfect as perfect can be. Nothing may be more misleading.

A boy going to Mass and Holy Communion with a few others of his age may make the boy who has left such actions behind aware that he wishes to rejoin his friends. And so, without being aware of it, you exert an influence for the welfare of others. You may, perhaps, attach very little importance to the value of your monthly Holy Communion as a source of edification for others; still it is very, very important. God will in His own good time and way grant you a reward for this good example, far surpassing your expectations.

Important as monthly Communion is from the standpoint of your society, it does, by no means, imply that you should never receive Holy Communion outside of that Sunday. It, may, at times, be necessary or advisable to go to Confession and Holy Communion outside of your monthly Confession and Communion.

You would never think of working hard for a week, or two, or three without wanting your pay. It is no more than right that you should have your wages after you have done the work. And yet we find any number of boys working for nothing. They may say some prayers, may keep the

Fridays and go to church on Sundays, may do works of charity, and yet do them for nothing, because they live in mortal sin. They may have had the misfortune of committing one the week after their monthly Confession. Hardly realizing their serious condition, they will say: "Oh, never mind; in three weeks I will again go to Confession. That long I can certainly wait!" In the meantime they work all in vain. Whatever good they may do will not be of any merit for heaven.

We live for nothing, work for nothing, pray for nothing, suffer for nothing when we live in mortal sin. The sooner we return to the Father, the better it will be for us. If your father's house were burning, would you say: "Let us wait a while till the fire is half over?" No. You would try to put out the flames as quickly as possible and save all you could. To give the flames more headway might mean the loss of the entire house. If you were sick and the doctor told you to take your medicine every two hours, would you take it every two weeks, or two months? You would not. You know your health is at stake. That medicine is to check your sickness. Unless it is taken as often as the doctor orders you to take it, your sickness would get the better of you easily, and, after it has gained headway, the strongest medicine might be unable to check it. It would then be only a question of days for the end to come. Your soul is exposed to as many and more dangers than your body. The soul has its ailments, its suffering and sickness as well as the body. Hence we must take the same precaution for the ailments of the soul that we have for those of the body. Nay, more; for, as the soul is of more importance than our body, it stands to reason that we must exercise more care in behalf of our soul than in behalf of any bodily infirmity.

Prevention, they say, is half the cure. It is far easier to prevent sickness than to cure it after the symptoms have become alarming. The same rule holds good regarding the

29

infirmities of the soul. And this very principle of prevention is the fundamental reason for frequent Holy Communion. What care will be taken to prevent sickness? We will avoid places where any so-called catching sickness prevails. We make use of vaccination and disinfectants to remove all danger of contracting a like sickness. We are told to beware of ice water when we are overheated.

We can, in like manner, prevent many infirmities and ailments of the soul that, in course of time, might be difficult to check. And the means of preventing these sicknesses of the soul is frequent Holy Communion.

All of us are tempted in the most vulnerable spot. The devil, like a prudent general, will never attack us where we are best prepared or fortified to the best advantage. But where an attack is most likely to prove disastrous to us, there the battle will be raging without mercy or quarter. As there are no two leaves alike on a tree, so each one of us has his own disposition, strong points and weak points, each one has a peculiar inclination and failing. The devil has made a study of each one of us. Hence all his attacks will be directed against the point that is least able to resist. To strengthen those weak spots against the attacks of the devil we have one remedy: frequent Holy Communion. Your most violent temptations may be against holy purity, the virtue of faith; it may be of pride, of revenge. The very fact that you have yielded to a certain temptation for a number of times is proof that the devil not only knows your weak spot, but that he makes very good use of his knowledge by causing you to fall time and again. Unless we are willing to let the devil win one point after another, we must try to stop him; must make the very points he attacks so strong that he will never defeat us again. Of our own power we are unable to resist him. We must have recourse to Jesus in frequent Holy Communion. There can be no doubt about the outcome of the conflict when we have Jesus fighting with us. And so Holy Communion is like a medicine that must be taken frequently and regularly.

But why should we wait at all until the devil has shown us, to our regret, at which point we are weakest? Would it not be more prudent to make use of prevention than of cure? Prevention is much more easy and certain. Hence it follows that we should receive Holy Communion frequently to prevent us from showing the devil our weak side. Frequent Holy Communion will lessen the inclination towards evil and make us stronger at the very point the devil selects for his attack.

From this, then, you will understand how necessary frequent Holy Communion is to wage the warfare against the devil successfully. He dreads nothing more than frequent Holy Communion because he realizes that with it his power for evil is broken. For that very reason he wages a relentless warfare against it. The most treacherous objection the devil has against frequent Holy Communion is to make us content with what little good we may do. He calls our attention to others who, he says, are not half as good as we are; that we are good enough to satisfy ourselves, and that "we should let well enough alone." Such are the suggestions of the devil.

On the other hand, Christ says this: "Be you perfect because your Father in heaven is perfect." And, again, He says two words full of meaning: "Follow Me!" Jesus, the most holy, the most innocent, the spotless Lamb of God, asks us to follow Him! He holds up to us His sinless life and asks us to imitate it. Does that mean that we are good enough at the present time? That we have no more faults to overcome? That we need practice no more virtues? Even though we be just, the Holy Ghost admonishes us to become still more just. If we have reached holiness, there are degrees in that as there are degrees in heat and cold. We may and we should be still more holy.

Who, then, do you think should be believed? Should we believe God, who, in His boundless wisdom, wants us to become more perfect from day to day, or the devil, who would make us think we are as good and even better than we might be?

There is, indeed, a reason for frequent Holy Communion. Without it there can be no true holiness. Our dear Savior, wishing us to be just and holy, wishes us to receive Holy Communion frequently. His Church, in carrying out this sublime mission, employs, I might say, numberless means to gain this purpose. There is hardly a month passing by but one of its thirty days is some feast day. Each age, sex and station of life has at its disposal a number of devotions best suited to their various demands. There are the six Sundays in honor of St. Aloysius, the devotions to St. Stanislaus Kostka, the nine Fridays, and many similar feast days. You may make novenas for some certain grace, then there are retreats, missions, Forty Hours, and many other devotions. All these devotions and pious exercises have some object. Each and every one of them points to the very center and core of our holy faith, Jesus in the Tabernacle.

Remove the altars, and we are without priesthood and sacrifice.

Without them we would be as helpless as are Jews and Protestants, whose churches, so-called, have two features: a grand organ and the facility of turning the church into a concert hall or a moving-picture show. It is by virtue of Christ Jesus upon our altars that the Church is what it is--the Ark of the New Covenant, leading God's chosen people to victory over death and sin. Hence the many feasts, devotions and holy practices of the Church are as many invitations to receive Holy Communion more frequently.

Our divine Savior has prepared a banquet for our souls. The honor of attending it is so great, our unworthiness so abject, that, unless the invitations were tendered in the spirit of the undying love of God, we should hardly dare to approach this feast of the soul. The love of Jesus, however, makes us bold; we accept His invitation whilst He in His unbounded love makes up for our many shortcomings by healing and strengthening our souls.

It may practically be out of the question for most of you to receive Holy Communion every day. But I do not know of any of you who could not be at the altar railing every Sunday morning, provided you were willing to make a little sacrifice.

I had the happiness of knowing a doctor who made it his rule to receive Holy Communion as often as he had to perform an operation. Since he was very, very successful, he had to perform from three to five each week. This saintly doctor is now dead. For some months before his death he knew there was no hope of his ever being well again. From that time on he was preparing himself for death by receiving Holy Communion every morning. His death was as saintly and edifying as was his life.

We have thermometers to know the degrees of heat and cold. If we wish to know whether our faith is dead in us or living, whether it ails from worldliness or enjoys the health of grace and love of God, we have only to ask the number of times we receive Holy Communion. Its frequency will be a sign of fervor and zeal.

CHAPTER VI. PIETY

If I were asked which virtue, apart from the virtue of purity, I consider the grandest virtue of a boy, I should answer without hesitating, the virtue of piety.

The boy saying his daily prayers is a little hero. This does not mean that the virtue of piety is so very difficult to practice or still more hard to acquire, but that somehow or other it has become a rarity with most boys. When you were still going to school, prayer and work were inseparable. You prayed before you began your recitations, you prayed when the work of the day was done. You prayed the Angelus, and recited some short prayer before and after each recreation. That was training you to be always ready and willing to raise up your hearts and minds to God. After you left school you took up other work in a shop or factory. There is no prayer said there. Instead of prayers you may have heard cursing. In course of time, being exposed to so many temptations, you may even have forgotten the prayers at the beginning and end of the day.

It was easy for every one of you during your time of school to think of God and to pray. You took pleasure in it. Now it is the hardest task for many of you to give to God five minutes of each day! In the morning they must stay in bed till the last minute, then rush for their breakfast, and then to work. At night they come home from work, read or visit, or go to some entertainment or party. They come home late, but tired, and fall asleep without as much as even saying "good night" to God.

34

All of which goes to show that the boy who says his daily prayers is worthy of praise.

If our school had only accomplished the one result of making you resemble tubes filled with so much percent of arithmetic, so much percent of history, grammar, geography and the like, our aim would have been a vain one. The only object of the school is to teach you to train yourselves to round out and perfect your lives according to the holy will of God. The frequent prayers in our schools are intended to train you to say your prayers in future.

You would never think of playing a game of ball, the outcome of which would mean a great deal for you, without practicing for days and days before the game was to take place! You would say you could not be in a game like that without training.

If training is so necessary for a game of ball, how much more will it be necessary for the important works of life? For these, too, you must train, Now, prayer is necessary. You began training in prayer when you went to school. Keep up this training and say your prayers every day.

I think the world of a boy saying his daily prayers. He may have his faults like the rest; where others will get deeper into them, he will try to get away from them. Not only will his daily prayers keep him from a great many pitfalls, they will, moreover, help him to cultivate many virtues. Piety is never isolated from other virtues. Wherever you will find solid piety you will find other virtues as well.

Some boys have a vague idea of the importance and necessity of prayer, thinking that it is necessary for some and optional for others. And, not to be either too lax or too severe, they consider piety much like their Sunday clothes. You wear your Sunday clothes when you wish to be at your

35

best. Then you brush them and lay them aside for the following Sunday. That is exactly what some boys do with their prayers. During the week they act like pagans. Sundays they say a few prayers, thinking that will do for the rest of the week!

And yet, there is nothing more necessary than daily prayers. Prayer is as necessary for our soul as breathing is for our body. Could we keep alive if we stopped breathing? We could not. We must fill our lungs with fresh air day and night. In like manner we must fill our soul with graces. Breathing, as long as we are sound and healthy, comes natural to us. We breathe without being conscious of it. We never for a moment stop breathing in our sleep. In like manner prayer should be natural for us. It should cause us no effort to pray. When breathing becomes painful to us, we know there is something wrong with us, and we call for a doctor at once. When prayer becomes painful to us, it is a sign that our soul is sick, and it, too, should have the advice of the doctor of souls, the priest. We can scarcely turn a page of the Holy Bible but we find some remark about the necessity of prayer. Our dear Lord, as a rule, never repeated an instruction. But three words He repeated ever so often: "Watch and pray!" We need graces every minute of our lives. For that reason we should pray and pray.

Our whole life, then, should be a constant prayer. While there are certain times each day, at morning and at night, when we should raise up our hearts and minds to God in a special way, it should be equally as easy for us to think of God at all times of the day. At the least sign of danger a small child will run into the arms of its father or mother. So we, too, should seek shelter in the arms of our heavenly Father at the least sign of danger of sin.

Our morning and night prayers should help us to think of God frequently during the day. Hence there can be no reasonable excuse for falling short in this most sacred duty. A great many boys will say some kind of a night prayer. At night, they are all alone with God, and they have some blemish upon their soul that makes them fear for the night. With the dawn of day that fear passes. The rest of the household is up, and they forget that the same God is still alive. Now, there is no excuse for neglecting your morning prayers.

If, for some reason, you may not have the time to kneel down for five minutes, say your prayers on your way to work, it will be far better to pray on the way to work or school than to spend that much time in sinful talk. I knew a student who said the Rosary daily going to college. Swinging his books in his right hand, he had the left in his pocket holding the beads. No one ever suspected that this boy that otherwise could be in all kinds of innocent mischief, would be so fond of saying the Rosary.

The boy who says his daily prayers, and says them well, will, in the course of his life, be tempted as much and, perhaps, more than another. But because of his prayers he will receive more graces and, like Joseph of Egypt, he will in time of temptation think of God where others are simply overwhelmed and overcome.

Because prayer is so important, God is willing to offer us some inducement besides the many favors and graces coming to us through prayer. God is more anxious to have us pray and to listen to our prayers than we can ever be to receive a favor. Hence, we should be more zealous for a life of prayer.

Have you ever considered that the company we keep leaves a mark upon our character? We may admit it, or laugh it off. The people with whom we associate will

37

influence our thoughts, words and actions. We adopt the favorite sayings, words and phrases of our friends, whether for good or evil; we follow their actions, and actions speak louder than words. For that reason Holy Writ says: "Tell me with whom thou goes and I will tell thee who thou art!" Every language voices the same sentiment. So our language has this old saying: "Birds of a feather flock together."

Company, whether good or bad, wields a powerful influence over us. And now, let me ask you, what better company could we have than God?

By praying, we are in God's company! It is natural for us to assume the ways, manners, thoughts, tastes, ideals, feelings and desires of those in whose company we are, and can we do better or spend our time more profitably than by remaining in the company of God as long as it is possible for us to do so? Whose thoughts and desires can be purer or holier than those of God? And these very divine thoughts and desires, if we keep company with God in prayer, will gradually become our own.

We have been told so often that the sinful world and God can never agree; that what God likes the world dislikes, that what God commands the world will laugh at as folly. This warfare has been carried right into our very hearts, and, if we prefer the company of the world to the company of God, we shall feel like siding with the world. We imagine that the holy Will of God is very, very difficult to follow; we imagine that what the world can offer us is far greater than anything in the power of God. We look up at the examples of the saints, and we find the very opposite. The ways of the world were not theirs. They saw things in an entirely different light. The world had no inducements for them. Its pleasures, its honors, amounted to nothing in their sight. They simply saw things from the standpoint of God. They hated iniquity and loved justice, because God hates iniquity and loves justice. The saints, because they loved prayer, kept God company and for that reason gradually began to think as God thinks, loving what He loves, and hating what He hates.

Believe me, we would look at things in an entirely differ-ent light if we prayed more often. We do not pray often enough and not well enough to make the effects of the company we keep with God more telling. Like the saints, we could not help seeing things the way God sees them if we were more desirous of keeping Him company in prayer. The saints kept God company by their prayers. We not only can, but should, follow their example. The company of God will mold our character as it has molded and elevated the hearts and minds of the saints.

I cannot think of closing this chapter on piety without telling you of a deathbed scene it was my blessing to witness. When I was a student at St. Mary's Seminary, Baltimore, Md., I had the happiness of knowing a saintly young man, a fellow student. It had been decreed in the divine Providence that this young man should die before he could realize the supreme happiness of standing at the altar of God. When this young man fought with death he thought of nothing else than prayer. Oftentimes, it is true, his prayers were confused; he would recite part of a litany, and end with a song in honor of the Blessed Virgin Mary or of the Most Blessed Sacrament. But pray he would. When people are in delirium, they will usually speak of what is uppermost in their mind during their time of health. Some will talk of their business, others of their troubles, their likes and dislikes. Think of what a saintly disposition this young man must have cultivated throughout his life, how he must have prayed day after day so that in his suffering he forgot home, pain, study, friends, and all that the world holds in store for us--simply praying, praying.

39

A few minutes before his death he regained consciousness long enough to ask to be excused from taking any more medicine. "I want to die. And please, bury me in cassock and surplice." After another pause, he said: "Pray for me !" His mind began to wander again. He started to sing the "Ave Maria Stella." Before he could finish the second verse of that song in honor of the Blessed Virgin Mary he had passed away.

I only hope, my dear boys, that your death and mine may be as happy as was his. It will be if we learn to pray as fervently as he prayed. Throughout your whole life take care of your daily prayers. Daily prayers will take care of you when you come to die.

CHAPTER VII. VOCATION, IT'S MEANING

From the smallest flower up to the tallest tree, from the tiniest animal up to the circus elephant, from the kernel of sand up to the highest mountain crowned with clouds and snow, from a drop of water up to the wide ocean, everything has been made for some certain object or purpose. God has pointed out some certain work for all things He made. Moreover, all things are made so harmoniously, and all things are so fitting, that the whole of creation is like a giant clock. The sun, for instance, is so perfect, the trip of our earth so exact, that our many watches and clocks are regulated according to the revolutions of the earth on her own axis and her revolution around the sun.

In this wonderful plan of God, man is not to be a spectator. He, too, has been assigned his place and work. Nor need we be surprised at this plan of God. We could hardly think that the God who made the smallest insect live for some purpose would overlook His most perfect piece of work, namely, man, and permit him to be without aim or purpose. If God had some purpose in view when He created the little worm, He must have had a purpose in mind when he made man to His own image and likeness. If God has a task for the little worm, will He not have an even greater task for man? Each one of us, then, has been given a certain life's work. Either we must perform it well, or, failing, face the consequences. Nor can we hire a substitute to do our share of the work, like men who shrink from going to war. The talents God has given us we cannot give to another. Each one of us is held responsible for the talents he has received.

We may, for the time being, feel elated over the honor God has bestowed upon us by taking us to assist Him in carrying out His aims. The responsibility, however, is equally grave; so grave, in fact, that, unless it were for the sustaining power of His Love and Mercy, we should feel crushed to the ground.

From all eternity God has known us. He has designed and set aside for us a certain set of graces and talents to fit us for the work He has intended for us. And then, when in His all-wise Judgment the time had come for our entrance into this world, He shaped conditions and circumstances that, with the graces and talents intended for us, we might perform our life's work faithfully and gain heaven.

One day our dear Savior said to the Apostles: "You have not chosen me, but I have chosen you." The Apostles, it is true, followed our Lord and Savior freely and gladly; yet they could not have followed Him unless they had been asked to follow Him. That gives you the true meaning of "vocation." The word itself is taken from the Latin, and means "to call." Your parents may call you from your play or favorite work and ask you to do something for them that may not be as agreeable as the work or play you leave at their call. If anyone else would have called you, you would have reasons to ignore him. But since your parents call for you, you know you should obey. Your very obedience may mean a sacrifice on your part; still, you never think of refusing, because your parents have a right to ask services of you that others have not.

So God calls every one of us for some certain work. Since He is our Creator, He has a claim upon our obedience. Since the plan He has in view with us is the most perfect that divine Wisdom could shape for us, the life-work He has decided for us is more fitted for our capacity and better adapted to our needs and desires than any other we might choose for ourselves.

God wants some of you to be plain, every day working men. Others of you He will want to see in stores, shops or factories. Some He will want to see in offices. Some He may want to see earn their bread as lawyers, doctors, or priests. Some of you He may want to see in a convent or monastery. All we can do is to be prepared for whatever work God assigns to us and, like young Samuel, say: "Speak, Lord, Thy servant heareth!" We consider the days of childhood the happiest of our life. Did you ever think why? These were days free from all care and worry. What little sorrows and troubles you did have were like sun showers. Before the tears were dry on your little cheeks, laughter over something else made you forget them. These days, however, are no more. Life, a severe master, stands before you now; and he demands work, work, work.

You see your fathers going to work every morning. It may be hot or cold, the sun may shine and invite them to take a day off and rest, it may rain or snow so that one would hardly want to send a dog away from home. Your father may feel as though he should spare himself, or feel hardly able to work, but you see him going to work without saying a single word of ill will. Time was when your father was a boy of your age; time was when he was free of care and sorrow; time was when he had to follow the call of God to work and in a spirit of obedience to that call of God, that vocation, you see him working every day. Now it is your turn to follow the call of God and do the work He has decided for you.

Doubtless, you have asked yourself this question more than once. I hope you have.

43

A hint of your calling may have been revealed when, in play, you imitated the work and actions of grown people. Some children, in playing, act like teachers, others as musicians, others as doctors, others show wonderful preference for some tools, like hammers, saws, or lathes; others imitate the priest, climbing upon a chair and speaking to an imaginary audience. Now, this favoring of some object or other, which to some extent seems almost instinctive, will very frequently indicate the direction in which the future vocation will have to be found. From my own experience, I might say that playing priest was one of my great hobbies when I was a little boy.

Each one of us is in duty bound to ask himself: "What is my vocation?" It is not the question of doing some work on earth, but doing the work God has intended for us. If the choice depended upon us, we might make dreadful blunders.

Years ago, in most European countries the young men, as soon as they reached the age of twenty-one years, had to appear before the military authorities to be examined by them. From that time on until they were discharged they had to serve in the army or navy, as the authorities saw fit. Some of these young men were assigned to the cavalry, others to the artillery, others to the infantry, others to the navy. Some were assigned to the commissary, some to the engineering, and some to the hospital department of the service. The peculiar fitness of each one was considered before a choice is made. As for himself, the young man had little chance in determining to what branch of the military organization he would like to belong. His capacity and fitness decided for him. One might be an excellent sailor, but a very poor horse man; another might be a poor man for infantry, yet a wonder of bravery with the artillery branch of the army, and so on. Still, there was another reason for assigning each one to some special post. At the head of the army there was a leading staff, defining exactly how strong the infantry, cavalry and artillery must be. It would be poor policy to let one branch expand at the expense of another. Each one of them must be calculated to effect the various plans of attack and defense that may become necessary. This subtle balance of power and strength might be lost if each young man could join the branch he prefers. In time of war that mistake might be fatal for the welfare of the entire country.

Almighty God, foreseeing what chaos would result if each man could do as he pleased, has wisely assigned to each of us a certain post of duty along the line of our fitness, that all work on earth might be carried on to the best advantage. It is His holy will that all trades and professions should be filled so exactly as not to destroy that balance of strength and power that is so necessary for peace and happiness of the world.

Paradise would, to some extent, be restored this very day if every one of us would try to do the work God had intended. But we find people trying to fit square pegs into round holes, or fitting round pegs into square holes. Our temporal as well as our eternal happiness depends upon our conformity with the holy Will of God. And why do we see so much misery, misfortune, so many tears and sorrows in this world? Why are there so many failures and disappointments in life? Simply because so many people will enter upon vocations for which they are neither called nor fitted. They act contrary to the plans of all-wise God. It does make a great difference all around whether we obey the holy Will of God, or whether we only seek to please our own whims and fancies. God is, by no means, indifferent or careless about whether we serve Him or not. If we obey Him, so much the better for us; if we fail, we must suffer the consequences. With these thoughts impressed upon your minds, you will understand the importance of making the proper choice in matters of vocation. Your choice will spell happiness or failure for the rest of your life. Nay, more; it may mean heaven or hell hereafter. God has shaped and arranged the graces to the calling or vocation assigned to us. Hence, if one dares assume a vocation for which God did not intend him, he will find himself short of the graces proper to that very calling. The graces and talents he has are not adapted to the calling. You certainly would not want to lead a life of misery and disappointment if it were in your power to choose success and happiness. As for myself, I desire nothing more than your temporal and eternal welfare. For that reason, I will tell you how to go about it that you may make a happy choice that you may find out and follow the vocation and do the task God has given you to do.

The very first and most important means of learning what God wants us to do is prayer. Pray earnestly, especially after each Holy Communion, that God may give you His holy Light to see the way. Never for a moment think that, because in all probability, your life-work will be that of the ordinary, everyday working man, you need not exercise as much care as though you were to decide about a higher calling. In the sight of God every work is important and holy, provided it is performed in a holy manner. I remember having seen three stained glass windows in a church. The first showed St. Isidore, the farmer; another, St. Margareth, queen of Scotland; and the third, St. Wendelin, the shepherd boy. Here are three saints, two of whom were very poor and plain people. Their vocation was a very low and common one, as the world would judge; yet, in the sight of God, they 'are on an equal footing with saintly kings and queens. No vocation and no work is to be despised. No matter, then, what your vocation may be, whether it be of the lowly or of the very highest, pray and pray fervently. After you have prayed, take a mental inventory of yourself, compare the various callings about which you may wish to decide with the talents and gifts you find in yourself. You may even consult your very first impulses, your earliest games or playthings. Ask yourself calmly in which state you would wish to die. That state will, in all probability, be the state in which you should spend your life.

Secondly, you should consult your parents. Their experience as well as their good will towards you will usually prompt them to give you the best advice, help and encouragement. If, however, you have arrived at some definite conclusion; if, before God, you think you have decided rightly and for some unaccountable reason your parents should try to talk you out of it, remember: we must obey God more than man. For some reason parents will, at times, show opposition when a child of theirs wishes to enter a convent or become a priest. If you are hampered in this manner, be willing that the holy Will of God be carried out on earth as it is in heaven. Many are the saints who suffered under the very same difficulty. There is still another whom, at times, you may overlook or forget. This man is your most intimate friend, a friend who knows you better than you do yourselves; a friend who will be truthful and candid; a friend who may not always tell you what you like to hear, but what will be of benefit to you. His judgment is the result of years of study, observation and thorough knowledge of the human heart. Hence, his judgment will he true and impartial. And this friend is the priest to whom you go to Confession. If you are wise, you will pick out some certain priest to whom you take a particular liking, and always go to Confession to him. In a very short time he will be able to advise you in the most important matters. Ask the advice of your confessor. If you have made a choice, he will be able to tell you whether your choice was a prudent one; if you are undecided, he will be able to guide you where, without his helping hand, you would be sure to stumble.

Outside of the religious, the clergy and a few chosen saintly souls in the world, the importance of the judgment of a confessor is hardly appreciated as it should be. Yet the saints have at all times considered the decisions of their confessors as the holy Will of God. At times God lets people know by means of miracles what He wants them to do, as, for example, in the conversion of St. Paul. As a rule, however, God makes use of natural means to let us know our calling. And one of the most important means of letting us know His holy Will is the confessor. Hence the voice of the confessor is the voice of God.

You may search the whole world and you will not find a single sister, or monk, or priest who have embraced their vocation to please themselves only. If you could look into the life of a religious or a priest you would be more than surprised at the many prayers they said, the Holy Communions they received to learn their vocation. And you will find that they humbly asked the advice of their confessors. Only then, when he gave his consent, and not before, did they make up their minds to take that important step.

People, as a rule, would meet with much more success, even in temporal matters, if they would treat their confessors as their personal and most intimate friends, asking their advice and following their judgment and ripe experience.

CHAPTER VIII. VOCATION, PRUDENCE IN CHOOSING

The question of a vocation may be ever so serious with some well-meaning boys--there are as many, if not more--with whom it means the solution of one only question; "What is there in it for me?" Little do they care for the holy will of God in their behalf. The very calling God may have determined for them is disregarded because they do not find enough honors, or money, or pleasures in it to suit their wants or tastes.

If vocation meant nothing else than so many dollars and cents, the question could easily be settled by looking up the earnings of the various vocations and picking out the one by which we can get the most money in the easiest manner. If, for example, the most money could be made by running railways, and you, and I, and all the rest had their own railroads, where could we get the people from to travel on our roads?

If vocation meant nothing else than getting all the honors that are within reach, we would all of us have to go into the king business or become great presidents. Even then it would be doubtful whether we could enjoy all the honors we would crave. But supposing each one could be a king, or president, or emperor, who would there be left to give us the honors due?

If vocation meant nothing else than getting all the pleasures the World can give, we would have to strive for nothing but pleasures. And how could we ever make ends meet? For the pleasure we take means work for many others, who in their turn could want to have nothing but pleasures for themselves. You see many a boat passing up and down the river. The decks are swarming with people who are having a good time. About twenty feet below the deck you will find sweating stokers working half stripped, covered with dust and dirt. They must feed the fires for the benefit of the excursion party. What pleasures have the stokers in their work? Besides the stokers there are the oilers, mechanics and engineers in the engine room, watching every movement of the complicated machinery. Where does their pleasure come in? Then there is the man at the wheel, the captain on his bridge. They do not leave their post for a moment to join in the pleasures of the passengers. To say that we are made for nothing else than pleasure is therefore nonsense.

Vocation, then, means nothing else than carrying out the holy Will of God. The very first answer of our catechism gives us this much to understand. We are made to serve God in this world and be happy with Him in the next. To serve God as He wants us to serve Him, we must serve Him in the vocation He has mapped out for us.

To choose the vocation in which God wants us to serve Him, and for which He wants to reward us, we must be guided by prudence. We must not ask ourselves, "What is there in it for me?" but "What is the holy Will of God." For that reason our dear Savior said: "Seek ye first the kingdom of heaven."

Prudence, then, will demand that we please God rather than our fancy. You may turn and twist a compass as you like, the needle will point due north. Neither should the pomp and glitter of this world be able to turn you from your aim and purpose--the holy Will of God.

In His infinite wisdom, almighty God has so shaped each vocation that, besides our daily bread, it will give us some little honor or pleasure. God did not intend to offer us good times at little or no expense. He knows our weakness far better than we ourselves. And out of pure love and mercy for us He has added some little honor or pleasure to each calling that we might not find its burden and responsibilities too hard to bear. Moreover, this consolation, the little honor or pleasure incidental to each vocation is what the dessert is to the whole meal. The dessert is always the smallest portion of the meal. So, likewise, are the pleasures and honors of each calling. Again, the dessert is the last course. So, too, the little honors and pleasures of a calling come at the end of life--if they come at all. A life work with all its efforts and trials, sorrows and cares must be completed before we can be given this dessert. Indeed, it must be appropriate, or it will not taste right.

To choose a vocation, regardless of what prudence would demand, will mean a life of sore disappointments.

The greedy boy, hungering for nothing but money, may notice a doctor. The doctor is well dressed; he makes the rounds of his patients in his automobile, enters the homes of the very richest, and has a nice home of his own. Says the boy: "I will be a doctor; for a doctor has a nice life of it and makes much money." We will suppose the boy studies medicine, passes all his examinations, gets his degree, and hangs out his shingle. Will he be happy? That is another question. Will he be ready to go out day and night, to be at the beck and call of every man? Will he be ready and willing to tend to patients whose sickness is so loathsome that relatives and friends are driven from the bedside? Will he be willing to wash out sores and ulcers, the very sight of which tends to turn a person's stomach? Will he be ready to risk his life to save others? His reason for being a doctor was not to do good, but to make money. As a doctor he will be a total failure; as a failure he will be unable to earn the money a doctor earns. His life is ruined and wasted. He could make more money digging sewers.

The ambitious boy will thirst for honors. He sees a priest and would like to receive the honor and respect shown to the priest of God. The ambitious boy makes up his mind to become a priest. Little does he know of the many daily sacrifices the priest must make. Like the doctor, the priest, too, must go to the sick. The obligation for the priest is still more binding; he must go, even though a doctor would have reason to stay away. The life of a priest is a life of self-denial, a life of the Cross. Only on the day of the Last Judgment will the world learn to know the sorrows, trials, sufferings and sacrifices that are the lot of faithful and zealous priests. It is not customary to dwell upon this side of the priestly life. Every priest, if he wanted to, could tell you that the little honor that is shown--and that at times so sparingly--is by no means a recompense for the burdens and responsibilities of the priestly office. If a man were to enter the priesthood with this one purpose of getting for himself all kinds of honors and distinctions, he would be the unhappiest of men.

A shallow boy may be without enterprise or ambition. In choosing a vocation he will look for something that is unusually easy. The work that would suit him best would be putting his feet up on some table in some office, doing no work, dressing nicely, take in every ball game, and get immensely rich. The discoveries and inventions up to date are great and manifold. But this kind of trade has not been discovered as yet. Every vocation means work. When God told Adam that he was to eat his bread in the sweat of his brow, you and I were meant as well as our first parent.

From this, then, you will understand why there is nothing more foolish than looking for money, honors, or good times, The boy who wants to follow some vocation simply for the money, honor, or pleasure there is in it will be sadly disappointed; his very act shows that he is dishonest; he wants something to which he is not entitled.

We call a boy a prudent boy when he reflects upon an action before he decides; who takes all things into consideration, weighs all the reasons for and against before he decides one way or another.

Such prudence should be yours in deciding upon a vocation. A prudent boy will reflect long and seriously, will weigh all the reasons for and against the calling he has in mind, will not be dazzled by the bright side, nor discouraged over the hardships that follow. He will understand that God wants him and nobody else to do the work intended for him. Hence he will pray earnestly and receive Holy Communion frequently; he will consult his parents and his confessor. God seeing his good will shall not permit him to grope in the dark. If you boys choose your vocations in this manner, you cannot go wrong. The choice you will make will mean happiness and contentment for you. You will not take upon yourself more than you can bear. You will never try to raise five hundred pounds, when all you can lift would be one hundred; nor will you take less upon yourself than you can bear. If you are determined to follow out the holy Will of God you will not want to content yourself with only twenty pounds when you can carry two hundred. The burden that is made for your shoulders will, indeed, be heavy enough at times. Like Christ, you, too, will sink beneath the burden of your cross; but God will not forsake you. His grace will make you strong, and you will find your yoke sweet and your burden light.

In considering the advisability of this vocation or that, there is one point that is frequently overlooked. Prudence demands that this one point be seriously

53

considered. This point, which gets no consideration whatever from many, is faith.

If you determine upon a calling or a work in which you run a great danger of losing your holy faith, it can never be the Will of God that you adopt it. It is true, we can hardly go anywhere at the present time without being compelled to listen to foul talk, to talk against religion, particularly against the Catholic Church, her priests and her institutions. There is hardly a shop or factory but some big-mouthed man will be found there talking against God. To make up for the lack of brains, he will use that much more lungpower. Ordinary people, not knowing the difference, will consider such a man very, very smart. And yet the Holy Ghost tells us: "Only the fool says within his heart there is no God." Any man with the least brains knows better than such an ignoramus who makes impertinence stand for brains. And such are only the ordinary everyday dangers to your holy faith. There are other places where you, as Catholics, are not even wanted.

Now suppose you could find work in such a place, even get rich, prosperous, influential, what will it profit you?

What will it profit you to gain the whole world! Look at the price you pay for it! For the few years of glory in this world you give your immortal soul. On the one hand, there is God who wants your soul. Give it to Him, and He promises to give you heaven for it. And this heaven is everlasting. On the other hand, the world, too, wants your soul. It can give in return only a few pleasures, a little money or some honors for a short time. Even if we had the whole world laid at our feet, we would be cheated in giving our souls for it. And now think what a little slice of the world people do get! And for that little bit they throw their souls away! A few thousand dollars, a little office, is all most people get. And for that they give their souls away! What would you think of your father if he sold his home for five cents? You would think he was not in his right mind. Yet, heaven is more than your house and lot; and what you get in return for heaven is not worth five cents in comparison. Never take any work that prevents you from going to holy Mass on Sunday. Missing holy Mass on Sunday is the first step to losing your holy faith. Look for such work only in which you are at liberty to have the Sunday for yourself. If you must leave home to work in another city, be sure there is a Catholic church there and let your first walk be to the priest's house after you have paid your respects to our dear Savior in the Tabernacle. Introduce yourself to the pastor of that church. No matter who he may be, he will respect you all the more for it. If the little town or city in which you would want to work has no church, my advice will be to keep out of it. In the first place, I doubt whether you will find one good Catholic family in that whole town. Instead you will find a number of indifferent Catholics, whose lives may not be as edifying as you might wish for. Those not of our holy faith that you will find in that town may be exemplary people in their way. Unfortunately, this may not prevent them from having deep-rooted prejudice against you for the reason that you are a Catholic. To keep up your holy faith in such a surrounding is very, very hard. For many it is impossible; you may be of that number. For your own peace of mind it will be advisable to stay away from such places.

It may be that, by following out these rules, you will lose money, that you will be obliged to let great opportunities slip by, lose them for the sake of your holy faith! God is rich enough to pay you back to cover the loss. Think of the great sacrifices others have made for the same holy faith you call your own! What are a few dollars in comparison to the lives that martyrs have given for our holy faith. Life was as dear to them as ours is to us.

If we thought less of dollars and cents and more of faith we would spare ourselves many troubles and gather more rewards for the life to come, you face the future, expecting success and happiness. Exercise prudence that you may select the calling for which God has intended you. It will pay you to consider the obligations of your holy faith. Faith will show you the way. Faith will tell you that you should not be misguided by the glitter of this world, that you are not created for money, or honor, or pleasure, but to serve God and be happy with Him forever.

CHAPTER IX. VOCATION--NECESSITY OF PERSEVERANCE

Along the banks of rivers you will, at times, see the empty hulls of ships. These ships are stranded. Whatever was of value, machinery, furniture, freight, and the like, was taken out and the empty hull was left to rot on the banks. Had it not been for some accident, that now rotten hull would even today be a noble ship sailing on the lakes. It is stranded, and there it is!

Many a life resembles such an empty, rotten hull. Something went wrong, and the life is wasted. I cannot better explain this sad failure of life than by giving you a real example of a life gone wrong.

A short time ago, a young man entered an engraver's shop to learn the trade. As, perhaps, you know, this work pays well after one has learned it thoroughly. The work, too, is difficult. One must be able to write and draw beautifully with pen and ink. It requires about four years to learn the trade. During that time the wages are very, very little. However, after one has mastered the trade, the wages are better than those of many other trades.

Well, this boy had been with a firm of printers for three years. One day a friend came to the boy, and asked him what wages he earned. He was almost ashamed to tell he got about fifty dollars a week. "Why, you foolish boy!" the other said. "Why don't you come with me and learn the cutters' trade! It takes you only a month to learn that trade, and from that time on you get four hundred a month!" That seemed very tempting to the boy. "Who will teach me that trade?" the boy asked. "I will," the other young man replied. "I have spoken to your folks, and it will cost you only forty dollars to learn. And in a month's time I guarantee you will be a cutter!" The next day the boy gave up his work in the shop and learned cutting goods for clothes. At the end of the month, it is true, he could cut out the pattern of a suit of clothes; but he had found no one for whom to cut them. All the tailors were supplied with cutters for years to come. He had no means to go to another city to try his luck. He was too proud to go back to the first shop. He had bragged so much about being a cutter and making so much more money than an engraver that he feared he would be laughed at should he apply again.

And so it happened that the boy spent many an idle week. He did get some work to do during the rush of the season at spring and fall; but these few weeks of work could not tide him over the balance of the year. After nearly a year he gave up the idea of being a cutter and began working in a drugstore. All he could do there was wash bottles and to sell hair oil and the like. He had neither the inclination nor the means to study pharmacy, and so he could never be a licensed or registered druggist. There was no future in store for him in that business unless he would have been content with being the head soda jerk at a soda fountain. Washing bottles did not pay, and so he left. After that, we find him in the shipping department of a big factory. For a time he was liked, because he could print the names so perfectly on the boxes and crates. But the work was not to his liking. Moreover, he was not able to handle the heavier freight. And so he left that place in the nick of time before being told to go. After being idle for a few more months he became a waiter in a cheap hotel. He was rebuked a few times by the management and guests, and that was the end of his hotel life. After that he tried a few more stores and shops. Now he is a man of thirty and he drives a grocery wagon. Whether he will be able to keep this work long is a question.

The life of this young man, sad as it is, is seen repeated hundreds and hundreds of times. His is a blasted, ruined life. How many boys and young men drift from factory to shop, from shop to store, and from store to some other factory! And it is all done with the view of getting more money for less work.

All work is hard, and all work has something about it that makes it, to some extent, disagreeable. Such, however, is the plan of God. Since the fall of Adam, work is intended as a penance for us, not a pleasure. In Paradise work was pleasure. Since, on account of sin, we are no longer in Paradise, work is penance. Such is the plan of an all-wise God. Bearing this in mind, you will see how utterly useless it is for us to look for some work that has with it nothing but pleasure. The wildest dreams of socialists will never be able to overcome this one fact of work being a penance. Nor can we find happiness in anything--so far as earthly happiness goes--but in working according to the holy Will of God.

In spite of the fact that our happiness lies only in the direction of the work designed for us by almighty God, we find so many boys who shirk earnest effort. They are drawn this way and that; try this work, then another. In fact, they never know their own mind from day to day. And, as time goes on, they are nearing their twentieth year without knowing a trade.

A sick man may realize that he ought to call a doctor; but there are a number of friends calling upon him and each one has a favorite remedy. One neighbor will give him some tea. He drinks this tea. Another comes and gives him some powders. "They did me so much good when I was sick, and I don't see why they shouldn't help you." So powders it is for a few days. Another friend comes along with porous plasters. They are advertised to do wonders. And so the sick man drinks tea, takes powders, and has himself covered with porous plasters. Next day another friend comes. He makes him tear off his plasters, stops the tea and takes away the powders. He has some wonderful pills. One pill will make one feel better, a box makes one well, and two boxes could bring a man back from the grave. So it is pills for some days. Then another friend comes with some patent medicine. The pills are put aside and the sick man begins emptying a bottle of that patent medicine. By the time the bottle is half empty the sick man feels that unless he calls the doctor at once, they may have to call the undertaker instead. Had he followed his very first impulse and called for a doctor at once, he might have been quickly cured; as it is, it may now take him weeks and weeks before he can get well.

The fickle-minded boy is exactly like this sick man. Instead of following his better judgment, he follows the advice of every Tom, Dick and Harry coming along.

Indecision is a great mistake for a boy. The sooner he can make up his mind and decide one way or another, the better it will be for him. The reason is not hard to find.

Up to a certain time of life, learning is easy. After that it grows harder each year. Gradually it becomes almost impossible to learn anything. It is generally taken for granted that the age of from fifteen to eighteen or nineteen is the best time to learn a trade. To remain undecided for even two of these important years means a drawback that may tell upon the rest of life. Weeks, months and years pass by, whether you work or not. But why should you let these precious years slip by? There is no reason for it. You do not want your lives to be failures. You must, then, make up your minds to do some work and persevere in it. It pays to stick to your trade.

To be hesitating, and doubting, and trying one work after another is a loss of time and opportunity. At your age it seems perfectly natural that you should learn a trade. What would you say if a man of over twenty-five stood beside you, learning the same trade? The first thought that would come to your mind would be: "I wonder why he was so slow about it. What is the reason he could not learn the trade sooner." You will have your misgivings; so will the employers have their misgivings. As a rule, a man of over twenty-five trying to learn a trade will make a fizzle of it. He will not want to learn.

At the age of twenty-five, a young man will want to be somebody. He feels that he is too big to stand beside a mere boy to learn. It is a humiliation for him to have others consider a boy five years his junior as his equal. He will want to spend money like the young man who has learned a trade, will want to dress becomingly, will want to keep company with some young lady, as others do who have a way of making a living and, like the rest of them, may think very seriously about getting married. I pity the poor girl throwing her life away for a man who cannot support himself, much less a family. You may, at times, hear of how an office boy works his way up to become the president of the company by which he had been employed, or of a messenger boy who worked his way up to become the manager of some telegraph company. No such promotions are in store for the Jack of all trades.

Because some boys will switch from one work to another, trying this work and that, we have with us this class of unfortunate men whom we call Jacks of all trades. As a rule, they are masters of none. They know something about everything. That is exactly what spoils them. They would be far better off if they knew everything about something.

Where a carpenter, blacksmith, or engineer has steady work, the poor Jack of all trades hardly knows from one month to another where, or what, or for whom he will work.

Perseverance is called a jewel; partly, because it is found so rarely, and partly because it is so precious. Because it is so rare and so precious, it is hard to find it. One must fight with failure to get this jewel of perseverance. Unless we make our failures stepping stones for success, we will never acquire perseverance. Our lives, without perseverance, will resemble the empty, useless hulls you see rotting along the shores. Unfortunately, some boys are so sensitive, so thin-skinned, that one single failure will be enough to cause them to throw ambition to the winds.

The way to success is paved with failures. If the first failure had discouraged our great artists and scientists, the world would be centuries behind the times. Had Columbus been discouraged at the first failures, he would never have discovered the New World. He was laughed at for thinking the world was a globe. He simply let them laugh and persevered in his plans until he was able to show he was right.

Success, when attained too easily, is not always lasting. The lasting qualities of success resemble the various fruits. The fruit ripening early in the year, like the strawberry, will not keep very long. The apple or pear, ripening late in the fall, will keep perfectly through the winter. If success comes too quickly, we have reason to fear that it will be short-lived. If, however, it comes to us after many failures and adversities, then we may have reason to hope that it will outlive the short span of our life.

If, then, you wish to make a success of the calling God has designed for you, you must persevere in it. Your aim may be ever so lofty, your intention at the start ever so noble, yet unless you persevere in spite of all failures and adversities, your life will itself be a failure. The higher you have aimed, the greater will be your fall. Like countless others, you will meet with failures. Like countless others, you, too, must profit by your very failures, learning to do better with every following effort. You are bound to succeed if you persevere.

It would, indeed, be a profitable undertaking for all of you if, instead of some useless novel, you would pick up the history of some great man and read that. Read the life of Columbus, Washington, Lincoln, Garcia Moreno, Windhorst, or the life of any of the countless saints, if only with this one purpose in mind of studying how these men made failures the foundation of their imperishable glory.

CHAPTER X. VOCATION--NECESSITY OF DILIGENCE

Recall for a few moments the days of school and try to remember how discouraged you felt when you got your first workbook. You thought you could never learn to write. If, out of curiosity, you looked at the workbooks of an older brother or sister, and you discovered that their books were far more advanced than yours, you no doubt felt like saying: "It's no use trying; I will never be able to write as nicely as that."

Now, however, as you look back to those times, you know that you have passed through all the various workbooks, readers, spellers, grammars, geographies, histories and other studies without losing much sleep, provided you showed ordinary diligence in your studies.

To remain idle for months and then to work real hard for two or three days for an examination will be of little benefit to you in later years, even though you should be lucky enough to pass. Some of you may have discovered as much by this time.

The experience of the past will teach you two lessons: First, that knowledge is acquired by degrees; and, secondly, that it requires constant diligence to transfer the knowledge from the page of the book to your memory and understanding. In fact, the usefulness of our knowledge will depend upon the degree of diligence used in acquiring it. For this very reason the boy, brilliant in school, will frequently be a failure in later years. The other boy who, perhaps, never received the highest grade, will often excel the brilliant boy in later years in true worth and capability. The reason is not hard to find. While the brilliant boy will be inclined to indolence because study does not cost him much effort, the other boy, less talented, has become accustomed to earnest effort, since he had to work hard to keep up with his class. The one boy thinks he knows it all, and therefore need not try hard; the other boy, knowing his weakness, realizes that he must exercise his memory and understanding to grasp a lesson. The result is that he will often excel the brilliant boy in actual achievements.

Now, the same methods of acquiring our school learning holds good for the learning of a trade or profession. Our whole life is but a school. About the only difference is that, in later years, vacations do not come as regularly as they did when we were boys.

Never be foolish enough to think that with the last day of school your study is finished. Then it is that it really begins. During your years of school you laid the foundation of your learning. You cannot build a church on a foundation intended for a small cottage. Hence the importance of laying a good foundation while at school.

To make your life work a success, it will not be enough to simply persevere in it in a careless sort of way. To do any kind of work in a slipshod manner will not be much of a credit to you. You must be diligent in your work; as busy as a little bee. Working without diligence means work only half done. If you see a tree with little and stunted fruit, you do not think much of the tree. What would you say of a man who turns out work in a careless sort of way, never caring how it looks, how or when it is done, just so it is done some time and somehow! You would say: "Why, that man isn't worth much."

A great musician, when complimented upon his wonderful skill, answered: "Oh, that is nothing at all. Anybody can do as well." One of the bystanders then asked: "Do you mean to say that anybody could play as perfectly as you?" "Certainly," the artist replied, "three things alone are needed. The first is study, the second is study, and the third is, again, study."

If you had practiced writing only once a month, you would have never become able to write. You filled notebooks one after another; you used up reams of writing paper; you wrote day after day. Now it has become easy for you to put your thoughts upon paper. In like manner you cannot expect to become perfect in any trade or profession unless you work diligently.

A plow permitted to remain idle will soon be rusty. But one in active use will soon shine like silver. Such is the effect of diligence upon all things. Diligence is necessary for our own well-being. What would become of us unless we were diligent in our bodily exercises? If we stopped taking our regular exercises our muscles would become flabby and soft, the blood weak and poor. The shortest walk would seem tiresome, or even impossible to undertake. Exercise makes walking easy. Why, you could not think of playing ball unless you practiced throwing, catching and batting, and practiced hard at that. You had to train your memory that it might retain what once you have learned. You must train your will power, your understanding, to have them work properly. And all that means nothing else but diligence. Unless we keep our mind occupied we grow dull; unless we give our body constant exercise, strength will leave us as water is lost in sand. Diligence, then, is so plain a duty. It seems strange our attention should have to be called to it at all. Yet, because diligence is a duty, it grinds. Say what you will, we live in a superficial age. To counteract this, we must be indefatigable in insisting upon diligence.

Men are inclined to be shifty. Consult your own inclination in proof of it. Do you not continually look for that which is easiest? Do you look for that which requires little effort on your part? Even a game or play requiring much thought or effort will be avoided.

Since you notice an inclination to look for the easiest work, fearing that an effort on your part would be too much of a strain, you had better be on your guard against laziness. Unless you become painstaking and diligent in your work, you will be a failure for life. Did you ever notice a juggler on the stage how he can throw and catch four or more balls with one hand? It does look easy, until you try it! It took this juggler years before he could do this trick well enough to show it on a stage. No matter how plain or simple a work may seem to be, it requires effort to do it well. Tennyson was asked one day how long it took him to compose a short poem. Its words were so plain and simple that one would think they were written as fast as a pen could go across paper. Tennyson smiled and said: "These four lines took me two boxes of cigars to make them as they are." It took him weeks to write these four lines. They were written and re-written, changed and corrected, until they were perfect. Genius does not mean a very bright mind, but the capacity for infinite work and painstaking.

Trades and professions are overcrowded. Still, there is always room at the top. Diligent and reliable workers are few and far between. There is an old saying: "Practice makes perfect." Those perfect in their trades or professions are very few in number. The world expects diligence of us; the standards of workmanship are high in every calling. No one will be willing to pay a first-class price for a third or fourth-class piece of work. Our work must be first-class, or we cannot expect a first-class price for it.

The mechanic who turns out poor work at a price for which one expects good work, will lose his trade. You see, then, how it happens that while some business men keep their customers, others lose theirs. Diligence is the word that explains it all. A hired man may have all the good points but diligence; he may be sober, good natured, quiet; he may have all the good points of not smoking, drinking, chewing, cursing, or gambling. But if he is lazy all these good points will be of little help. They will not be able to hold his position for him. No employer can use a lazy man. To illustrate the advantage of diligence from another point, let us suppose your father is a carpenter who knows his trade from A to Z. His employer places all his confidence in your father. He lets him work as he knows best. He does not need to watch your father, as others must be watched, for he knows your father is diligent and conscientious. He will put your father to some work and tell him to go ahead. Now, if hard times should come, if work should become scarce, so that the employer will have to dismiss some of his workmen, will he dismiss your father with the first crowd? Indeed not. First he will discharge those who are inefficient. Your father will be the very last man he will think of sending away. He knows your father could get work anywhere. To lose your father would be a loss for him. It would hurt his business to let such a man go. Such a good workman is kept. A diligent worker makes himself indispensable.

The examples and illustrations of diligence I have shown you so far do not show you all the beauty and advantage of diligence. There are still other rewards in store for diligence.

Looking at the maps of the hemispheres you will have observed that neither water nor land is marked for the South Pole. Explorers have not explored that part of the earth enough as yet, and so the maps leave a blank space at the pole. It remains to be seen whether there is land or water below the ice. In like manner no trade or profession is fully known or understood. There is still room for explorers to learn more about each trade or profession. Inventions adding to or changing the work of millions are made every day.

You may learn some trade, or science, or profession, that millions have learned before you. They have not grasped it entirely; neither will you. You may know more than those who lived fifty years ago, but so will others know more who live fifty years from now. There is always room for new ideas, new methods, new machinery, new tools and new branches of work. What was new yesterday will be old tomorrow. How many thought of gasoline engines and automobiles a hundred years ago? Thousands of men work at these very machines. We see factories in every town turning out such engines or automobiles. Fifty years from now we may see as many factories building flying cars of some kind.

Who will keep up this march of progress? The idle and careless worker, or the man who is diligent and always willing to learn more about his trade or profession?

The road to success is a hard road. There is no bunting, no decoration, and no flags or welcome signs are found on the way. The road is hard, indeed, rough and steep. It means hard and endless work. Life is no Sunday school picnic, but a hard workday. For that reason be diligent, faithful, patient and untiring in your work that you may not work in vain.

CHAPTER XI. THE BOY AND THE COLLEGE

An experienced schoolman, after thoroughly examining our school and college system, passed the following criticism upon it: "America," he said, "makes a great mistake in training too many boys to become salaried people instead of wage-earners." Every little two by four brain is made to believe that it is made for something great; that the one desirable thing is to follow some get-rich-quick scheme; that labor is a disgrace and idleness a distinction.

As there are many girls afraid of doing housework for fear of disfiguring their beautiful hands, there are many boys going to college to avoid hard work. As a result, we have too many doctors, lawyers and other professional and semi-professional men whose success would be far more substantial if they had learned a trade, such as carpenter or butcher. The trouble with our high schools and colleges is that there is not enough sifting done to keep out the undesirable and unfit element.

It is by no means my intention to discourage anyone from seeking a college education when it will be to him of real benefit. If a boy is really talented and has the vocation, by all means, give him a college education. When, however, a boy is not sufficiently bright, when he lacks the necessary diligence, will-power, and perseverance, then the years spent at college are a waste of time, of effort and money.

An example from my experience will explain my meaning. A certain boy had passed in his high school examinations by a narrow margin. His father was a well-to-do business man, and, of course, the boy had to go to college. Nothing else would do. The boy had no more aim or vocation for a profession than the man in the moon. But he had to go to college. After spending a few years at college, and regularly failing in his examinations, it became at last plain to the boy as well as to his father, that the boy was not intended for the professions. The only branch in which he gave any promise was drawing. I suggested that he do newspaper work, until he could find an opening to do illustrations for some magazine. The poor fellow, however, lacked push and perseverance, his failure at college had thoroughly discouraged him, and had made him lose all faith in himself. Now he is a clerk in a cigar store.

This is only one of thousands of such deplorable cases, but with this particular case in mind I want to ask you two questions:

1. First. What good did this boy get out of the years he spent so uselessly at college? Those years were not only a waste of time; they were actually detrimental to him. He learned to hate and detest hard work. The years in which he might have learned some trade are beyond his recall.

2. The second question is this: Will he be even a success as clerk? He hates hard work of any kind, and, because he has no certain aim in life, I am afraid he will be a poor hand at earning his bread in any calling.

You will now better understand me when I say colleges are not meant for the majority of boys. The very fact that a boy passes his high school examinations does not imply that he must go to college.

And those boys who think that at college, life is easy, that there is no work to do, are sadly mistaken.

71

Persistent study is much harder work by far than manual labor.

And when boys think that the highest aim of a college or high school is to turn out professional football or baseball players, they are also mistaken. There may be some colleges that pay more attention to muscle than brain; but, after all, the real object of a college is to train the mind and to store the mind with knowledge.

Now, taking for granted that a boy is qualified to enter college, that he has an aim before him and does not go to college simply to waste time and shirk hard work, we may divide colleges into two varieties: those giving a business education, like commercial colleges, and, classical colleges teaching languages, arts and sciences.

Every boy intending to take up his father's business should acquire a business education. This comprises a thorough course in bookkeeping, general office work and commercial law. If your father has a business of his own and you wish to succeed him, such a commercial training will be necessary for you. Some hundred and fifty years ago it was common for people to make fortunes even though they could not write their name. These times are past. In our mad rush the system that was new yesterday will be old-fashioned by tomorrow. You cannot expect to carry on business as it was done by your grandfathers.

Commercial colleges do not only turn out typists, stenographers and bookkeepers. Young women are strong competitors in these branches. Not because they do this work better than young men, but they are content with less pay than a young man would usually demand for the same kind of work. In other colleges, there are also taught electricity, electrical engineering, civil engineering, forestry, horticulture and the various branches of machinery, and they all offer opportunities for bright and diligent boys. And

72

while many trades and professions are overcrowded, these branches of learning are usually not. The demand for civil engineers, electrical engineers and advanced machinists is often greater than the supply.

Besides such technical colleges, there is the classical college, teaching languages, arts and sciences, preparatory to courses in medicine, law, philosophy and theology. Boys who wish to enter upon any of these callings fit themselves for them by going to such colleges. It would be better for the standing of the professions in particular, and for mankind in general, if such a college course would be obligatory, as it is in Europe. Physicians and lawyers who graduate from a good classical college before they enter the law or medical school, are generally more successful than those of years ago who could boast of only a three-year course in some inferior medical or law school. The young lawyer, with only a three-year course in some law school, may have known just about enough law to pass an easy examination, but he had not the attainments of another who first went through college and who will command more confidence owing to his learning.

The young doctor who had no other training than the three-year course of some second-rate medical school did, of course, try and practice medicine. These get-there-quick doctors were often more of a help to the undertaker than to their patients.

In this rush of the present day, we are inclined to be superficial. To spend ten or more years in studies is too long a time for most men. Hence we have so many quacks in the professions.

When I went to college, I bought most of my books at a second-hand book store. To my great surprise I found most Latin and Greek authors almost in a new condition. In most cases I would find the first five, eight or ten pages somewhat the worse for wear, but all the rest of the book was as good as new. Evidently they had been the possessions of the many who made a trial at college and gave it up.

A little knowledge is a dangerous thing. To have only a slight knowledge of one science or another may prove a drawback for the whole life. The conceited man with a little learning can be more kinds of a fool in less time than the man of the backwoods who has only a district school training.

If you firmly believe that a college education will be of benefit to you, make sure you are right, and then go ahead with a push and a good will. A college education, whether commercial or classical, will be the best gift that is in parents' power to give to you.

And if you do go to college, bear in mind it is to develop your mind and to make you capable of success in your aim of life. Remember, too, that knowledge should not engender pride. The brightest minds the world ever knew were simple and unpretentious. Never for a moment think that, because you have an armful of books, you are by this very fact a better boy than the one you see going to work with a lunchbox in his hand. The boy with his little lunchbox may someday be a greater and a better man than you, in spite of all your learning.

CHAPTER XII. VOCATION AND IDEALS

These talks on vocation would not be complete without some consideration of the importance of ideals. Almighty God endowed us with memory, will and understanding, and in His infinite wisdom He deemed it advisable to give to these three powers of our soul the support of the gift of imagination. Hence every boy-- excepting the good-for-nothing variety--has his great ideal. His main idea, his principal thought will center around some thing or person connected with the vocation he has in mind. One day, he, too, hopes and desires to reach the goal others have reached before him. This is his ideal.

A locomotive, a steamship, a fire-engine, the uniform of a soldier, farm life, a doctor's, merchant's or priest's vocation, or any of the other thousand and one callings are as many ideals for as many boys. Whatever the ideal may be, the boy thinks and thinks of that only. He will imagine countless cases and emergencies and picture to himself how he would act in the various circumstances. His mind will come back to all these problems frequently and seriously.

The boy who wants to be a computer engineer thinks there is nothing finer than working a computer. His only surprise is that others do not share his sentiment. While another boy would grow tired and disgusted with all the many technical names of the various types of software, he thinks there is nothing grander than that study. Where another boy would get weary of figuring out the writing of the various programs with mathematical precision, he would rather miss a meal than give up the problem.

His whole life is wrapped up in this one ideal--a computer.

This boy knows, too, that it will require much hard work before he will be given the run of a software division. But he knows likewise that with every design he will have to draw he will come nearer to his ideal. This one thought encourages him, makes his work light and agreeable and makes him think that his work is the grandest work on earth.

The very fact that almighty God has given us imagination should be the reason for urging us to use it properly. Imagination need not make dreamers of us, forgetting the reality of life, our work and purpose. Properly trained and rightly directed, it is of incalculable benefit to us. It helps us to overcome the enormous difficulties we meet with in following out the holy Will of God--our vocation.

Did you ever notice a little girl playing with her doll? The little girl imagines that her doll is alive. Her doll must eat and drink and sleep. Then, again, the girl pretends her doll is sick and she takes care of her sick doll as though she were a real mother to that doll. Why is that girl so fond of her doll? It may be nothing but a bundle of rags. The reason she spends days and days with that bundle of rags is that her own mother, taking such tender care of her, is her ideal. She, too, wants to be a mother, thinking there is nothing better or nicer or grander than her mother. And in order to be a mother she must find something smaller and more helpless than herself upon which she may shower the same affection that she receives from her own mother. As she is told to be quiet, to sleep, to eat or drink, she thinks she must make the doll keep quiet, must sing the doll to sleep, and, if it should get sick, give it the same tender care the real mother gives. You might offer this little girl genuine diamonds and a string of pearls, she would never for a moment think of giving that bundle of rags in exchange for them. That doll has more value in her sight because it embodies an ideal. Now, our ideals may, at times, be nothing more or better than such a lifeless bundle of rags. Perhaps they may never be realized. Nevertheless we treat them as seriously as the little girl treats her doll.

As a rule, the higher we aim, the greater will be the obstacles that we must overcome. You may have determined upon some calling and you find everything against you. Your parents may not approve of your choice, you may not have the means in sight to carry out your plans, your boyhood friends may laugh at you for trying to climb higher than they would dare--if it were not for your ideal keeping your hope alive you would give up the struggle.

Talking of trials and obstacles that are set in our way at the start of life I must tell you of the experience of a boy whose one ideal was machinery. As soon as he was' old enough to work, he found work with some machinist. Nothing else suited him as well as that. An over-anxious mother, having heard and read of a number of accidents in which machinists were injured or killed, was not at all willing to let him learn this trade. According to her idea there was nothing nicer or cleaner than clerking in some department store. But the boy, having machinery on his brain, as his mother put it, was finally permitted to follow his inclination. He was by no means satisfied with simply learning the A. B. C. of the trade; he wanted to know all that could be known. He read books on machinery and soon knew more about the nature of forces than his master. He began constructing models of new machines and worked hard and faithfully. His boss, seeing that he could teach

77

him nothing more, though he disliked losing him, got him a place in some big shop. After a few years, this boy, now a young man, had changed the looks of that entire shop. By the models he had constructed he showed the firm that their machinery was behind the times. After a thorough test, the firm was convinced that the young man was right and he was told to go ahead. Old machinery was replaced by more modern motors, and the work of the firm thereafter was done at a great saving of time and labor. One day it happened that a professor of engineering at some university came to visit the head of the firm. The professor was shown through the plant. It was natural for him to take a great interest in the new machinery, and its simplicity and practicability astonished him. So the professor asked: "From which engineering school did your man graduate?" "Why," replied the head of the firm, "the young man never saw the inside of a college." The professor thought it could not be possible, but after being introduced to the young man, he had to believe what he heard and he warmly congratulated the young man upon his great success.

A boy who has no ideal will not amount to very much. He lacks courage and perseverance. He is without an aim in life, and aiming at nothing, he will accomplish nothing. He may feel like doing something or being somebody, but he makes no serious or painstaking effort, and when he realizes that he is a failure he will blame everything and everybody but himself for it. We find such people among tramps, loafers and cranks, and among socialists and anarchists. They should not blame the world, or man, or God, but themselves, that they are human wrecks. Their indolence, their lack of purpose, of aim and perseverance, their lack of an ideal, their hatred of real work, has made them wrecks on the ocean of life. But as it is in human nature to put the blame for our misfortunes upon others, so these unhappy people blame others, where they should blame only themselves.

Therefore, boys, have your ideals! Weave a halo of light around the trade or profession you wish to follow. Look up to the lives of great men who had their ideals, as you have yours. The highest positions in life fell often to those who, as boys, had little or no chance of getting an education. Pope Sixtus V, as a boy, had poor prospects. He drove hogs. St. Patrick was a slave boy. One of our presidents was a mule-driver along the Miami Canal. But all of them had lofty ideals and did not remain what they were.

One day, a Franciscan Father, who had lost his way, sought direction from a little boy who was driving hogs. The boy answered all the questions nicely, and was so polite and showed so much good sense that the priest took a great deal of interest in him. Learning that the boy's parents were poor and that he wished to become a priest, the Father took charge of him, brought him to the convent to study and the poor boy was made a priest. He succeeded so wonderfully in the trust placed in him, that he rose higher and higher, and in course of time he was elected pope, and took the name of Sixtus V.

Our Holy Father, Pius X., was likewise the child of poor parents. Little did he think, when he went to school, that one day he was to hold the highest rank on earth. But he had a lofty ideal. His ideal was to become a faithful and zealous priest. It cost him many efforts and trials, hardships and sacrifices; but that ideal was before him and he overcame all obstacles. He preserved this same ideal during his priestly life. Now he has been raised to the highest honor and dignity a man can receive, a canonized saint. He was the faithful and zealous high-priest, the Vicar of Christ according to the heart of God.

The life of every great man offers us a lesson in showing us how ideals should be fostered and carried out.

Pick up the life of any of the saints, the life of any of the great men of the world, of this or any other country and you will learn that it was the lofty ideals they upheld that made them great. Reading history, you can likewise learn how men will fall when they lose sight of their ideals. Benedict Arnold forgot his great ideal of patriotism. Like Judas, he became a traitor. You find monuments erected in honor of all the heroes of the Revolution; but the name of this one traitor is never mentioned. His name and honor would have never died had he not turned a traitor. He forgot his country and his ideal, and now his name is an object of contempt.

In one of the halls at West Point, every American general has a memorial tablet inscribed in his honor. Among that number there is one blank tablet. Visitors are told that that tablet was to have been reserved for Benedict Arnold had he not turned traitor. It is kept blank to show that his name should be forgotten. And like him, many have miserably failed, because they lost sight of the ideal they once had.

Remember, then, how important it is for you to hold fast to your ideals. God and the world place great confidence and great hopes in you. Do not disappoint them. In our own grand country success is open to every boy. It is open to you, if you but try.

CHAPTER XIII. FORMATION OF CHARACTER

Who is there that does not enjoy a few days out in the country during summer time? To see the fields ready for harvest, to see the trees laden with fruit so that the branches must be propped up to keep them from breaking down with the weight of the fruit they hold. Pleasing though this sight may be, it all is the result of hard work. In spring the farmer must be out in the fields plowing, cultivating and sowing. The fruit trees must be trimmed and sprayed. Had the farmer been careless and idle, the fertile fields would be desolate wastes; the fruit trees now laden with fruit would be bare. The farmer, then, cannot expect a plentiful harvest unless he works faithfully in the spring.

In a similar way, our life is divided into seasons. Youth is the springtime of life. Unless you are busy now, your summer of ripe manhood and your winter of old age will be dismal failures. A few years hence you will be young men. It will not, however, do to be men in looks only, and mere children in actions. To be nothing but an overgrown baby is nothing to be proud of. The fact is, we have such over-grown babies. Some boys grow to young manhood without developing their character. As none of you want to be overgrown babies, you will have to develop your character.

Cement, before placed into its mold, can be given any kind of shape. But after it has been placed into its mold it becomes hard as stone.

At the present time, your minds and hearts are soft and pliable, but you will be fashioned after the mold you will select. You will become fixed and set in your ways for better or worse. It is useless to try and give the cement block another shape or size. It will be equally useless to try to give your heart and mind a different cast after you are once set in your ways. From this, then, you will see how important it is that our hearts and minds are given a proper training. If a serious fault is committed in that regard all the efforts in the world may not suffice to remedy it.

This suitable training of mind and heart we call developing, or building up the character. We speak of good and bad characters in as much as this training was either good or bad. We may speak of a person as being a grand or lovely character because his goodness of heart and mind outweighs everything else. Of others we may speak as being bad or dangerous characters because they are always inclined to do wrong. The thief, the drunkard, the liar, the backbiter, or the unchaste person, such people are called bad or dangerous characters, and with very good reason.

Developing character, to a great extent, may be likened to the work of the architect. He first sees the building in his mind. Then, after he has fully thought out the plans, he brings them to paper. The masons receive their plans and specifications and are told how the various stones or bricks must be placed. The mason may not realize the greatness of the work. It is not necessary. All he has to do is to make his work agree with the plans before him. The beauty of the building will then take care of itself. All he must do is to put up the bare walls; others will finish the work.

In forming your character, another has made the plans long before you ever thought of character. The plans for your character were drawn up by none other than almighty God Himself. He gave them to a helper to have your character built up for you. The Catholic Church is this helper and she does this work of building up your character by her teaching, by her parish school, her societies, and, last but not least, by the aid of your parents. You yourself are the workman. As the bricklayer may not realize the magnitude of the work as he lays stone upon stone, so neither may you realize the loftiness of the character you are building up by following the plans of God. Your early instructions at home, your training in school, your instructions prior to your first Holy Communion, they are as so many stones and bricks. With them you have laid the foundation of a living temple of the Most High. And now that the foundation has been laid, you must not think of stopping. As members of the Church, you continue this building up of your character. The conferences, the rules of the Church, daily prayer, the frequent reception of the Sacraments are as many more building stones. If you place all these stones as they should be placed according to the plans of our heavenly Father, you may be sure you are building for yourself a fine character; a character pleasing to God, to His holy angels and the saints.

Here again, you find an explanation of the purpose of the Church. Its aim is not to get a nickel or a dime out of your spending money, but to help you systematically to build up your character. Boys that do not belong to the Church miss more benefits for their later years of life than they may realize at the present time. And, what is more, the loss is lasting. The future will never return to you your youth.

The masons having finished the bare walls of a building, others come along to finish the work and make the building complete. To finish the building of your character according to the plans of God, you must carry out

83

all His directions to your best ability. This finishing of your character building is carried out in a two-fold way.

With original sin, we inherited the inclination towards evil. This inclination is towards evil in general and some certain sins in particular. It is sometimes easier for us to lie than to tell the truth; easier to be idle than work; easier to stay away from church than to attend it; easier to be self-willed and stubborn than obedient. This is the general inclination towards evil, and it is bad enough, but there is still more reason for apprehension. There is the particular inclination towards some certain sins, some pet vices of which persons are guilty more often than of any other sin. Some certain sin is their specialty. One boy may be habitually foul-mouthed, another naturally lazy, another abusive, another quick-tempered and given to hatred and revenge, another indifferent towards religion, and so on.

We need never think of building up a good character according to the plans of God if we permit such pet sins to grow stronger. Before you are aware of it, your youthful hearts and minds will be set in their ways and then it will be too late to mend. The warfare you must wage against evil inclinations is different from any other. When two nations are at war they will stop fighting after they have had enough of it. Peace is declared and they enter upon agreements as though there had never been the least difference between them. If we could but say the same of our warfare against our evil inclinations! If we could only say: "Now this must stop. You have been beaten fairly and honestly so often that to fight longer would be useless." Alas, we can never say this. This battle will only end with our last breath. No victory of arms is so crushing as to force this enemy to surrender. We may gain a glorious victory and the very next moment be attacked again. We may gain a thousand victories, but lose the last battle and we are lost forever. For that very reason our dear Savior said repeatedly, "Watch and pray."

Therefore, to hope to crush our inclination to evil with one mighty blow would, indeed, be foolish. It can never be done. To build up our character systematically, we must aim the strongest blows at our pet sin. That means strengthening our weak point. Frequent Confession will show you your pet sin without much effort. And this pet vice must be stopped by all means, if you wish to be victorious at the end. With the grace of God we can overcome evil inclinations. Without Christ we can do nothing; with Him, everything.

Sad though the aspect of a predominant sin may be, there is the consolation that we have also an inclination for some certain virtue. Our heavenly Father has so shaped our disposition that some certain virtue will appeal more to us, and seem easier to practice, than another virtue. Your training and environment have much to do with this. This idea we see brought out in the lives of the saints. The saints, it is true, practiced all virtues, still they made one particular virtue their specialty, and practiced that in a higher and more heroic manner than other virtues. Where St. Francis excelled in humility, St. Elizabeth of Hungary excelled in patience. St. Francis of Sales excelled in meekness of heart, St. Aloysius excelled in purity, St. Wenzeslaus excelled in zeal for holy faith. And, so, we might go through the entire list of saints and find each one of them excelling in some certain virtue, as star differs from star in brilliancy.

We, too, have the germ of some certain virtue that should be a part of us. Some certain virtue will appeal strongly to us; we will prefer it to others. That is exactly the very virtue we should try to cultivate. One boy, for instance, is very charitable, always willing to help, even though it

85

may inconvenience him. Another boy is particularly modest and abhors the least improper word. Another is inclined towards prayer. Another is zealous for the glory of God and the salvation of souls by bringing back to the true fold boys that had gone beyond the influence of even the pastor. Another boy is very zealous for the holy faith, defending it fearlessly where others are afraid of saying a word. Whatever the virtue may be to which you feel yourself drawn, practice it faithfully. The other virtues will follow in due time.

Our character would, furthermore, be developed only insufficiently if we tried merely to avoid evil. As we are unable to overcome evil with one blow so neither will we be able to practice all the virtues at once. To develop the good disposition we have, we must practice the virtue to which we are most drawn. Having mastered the first virtue, the one we admire most, we begin practicing other virtues till in the fullness of God's own time, we have finished the building up of our character and receive a crown in exchange for it.

Character is to disposition what vocation is to work. In each, we should endeavor to draw out and develop the best that is in us. In choosing our vocation we try to use our talents and gifts according to the holy will of God. In developing character, we try with His grace to overcome evil impulses and practice the opposite virtues, so that we may at all times think and speak and act in a way pleasing to God.

CHAPTER XIV. THE IMPORTANCE OF TRIFLES

Many boys, in building up character, overlook the importance of trifles. In their boyish eagerness, they will strive only for what seems big and important to their minds. All matters that do not come up to these great things of life are considered of no value. Yet life is made up of a chain of trifles, and as a chain is as strong only as its weakest link, the most carefully made chain will amount to nothing if it has one weak link. So may our life be ruined by one trifle.

No man is made a saint or sinner in one day. The progress in either direction is slow; so slow, in fact, that it is almost imperceptible. Trifles pave the way to virtues and to vices.

One unkind word may not mean so much, it may be only a trifle. But if it is followed by others, there will soon be a fault-finding, nagging and quarrelsome disposition. And that is by no means a trifle. One little theft may be the outcome of some boyish prank or frolic; as, for instance, boys will go into a field or orchard to help themselves. Of course, they would not for a moment want to appear as thieves. Boys do not call it stealing when they enter the field or orchard of another man. Now, however, if you go to prison and ask any of the convicts, they might tell you, if they wished to speak the truth that their thefts started in just such little pranks. So does a jocose lie not mean very much. It is a trifle, people will say. Still, lies will grow. The backbiter, the slanderer, the murderer of fair reputations, they all began by telling "white lies."

Rightly speaking, there are no trifles.

To bring this lesson of the importance of trifles home to you, I can do nothing better than give you an example from life. Some years ago, a certain old man became a regular caller at the rectory. He was a smooth talker, and there was something about him, his way of speech, and his general bearing, that made me feel that he must have seen better days. This old man would, for a time, come once a week with a supply of lead pencils and notebooks, selling them at about double the price one would ordinarily have to give for them. Still, because he seemed poor, I did not feel inclined to bargain with him, because he seemed to make an attempt at supporting himself, instead of depending entirely upon charity. Then, again, months would pass, when the old man would not call. All of a sudden he would bob up again, with pencils and little notebooks, and opportunities of practicing charity. One day I asked him his name. He muttered some words I could not understand, and left the house. From that day on I never saw him again.

Sometime after, the daily papers told of an old man having been caught forging a note. The description of the man tallied exactly with my frequent visitor. Before sentence was pronounced, the court asked whether he had anything to say. The words of that old man were printed in full, because they conveyed a profound lesson. He stated that he had given a fictitious name, because he had agreed not to humble the name of his family. Then he told the story of his boyhood. Being the son of wealthy parents, he thought work was a disgrace. At school he was too lazy to study. To get along with his class, he copied his lessons from others. All this was overlooked, because he was the pet at home. In the course of time, he went to college. There he was caught at cheating and dismissed in disgrace.

Forging lessons at school was a trifle in comparison to cheating in an examination at college, but that trifle led him to disgrace.

His dishonest practice of cheating the teacher at school did not remain a trifle. It grew larger at college and still larger in later years. He became a cheater and forger, and there is hardly a prison on this side of the Mississippi River that did not harbor him at one time or another, At the end of his sad story, he cursed his parents for having been too lenient with him; he cursed his teacher; he cursed himself, and the day of his birth; he cursed the day of his first theft. His tragic story deeply moved his hearers, and they looked on him with pity as he was led away to imprisonment.

By this time, this unhappy man may have faced another judge. Let us hope that God's mercy was his in abundance.

This old man might have been highly respected. His fellow citizens might have given him offices of trust and honor. He might have had a beautiful house. He might have had a happy family, a good wife, and loving children. But, instead of all that, his life was a life of misery, And all the misery of that old man was the consequence of a trifle. Had he been honest enough as a boy to consider the forging of lessons a dishonorable act, he would not have been guilty of copying examination papers in college. Had he passed through college successfully, and had he kept a clean record, he would have been an honor to any profession. It was a trifle that brought about his downfall, and you may go to all the prisons and halfway houses, asking the Inmates the reason of their downfall, and they will tell you a similar story. Many of these unhappy people had homes as happy and as sweet as yours; they were at one time as well-meaning and as well-disposed as you are today. That, however, did not prevent them from falling into the snare of trifles.

Never think for a moment that you can taste of the forbidden fruit just enough to know what it tastes like, thinking yourselves strong enough to withstand later on. You will not. Others thought so, too. They fell.

As some trifles lead to crime, others lead to virtue. And, although it is natural for well-meaning boys to maintain high ideals, it is equally natural for them to overlook the trifles that lead up to them. Hence, the highest praise a successful man may receive will be to be called a master of detail, a master of trifles. To master trifles means to master one's self. Success is only found in mastering trifles.

To say a kind word for an absent one when others speak ill of him, may not mean much in itself; but every such word helps to build up a noble character. To do a little favor, especially when one knows that he will receive nothing but ingratitude in return, may not be more than a trifle of itself; but each act of this kind helps to make our character lofty. Not a day passes but offers us countless opportunities of doing good. These actions may be nothing but trifles as far as the world judges, but each and every one of them helps us to become more noble and virtuous.

No doubt, you have seen mosaic floors put together with thousands of little stones. One of these little stones will not make a showing. You must have a great number of them, place them side by side, according to a definite plan, and you get those wonderful pictures and designs produced with mosaic work.

In a similar manner, our life is made up of trifles, which, if placed carefully after a good plan, will make life a success.

Misplacing one single little stone of a mosaic composition may spoil the effect of the design. So, in like manner, one trifle may oftentimes undo a life work. We would, no doubt, take better care of trifles, if we could but know the far-reaching result they have. The future only can show us the relation and proportion of the various trifles to each other and their effect upon our life. It is only when we look back upon the past and recall the various little instances and trifles, that have had a bearing upon our course of action, that we begin to realize their importance.

I remember an instance in which a trifle was the means of a boy becoming a priest. This boy had the desire of being a priest, but his parents were opposed to his vocation. It happened that the pastor was sick and the assistant priest gave the instruction to the first communicants. The lesson was Holy Orders, a study which for this boy held great interest. When the priest returned to the rectory his pastor asked him how he liked the class. "Very well," he replied, "but one of the boys should become a priest. This boy not only answered every question about Holy Orders, but he explained the answers so intelligently that he evidently is very fond of the subject." Through the help of that assistant priest, this boy became a priest. One trifle, little though it seemed in itself, was the key to his success in gaining the object of all his desires.

Therefore, do not lose sight of trifles. A trifle, be it ever so small--if it leads to sin--must be shunned. It is enough for us to know that just such trifles have brought ruin and disgrace upon others. Do you wish your lives to be held up as a warning to others?' Will it not be far better for the world and ourselves if our lives serve as a model for others to imitate? It is advisable and necessary to keep our gaze on the lofty ideals. But, at the same time, it is indispensable to look where we are walking so that we should not fall. What would it profit us if we gazed at the stars and by a misstep fall into an abyss!

As you should shun the trifles leading to sin, so you must profit by the trifles that lead to good. Every day, some little trifle will help to make you more perfect in virtue, and more pleasing and lovable in the sight of God. Unless we are faithful in little things, we shall not be faithful in things of importance.

CHAPTER XV. THE MANLY BOY

Now that we have considered the building up of character and the importance of trifles, let us consider some of the usual traits of boys, good traits and bad traits, in a particular way. The conferences upon these traits will show us the plan of our character building in what architects would call detail drawings.

The trait that may be considered one of the most important is manliness. Hence, we will, for today, consider the manly boy.

There is hardly a word in our language that is given so many meanings, many of them mistaken, as the word "manliness".

Some consider as "manly" the boy who has a chip on his shoulder from morning to night, spoiling for a fight at all times. Such a boy is very careful in sizing up his antagonist, and, when he thinks he has found an easy mark, goes for him without mercy. And, because he can overcome so many weaker ones he is admired by many as a manly boy. Others there are who see manliness in stubbornness. Some boys are as stubborn as mules. To argue with such stubborn boys does as little good as reasoning with a stone wall. And such stubbornness, that will not listen to reason, is looked upon by some as manliness.

True manliness, however, does not consist in any of these things. So far as bodily strength is concerned, many

93

animals are stronger than man. Yet no man will, for that reason, consider such animals superior to man. Strength is a gift that God has distributed among men very unevenly. And, often, it happens that giants in bodily strength are dwarfs in regard to brains. As a rule, great scholars and artists would not last for one round with a prize-fighter. Neither can prize-fighters usually pass a high school examination. The man with the strength of an ox may not have an ounce of manliness about him; he may be nothing but a brute.

As manliness does not consist in mere bodily strength, neither is it mere stubbornness of the will. The boy who wants his way, even when his judgment tells him he is wrong, is not, for that reason, a manly boy. Indeed, he is anything but that. We find stubbornness in mules, but we do not for that reason hold them up to the world as models of manliness.

In what, then, does true manliness consist? True manliness consists in strength of the soul, rather than in bodily strength or stubbornness.

Such strength of the soul will influence and guide the will to do what is right, no matter what the consequences may be. Hence, when we speak of a manly boy, we do not mean a young prizefighter, or a bull-headed boy, but a boy who lives up to his convictions, always thinking and saying and doing what his conscience tells him is right.

We will, for the present, leave religious convictions out of consideration, because that subject will be treated fully when we come to consider our duties to our holy Faith. For the present, we will consider strength of soul in our everyday conduct.

A crowd of boys has gathered and they are talking about an absent boy. One says this, another says that, and nothing very complimentary. All have their little hammers out, knocking unmercifully. Have you the heart to speak up and say; "Boys, you should not talk that way. If what you say is true, you have no right to expose his faults, and if what you say is not true, you are guilty of slander." "Oh, I cannot speak up like that," you may say; "why, the whole crowd will go for me, if I should call them to task in such a way."

If such is your way of looking at it, you are not a manly boy.

You will permit a wrong to go on for fear that some might take offense at your doing what in the sight of God and man would be just and right. A manly boy will understand that such boys can never be true friends. If they talk in this manner about others what will prevent them from speaking about you as soon as you have turned your back? And if by being manly enough to stand up for right a boy loses the friendship of such companions he must know the loss will not be great.

Suppose you have been guilty of a wrongful act for which another is made to suffer. Are you manly enough to own up to your own bad conduct, or are you going to allow another to suffer for your misdeed? If you are not manly, you will have no feeling for the innocent sufferer and, rejoicing that suspicion does not point your way, you may even try all you can to shift the blame upon others, and possibly employ unfair means to shield yourself while another suffers innocently for your bad conduct. Such behavior is not manly. If you own up to your guilt, you will be a little hero in the sight of all that know you. A great many faults are overlooked if we own up to them manfully. On the other hand, to permit others to suffer for what you have been guilty of is mean and cowardly. As the truth is bound to come out some time, cowardice will be made known, and then you need not expect pity or mercy, because you do not deserve any.

Years ago, out West, an innocent man was sentenced to death. Circumstantial evidence was so strong that he was declared guilty of having murdered two girls. The unhappy man, when placed under the gallows, declared that as he was about to stand face to face with a higher judge, and as he would never think of appearing before God with a lie upon his lips, he would affirm with his last breath that he was innocent of the crime and that he died for the crime another had committed. A few years later a relative of these two girls died. On his deathbed he confessed that he had murdered the girls and that he had sworn falsely in order to fasten the blame upon the innocent man. This cowardly murderer had saved his reputation for a short time. He was able, by swearing falsely, to deceive the judges of this world. But, now he had to appear before another judge who could not be deceived. He could not fool God. What reputation did this cowardly murderer leave behind for himself and his family? And an innocent man had to die a shameful death for this cowardly murderer, an innocent family had suffered disgrace.

Manliness is also manifested in fearlessly saying our mind when we are thoroughly convinced of the right.

It is impossible to avoid all misunderstandings and all of us are liable to make mistakes. Nor are we able to fathom all the thoughts or intentions of others when, at times, we do not even know our own minds. For that reason we are sometimes likely to see slights and insults where none were intended. We know very little of the troubles and sorrows others may have. We cannot expect that the faces

96

of our friends should always be happily smiling when they see us.

To illustrate this, let us say, two boys, James and John, are chums. They have known each other since they were children and now they go to work in the same shop. One morning James had some little trouble at home. He was so taken up with the thought that he did not hear John say good morning to him. That made John wonder greatly. He tried to think what James could be angry about and finally thought: if he cannot return my greeting, well, I shall not bother him hereafter. The next morning James had forgotten his little trouble. He spoke to John but John had no answer for him. Then James begins to worry, wondering what went wrong with John and resolved never to speak to John until he speaks first. Now the two boys are at odds. Neither knows the reason why. They avoid the company of each other, suspecting each other of things of which neither is guilty. Neither of them knows why their staunch friendship has come to a sudden end.

You will admit, boys, that such conduct is certainly foolish. That James may have had some little trouble at home, is perfectly natural. That the thought of it must have worried him and let other things escape his notice is equally natural. Now, if John had been a manly lad he would have said at the first chance "What's the matter, James, I said good morning to you and you never answered. Something must have gone wrong else you would not act like that." And then James would have told of his trouble and both would be the same fast friends. And if James had been manly enough the following day, he would have asked John why he did not answer. Then John could have explained. But neither of the two was manly enough to speak up and as a result they are enemies, perhaps, for life.

97

What use is there of a watch that will not keep correct time? That watch may bring us into all kinds of trouble if we must do work that demands punctuality. What is the use of having the will, when we are afraid of acting the way we should.

You cannot keep up bodily strength without proper exercise. Neither can you acquire, nor keep up, strength of soul without proper training. What dumbbells, punching bags and Indian clubs are for the strengthening of the body, that is what conscience will do for the soul.

And since you wish to be manly boys, everyone of you, exercise your soul by following your conscience. Conscience is the voice of God. Never think or say or do anything for which your conscience would reprimand you. Remember, you may have the strength of a young lion, and the stubbornness of a mule, without having the least trace of manliness.

Always think and speak and act as your conscience tells you that you should and you will be manly. The world despises nothing more than a coward. And, unless you follow the dictation of your conscience, you will belong to that class of people so heartily despised by every right thinking man.

CHAPTER XVI. THE SNEAKY BOY

If you would meet with a snake on your path, you would either run away as fast as your feet could carry you, or you would try and render the reptile powerless to do harm. The sort of human being usually called a sneak causes the same feeling of disgust that one has at the sight of a snake. And, although it would be against all laws, human and divine, to kill such a person, a good tongue lashing or even a good, old-fashioned beating may be in order where flight would be ill-advised. (Editor's note: Originally written before WWI, attitudes have changed and beatings are not considered a choice today.)

You know how the sneak starts out. At school he is the "goodie-goodie boy" so far as appearances go. In spite of his pretense, he will be ready for the dirtiest work, provided he believes he will not get caught at it. He knows and practices mean tricks at the expense of others; he will steal and copy his lessons. He will try and appear bold and masterful to be called a manly lad; and timid and humble, if he can pass off as a model of obedience and meekness.

If some other boy should try to play an innocent and harmless joke, the sneak will go and tell on him. He will endeavor to get into the good graces of the teachers, in order to have more influence, and will be chummy with unsuspecting victims to harm them all the easier. As he grows older he will seek to become the pets of those that are older than he. Through their influence he will try and take advantage of those of his own age. And so he will go on until found out.

And, then, people will be shocked to think that this nice boy went wrong. Why, he was so good, so pious; why, he would not hurt a fly!

Really, however, there need be no surprise over the fate of such sneaks. They may be successful in concealing their wicked designs for a time; but, sooner or later, they are bound to be found out. Feel the paw of a cat. How smooth and soft it feels. Let the cat get up its temper and you will feel the ugly claws that are concealed in the pretty paw. The sneak is like such a paw. His talk is velvety and smooth, he appears as harmless as an innocent kitten, but there is malice concealed under the bland exterior.

As a rule, it does not take long to find out the sneak. Deception is so hard to play consistently that the deceiver often gets caught in his own traps; weary of wearing the mask continually, he shows his face in unguarded moments.

To protect yourselves against the mischief of the sneak, it will be necessary to lay down three rules for your conduct. In complying with them you may save yourselves untold worry and misery.

(1) Pay no attention to flattery or smooth talk. No one will ever think of flattering you unless he sees in it some benefit to himself. The sneak, in telling you of your great strength, your good looks, or of your brilliant talents, may have a hard time keeping his face straight; he does not mean a word of it. But, being a master of smooth talk he plays his part with great apparent sincerity. If you are easy you will believe him and give him credit for knowing enough to appreciate your talents, your looks or your strength, and

you feel that you have gained another true friend, one that really gives you credit for what you are and what you know.

As soon as the sneak has gained your confidence he will begin to make use of you to further his own purposes. There may be some dirty work for him to do; too dirty perhaps for himself. And he will get you to do it for him. He will manage to make it so agreeable for you, you will never suspect that you are his tool and his fool until it is too late.

Never listen to flattery, therefore. It is not meant for your benefit. Granted that what the flatterer says may be partly true, even then we should not find pleasure in it. The swan is a beautiful animal to look at as it swims proudly on a placid lake. But its feet are clumsy and ugly. There is so much imperfection in the best of men that flattery is always out of place. Flattery and truth are strangers since the fall of Adam.

Talking of flattery reminds me of a man who was governor of one of our states. For a time he was even mentioned as a presidential candidate. He had been a poor boy and worked his way up from the work-bench. He led a spotless life, was honest and fearless.

He was elected mayor of one of our large cities, and finally elected governor of the state. His reputation for honesty was known throughout the land. There was not enough money in the world to bribe him. He was fearless in enforcing the law, no matter how powerful the culprit. As great as he was, he was not without his weakness. His enemies found it out. This man, whom money could not buy, was open to flattery. By skillful flattery, one could get anything out of him. Some scoundrels made use of flattery to gain his confidence and good will; they were given appointments of trust and responsibility. These men had no love for the governor, their assurances of admiration and devotion were lies.

In the course of time they managed to cheat the state out of hundreds of thousands of dollars and to all appearances it seemed as though this upright and fearless governor had been the partner of these low grafters. For was it not he who had helped them to get these positions of trust and responsibility? Thus discredited and disgraced, the governor left the country when his term had expired and died shortly after. It is said that he died of a broken heart. Those he had considered his faithful friends had betrayed him and caused his disgrace and ruin.

Had this man been as callous to flattery as he had been to threats and bribery, he might even have occupied the presidential chair, with credit to himself and honor to his country. But his weakness for flattery put a sudden end to his usefulness, and his last days were spent in sorrow and anguish.

(2) Never allow anyone to talk to you about the faults of others. The same person will go and talk to others about your faults, true or imaginary.

The sneak will come to you and tell you what so-and-so has said about you. Perhaps it is true; often it is not. At any rate, he will get you worked up to a proper pitch of indignation and then you begin telling him what you know about this same so-and-so. That is exactly what the sneak wants. Then he goes to so-and-so, and tells him what you said. Very likely the story is improved upon for greater effect. As a result, you may have lost a true friend. Worse yet, there may be enmity resulting in all kinds of spiteful doings, and the sneak rejoices and chuckles at the quarreling. If you wish to save yourself trouble and worry, never pay attention to gossip, and never permit yourself to be drawn into it.

(3) The third rule to govern your actions in guarding against the sneak is this: Never allow yourself to expose the hidden faults of others.

Like a peddler, going from house to house with all kinds of articles, the sneak goes from one to the other peddling gossip. He will give you all the gossip you want to hear in exchange for the gossip you will give him. The sneak has studied his part well and he will know how to handle you to get the information he wants. He will put questions and make suggestions so cleverly that, before you are aware of it, he has trapped you in some manner. And then you will either tell him the rest, or he guesses it. It will not take him long to put two and two together, and, with what you have said and what he knows, everything is now in readiness to make trouble.

The sneak may find it hard to win you by flattery; he may not be able to get your ear for his gossip; but this third rule, never to permit yourself to reveal the hidden faults of others, will be the one he will seek to make you break for his benefit.

The reason why this trick of the sneak is so dangerous is that it appeals so much to human nature. Say what you will, in your heart of hearts you are conscious of your faults and shortcomings. We are all alike in this. We hope that our faults may remain hidden to our dying day. We want to keep them hidden by all means. To keep them covered up, we will always try to appear at our best. If, by speaking of the faults of others, we can keep our own reputation from close scrutiny we are tempted to sacrifice charity so that we may appear in a better light.

The one weapon we have against the sneak is-manliness. Observe and practice these three rules that I have just laid down, in a manly way. You will then be feared by the sneak, and admired by every honest and well-meaning boy.

In dealing with the sneak, it will not pay to mince words. Let him know that you can look clear through him; let him know what you think of him and of his methods.

As for yourselves, be at all times candid. Never be guilty of underhanded methods in your dealings. Never make the business of other people your business. If you properly mind your own it will keep you busy for the remainder of your life.

Time will come for the sneak when all his resources will be exhausted; when all that know him will have realized his mean character. When the enemies he has made will accomplish his exposure, then the sneak will reap what he sowed. All his life long he has sown discord, hatred, envy, jealousy and revenge. And so he will reap the enmity and retaliation of those he has harmed, and the contempt of all right-minded people.

CHAPTER XVII. THE BOY WHO SAVES

It used to be, when a boy began to work, he usually turned his earnings, little though they be, over to his parents. They in turn, if they could do so, gave him a certain amount of these wages as spending money. This custom, as observed in most families, is very reasonable. On the one hand, it is the boy's duty to help his parents along, not as though he could ever repay them, cent for cent and dollar for dollar, for what they have done for him, for that is impossible. It should be done as a mark of gratitude. On the other hand, it is also right that the boy should be given some spending money, because he is no longer a child going to school.

The question now is; what should the boy do with his spending money? Everybody will understand that your spending money cannot amount to very much, because the wages you earn are small. Still, is there any reason why you should be like a little child that runs to the candy store as soon as it has received a dollar? Should you spend all your money in the pleasures of one evening and then feel wretched for the rest of the week because you haven't a cent? Would it not be a far better policy to divide that spending money, allowing yourself a certain part of it each day, and laying something of it aside though it be only a dollar?

It seems as though some boys will never be able to save money. Their money seems to burn a hole through their pockets.

These very boys show, by their way of acting, that there is plenty of truth about the old saying of the fool and his money being soon parted. These boys can hardly realize that in a very few years they will have to depend upon nothing but their own resources. As long as they were children, they found their table furnished them with three square meals; they found a cozy bed to sleep in, and a furnace to keep them warm in winter. They scarcely ever realize that father and mother must provide, by hard work, all these home comforts. And, if by some accident, these boys should be left to themselves they will find out that life is by no means a picnic.

In spite of the fact that ours is a land of plenty, there are every day many people going to bed hungry. Riches and poverty are often next-door neighbors. To consider the various causes of poverty would take us too long a time. But one of the most frequent causes of misery in the midst of plenty is *extravagance*. Some people wish to buy all they see advertised. They want to live and dress as well as others who may earn double their salary or wages. Every show, picnic, excursion, circus must be taken in or they will not be happy. You cannot insult those people worse than by hinting that they ought to live within their income.

Now look at some of the boys and girls earning, perhaps, one hundred or one hundred and fifty dollars a week. All they earn is spent for adornment or pleasure. In case of sickness, there would not be a penny for medicine or doctor bills. Their rings or watches would have to be sent to the pawn shop. If they were to lose their position, they would not know where the money should come from to pay for the next meal. And then, if that happens, people will go and complain of bad luck, instead of mismanagement; they blame the world for the suffering that is entirely their own fault.

To show you the importance of saving I will explain to you two important business rules. The first of them is: It is hard to make money, but still harder to keep it.

You realize how hard you must work to earn a few dollars. You know, also, that with a nickel here and a dime there, your spending money goes faster than you earn it. You hear the grumbler say: "what's the use of saving a few pennies; shouldn't I have any fun at all? Those few pennies I am told to save will not make me rich!" In later years, this same grumbler will probably have the biggest hard-luck story to tell.

Will it pay you to begin saving at the present time? I say; yes! Suppose that on your fourteenth birthday you begin to lay aside a dollar a week and keep it up until you are twenty-one years of age. As the habit to save gets stronger within you, you will put five or ten dollars in your little bank. At the age of twenty-one, that saved money will amount to five hundred dollars or more. That money will be as good as found, because you never really missed it. It is true that this small amount is nothing in comparison to the fortune of a rich man; but for you it will mean a great deal. To you it shows the wisdom of economy and of self-denial. The lesson this saving has taught you is worth vastly more than the amount saved. Those years of constant saving will be the foundation of your future success. Many a time, when you put the few dollars aside, you may have felt like using them for some other purpose. But, with each little amount so put aside, you strengthened your habit of saving; your repeated acts of self-denial became easier in course of time, and, at the age of twenty-one, you will have learned what many others will never learn; namely, that we all must practice economy and self-denial if we wish to be successful, to become independent.

Hence, boys, save a little each week. Divide your spending money so that it will reach for every day of the week and leave something to put aside. Get the habit! Like every other good habit, though it may seem difficult at the start, it will become easier by practice. The habit to save will grow with your income. You will consider it a matter of course to save more when you earn more.

It will be absolutely useless to try and save by fits and starts. Unless it is done systematically, perseveringly, your saving will never be a success. You must make economy and saving a habit. Then you will be sure of having something for a rainy day.

The second important business rule is: *It matters little what you earn; it is what you can lay aside that counts.*

Many boys will not think it worthwhile to save a few dollars a week. That is all nonsense with them. Don't they want their fun? If they have to work so hard, shouldn't they have some pleasure out of it? Others will tell you they cannot think of saving anything at the present time. They are just about keeping even with expenses, but as soon as they get more pay they will begin to save. All this talk is just about as sensible as if a boy would say he will never go near the water until he can swim. No boy can learn how to swim unless he tries real hard, time and again. Nor will a boy learn how to save unless he tries hard, very hard.

How is it that many a man cannot save a cent though he earns two hundred dollars a week, where another man who earns only half of that finds it possible to lay aside two or three dollars a week. The former has kept on saying that he is going to save when he will earn more. His salary has been raised every few years. But as his salary kept growing, he felt he had more needs and wants, and, in trying to provide for them, he was just about able to keep out of debt and nothing more. If that man should ever earn three hundred dollars a week, there would be so many new wants that he would probably need all of it to provide for them.

Many a laborer earning only twenty dollars -a- day is able to lay something aside. Nobody need tell him his salary is small; he knows it. He knows, too, that nobody will look out for him when he is unable to work, and so he divides his money accordingly. He will not rent a house he cannot afford; his living expenses will fit his income; he will have a certain amount set aside for clothing, a little for pleasure-in which the entire family will take part, and what remains is saved. In twenty years it may easily happen that the two hundred-dollar-a-week man will be out of a position and penniless whereas the other, with his little earnings and savings, will own his house and a lot and have a few hundred dollars in the bank for a rainy day.

Which of these two men would you want to be when you are old?

You will prefer to be the man who earned less and was able to save, rather than the other who spent his money as quickly as he got it.

You are now in the period of transition from childhood to manhood. Unless you learn now to save you will never learn it. For the ways of spending money multiply with the number of years.

When you were little, your parents have granted you many a whim. But remember, you are little children no longer. Your parents might have enjoyed many a pleasure for the money spent on you, but they knew they had a duty towards you. Many things they have denied, and still deny themselves, because there were and are hungry mouths at home that must be fed. Now it is your turn to follow this very way of self-denial in little things. In the course of time,

109

you will have to make much greater sacrifices. Get ready to make them at their proper time, by learning to render smaller sacrifices at the present time. Many a show and circus will come to town in later years that you will not be able to see; many an excursion will go up the river and down the river that you will not be able to join; many a merry party you will have to miss; begin to practice self-denial now so that you may become strong when the time of trial comes; begin saving now so that you may acquire the habit of economy, and thrift, without which no one can be successful.

CHAPTER XVIII. THE SPENDTHRIFT

If you ever had to take care of a little child, you know that you could never give it all it wanted. Let a little child see a toy and it will kick and yell till it can get hold of it. That toy, however, will by no means make the child happy. The novelty soon wears off. When it sees another toy, the child will not be satisfied until it can have that new toy. The other has been cast aside. No amount of reasoning will make the child see its folly.

One oftentimes wonders that such small parcels of flesh and bone contain so much greed and self-will. Even before a child is able to speak, he wants to have his way about everything; he wants all that is within sight. And when cake is passed around, he wants the biggest piece. Nothing else will do.

This disposition of greediness grows in children if their wants and desires are not properly curbed. Such a boy grows up with the idea that he is entitled to the best there is, not because he deserves it, but because he wants to have it to satisfy one of his many whims. He has no consideration for the rights of others. His brothers and sisters, his playmates, are not considered. They are expected to give up their share to him, and he becomes ugly if someone puts in a claim to something that he wants for himself. This spoiled boy wants everything he takes a fancy to. All his spending money goes as quickly as he can lay his hands on it. The young spendthrift spends it without any benefit to himself. It could be easier for him to carry water in a sieve than to save even one penny. With these few remarks, my dear boys, you have been given an idea of how the first wicked impulses of a child, unless they are checked in time, will grow from bad to worse; you understand how it is possible that a man may become a spendthrift.

I once knew a bright young man who had been such a spoiled child. He finished his course in some business college. After graduation, he was given an important position with some big wholesale firm. Although hardly twenty years of age, he was made the equal of some, and the superior of others, twice his age. The salary he got in one week was more than many working men get in a month. But he found no difficulty in getting rid of it. It was his one ambition in life to be called a good fellow. He certainly succeeded wonderfully. For a time, he found it hard to gain the good will of his fellow clerks. No little amount of jealousy had to be overcome. His money, however, succeeded, and he became chummy with all the men in the office. After he had bought the good will of these people he became indispensable to them. No jollification, no party or picnic was complete without him. He was the life and soul of every gathering. His stories were the best; so were his cigars and the drinks he ordered for the crowd. He could not walk a block without meeting somebody he knew. The very first question would be: "What will you have?" And then "Have another!" And so day passed after day. After he had been with the firm for a few years, he met with an accident and had to go to a hospital for some operation. Then it was found-to the surprise of all-that he had not saved a single penny. All that was left for him was to be placed in one of the wards for the city charges. His hundreds of friends vanished like smoke. Not a single one even inquired about him. His friends had no time to look him up; they had to find another fool at whose expense they could eat and drink. After many months, that seemed to the unhappy young man like so many years, he was able to leave the hospital. His position with the firm was lost. His former friends knew him no longer. They knew he had no money and were afraid he might ask for a loan if they showed the least sympathy. Without means, without position, he had to take odd jobs. A cheap boarding house was all he could afford. He was down and out. He had neglected his parents in his spendthrift days and now in his distress he was ashamed to write to them, and so he went to pieces as fast as he could. One day, someone called on me to help get up a little purse for this unfortunate young man. We got enough together to clothe him from head to foot, and bought him a railway ticket. What a home-coming it must have been for him to face his parents, broken in body and spirit! What a heartbreaking lesson this was for that young fellow! If he gets another good position, will he be the spendthrift that he has been in the past? The lesson should open his eyes. Experience, however, shows us that the moth will seek the flame no matter how often its wings are singed. It will hover near the fire till finally the fire kills it.

The example of this unhappy young man should be a lesson to you.

A spendthrift is never happy. When he will most need friends and money he will be without both. This young man might have lived like a gentleman and yet put aside thirty or more dollars a month. Instead of that all his money went to show people what a good fellow he was. And that is always expensive. He had been a spoiled child, and that is something hard to get over, no matter how severe the experience.

There are two factors in the making of a spendthrift. One is an inordinate love of self. The selfish boy will want everything in sight. It matters little whether he is entitled to

113

it, or whether he can afford it. His one idea is to get what he wants.

The other is the inordinate desire to be prominent, to become popular. I do not wish to imply that the boy or young man should shun the society of others. A boy should mingle with his kind. He should make himself well liked by being pleasant and agreeable with all, kind and generous, prudent and pure.

A boy without the experience of worldly ways, and still wishing to be popular, may not be aware of the fact that there are two kinds of popularity. There is popularity and then there is popularity! After all, they are not so hard to tell apart. When a boy is popular among the good boys of the parish, when he is a natural leader for all that is good and noble in the Catholic boy, when he gains the esteem and good will of the rest of the Sodality, and others gladly follow him because they recognize his good qualities; then you have the right brand of popularity. That kind of popularity is genuine. It is one of the many rewards of a good, clean life.

If, however, popularity takes its source from the opinions of the evil minded who acclaim him as the best man, who sets up the most drinks and most cigars and tells the worst stories, then we know that it is not the right brand. Popularity, then, is judged by its source. It is either good or bad. To be good and genuine it must find its source in the opinion of well meaning people; it is bad, if it finds its source in the praise of those of ill repute.

The spendthrift will be satisfied to gain the popularity of idlers and loafers. Since he cannot earn popularity by excellent conduct, he will buy it, by being what the world calls, a good fellow. He makes a fool of himself by wasting his income that people may slap him on the shoulder and tell him what a good fellow he is.

Truly, the spendthrift pays an awful price for what doubtful pleasures he gets out of this life. He not only sacrifices his earnings, but his future, his career, his happiness. When old age overtakes him, it finds him without means. It happens frequently that even relatives ignore and disown such men. Look at the welfare lists and you will discover that fully two-thirds, if not more of the peole, now depending upon charity, were, in their former years, people of some means. But they spent their money as quickly as they made it. And now, when they might be well off and live comfortably, they depend upon charity for the bread they eat, and for the roof that shelters them.

Therefore, be wise in time. Despite the approval of those whose only object is to find an easy mark at whose expense they can eat and drink and smoke, remember that you will not always remain young and strong and healthy. The time will come when you will be old and feeble. To depend upon the charity of others at that stage of life will by no means be happiness or comfort.

It will be far more prudent for you to learn to deny yourself a pleasure here and there, at the present time. Do not spend your money for trifles. If you do not learn to deny yourself little pleasures now, the time will come when you will be compelled to deny yourself the comforts of old age. And I think you will agree that to deny ourselves unnecessary things now of our free will is a good deal less unpleasant than to be compelled to deny ourselves necessary things when we most need them in our old age.

CHAPTER XIX. THE HAPPY BOY

If you wish to be prudent in selecting your friends, you will not judge a boy by the clothes he wears, nor by the money he may jingle in his pockets. Neither wealth nor fashion are among the requirements of true friendship. We desire that a friend shall stand by us in our need, and that we may learn from him good qualities of which we may be deficient. If, then, you look for a true friend you will select one of whom you are sure that he has a noble heart.

As the sick man longs for health, so do we long for happiness. We like a happy boy; we like to make him our friend.

No doubt you know some such boys. There is no reason why you should not be one of those happy boys, spreading the sunshine of gladness and good-will wherever you go.

What is required to make a happy boy?

Money does not make people happy. I have known many wealthy people whose troubles increased as their wealth increased. Many a poor man enjoys his meal much better than the wealthy man who has the choice of the daintiest dishes. A drink of water tastes the same whether you drink it out of a tin cup or a jeweled vessel. Is it not strange that, in spite of all our efforts and of all the boasted wisdom of the world, true happiness is so hard to find? And yet happiness can be found if we look for it in the right places. Some try to find happiness in the possession of vast sums of money. Others think they can find it only in the boisterous company of the vulgar and wicked. Others think happiness consists in honors, in titles and offices, the high positions of the world. Others look for happiness in all kinds of excesses. These seekers after happiness, when arriving at the end of their lives, find themselves even further away from true happiness than when they started out. If you seek happiness in vanity, money or honors, or even sin, you will be as much disappointed as the countless millions that sought happiness in these things before you.

The secret of happiness lies in two things: contentment and innocence.

God wants us to be happy, both here and beyond. That is why He has created us. Nor does He want us to be groping in the dark. He has outlined a way for us that will lead us to happiness both here and beyond. All we need to do is to follow the path God has marked out for us. The way of God is the way to true happiness.

You will know the happy boy at first sight. He has a smile that knows nothing of a sneer. He is cheerful without being vulgar; pleasant, without being ostentatious. His words will be without a sting. Others may be richer, stronger, or more influential. That does not bother the happy boy. Others may be more talented, more successful. He is glad of their prominence. And the reason of it all is that the happy boy has contentment and tries to make the best of what he has. It is a wise saying that "if you cannot have what you like, like what you have."

The happy boy will always be able to look you straight in the face. He has nothing that he must try to hide from you.

Look out for the boy who cannot look you in the eyes. When a boy cannot look into your eye, it is almost a sure sign that he has sacrificed the purity of his heart for a silly, passing pleasure. All the money, all the honors, all the pleasures of this world cannot bribe a guilty conscience. Boys with a guilty conscience have their guilt written upon their foreheads. Ask them to be happy; they cannot.

You have heard me tell you much about the holy Will of God.

Its importance has been shown to you in many different ways. A diamond has many little angles. Each one of them has a light, color and sparkle of its own. The holy Will of God resembles a diamond. At each of its many angles we see a new light and charm we never noticed before. And we see a new light in the holy Will of God when looking at it from the angle of happiness.

It is the holy Will of God to give to each human being certain gifts and certain responsibilities. As our Lord told in one of His parables, God gives five talents to one, two to another, and only one to a third. To each He gives according to his capacity. It would be a hopeless task to try and make a quart measure hold a bushel of apples. In distributing His gifts, God is guided by His infinite wisdom. He knows our capacity for work, for suffering and responsibility, far better than we. He has weighed our strength and capability, and has given us neither more nor less than we can well stand.

The happy boy understands this. If God has given him only one talent, he will not look with ill-will and envy at another who has received five, but feel content and happy, realizing that if God has seen fit to confide to him only one talent, his responsibilities are correspondingly small.

It has been said that the world is a stage and we are the actors.

118

When selecting a play, to be given for the benefit of the parish, I must consider the various parts that the play contains and also the members of the club. There will be funny parts and heavy parts, large parts and others that may have no more than one or two lines. Now some of our amateurs may be good for a light role, a comedy part, others may do well in a heavy part. Some member may be good at selling tickets, another in getting advertisements for the program. And so on. Would the play be a success if I gave the comedy part to one who can only play a grave part, if I made the one who can get advertisements play the clown, and make the tragedian solicit advertisements? A play can be a success only if the parts are assigned according to fitness. And so it is in the world, in which God makes each one of us play a part. Some have a leading part; others may have hardly anything to say. Some play comedy parts; others undertake to suffer in heavy parts.

When tempted to discontent we should look beneath us. It is true, there may be many above us. But there are as many, if not more, that have received even less than we. If these, too, are asked to be content with their lot, we surely should be. It is a mistake for people to think that contentment means idleness. The man who received one talent was by no means content when he simply buried the little treasure. Contentment does by no means exclude proper ambition. The man of one talent was not supposed to earn two or five or more, like the others who were given more. Had he had enough ambition to work with that one talent to gain even one more, his reward would have been as great as the reward of the others. Contentment does not mean idleness.

To be content means to work faithfully with the gifts God has been pleased to bestow. It means not to crave for more than God has deemed prudent to grant, and not to look with envious eyes upon the gifts or talents of others.

The other requirement for happiness is innocence. Look how beautifully the sunlight is reflected from the pure waters of a lake. How the water glistens in the sun as though the waves were melted gold! An unsightly swamp does not shed that brilliance. In like manner, a pure and innocent soul reflects the peace and beauty of God in its life. The clearer the water the deeper will the light of the sun penetrate it. The purer the soul, the more profound will be its peace and happiness. Looking into the eyes of an innocent boy you look deep into his soul, and there is not a corner or hiding place that he is afraid of showing. He has nothing to fear, nothing to hide. But one cannot look very deep into swampy, foul water. The swampy water is covered with filth that prevents the sunlight from entering. It is a breeding place for disease and contamination. The eye of the guilty boy resembles that swamp. The sunlight of grace is prevented from entering his soul by the filth of his sins. His soul becomes a breeding place for vice.

The very fact that he tries to conceal something betrays such a boy. This constant dread of betraying himself, the constant effort of concealing makes the life of the guilty boy miserable. He may have the grandest mansion to live in, the finest clothes to wear, and yet he would gladly give you all these, if by their exchange he could again be a happy boy.

By all means, then, be happy boys. First of all, be content with the position and condition in which God has seen fit to place you. Be not deceived by people who promise to create a heaven upon earth contrary to the laws of God. If God had seen fit to make all people rich and brilliant and prosperous, and if such had been for the best of mankind, be sure He would have arranged it so.

Be content with the gifts God has given you; strive to work out the salvation of your soul as God wants you to.

120

Spread cheerfulness and gladness all about you as the sun sheds its light.

Keep your heart free from the stain of mortal sin, especially from the worst of all, sins against holy purity, by avoiding every danger to fall into them.

Then, indeed, you will be happy boys, you will be a source of joy and consolation to your parents and friends, you will be an honor to your Church and to your Country, and the pride of God and of His holy angels.

CHAPTER XX. THE CHRONIC KICKER.

You have, no doubt, come across that obnoxious specimen of humanity called the chronic kicker. And, when it is at all possible, you will try to avoid him. Usually, the chronic kicker is a lean, sullen-looking fellow who has fault to find with everyone he meets and everything he sees. If he plays his part well, he may, for a time, be considered a clever but much abused man. But soon it is discovered that he is nothing more than a false alarm. He is not taken seriously, though he thinks he should be. The chronic kicker is unreasonable and disagreeable. We are all aware of that. And, since it is so easy to find fault let us be on our guard not to join the ranks of chronic kickers.

To understand the chronic kicker in all his ways and workings, let us take him apart, figuratively speaking, to study his component parts.

First, there is his mind.

The chronic kicker has a very exalted and exaggerated opinion of his importance and his ability. He finds himself, he thinks, the only man of honor and righteousness among a lot of thieves, scoundrels and fools. He feels that, if it were not for him, the whole world would probably go to the dogs. But some kind providence has placed him in this world at the proper time and place and he will set the world right, he will save the world from the inevitable ruin to which it would come unless he stood in the way of its destruction. He finds fault with all parties and all men and there is no other right way than his. In his conceit, the chronic kicker imagines that he has cornered all the intelligence of the world. There may be many others that can look through a ladder as well as he; but he is too conceited to admit even that much.

His conceit prevents him from knowing what is imperfect in himself and what is perfect in others.

Then, there are his eyes.

The eyes of the chronic kicker are deceiving. They cannot see his own faults though they be legion; but the least fault in others, be it ever so small, will never escape them. His eyes are like the telescope that brings remote objects to his particular notice. When told of his own faults, he reverses the telescope to make them appear small and of no importance. He sees no beauty in all the wide world. Everything passes before him as in review, and in each and all he sees nothing but imperfection, hypocrisy, and every fault and blemish of which a degraded race can be guilty.

Then, there are his ears.

The ears of the chronic kicker are open at all times to listen to tales about the faults of others. The backbiter and the slanderer are friends of the chronic kicker. But his ears are likewise open for flattery. He drinks in every word of cajolery as eagerly as one who has suffered thirst drinks water. The flatterer is the one man, the chronic kicker feels, that has enough good judgment to appreciate him.

If one, however, dares to speak a kind word in behalf of another those ears are deaf. And one might as well speak to a lifeless statue as to the chronic kicker if one dares to hint at the existence of a few faults. To argue with the chronic kicker in order to convince him of his errors is as hopeless a task as washing a crow to make it look white. Truth and the chronic kicker are not on speaking terms.

123

Then, there is the tongue of the chronic kicker. That tongue is poisoned and will have nothing good to say of anybody or anything. All the wicked news the ears have taken in passes through a vicious imagination, and is given out as gospel truth. This slanderous tongue wags from morning till night to inform the world of manifold and glaring wrongs. To change the monotony, the chronic kicker will on the other hand spare no efforts in self-praise; he is prepared to show that he is the one true and perfect being in the world and will demonstrate that, if the world will only accept him as its guide, philosopher and friend, he will reform the entire creation. If his advice is heeded in time, he can change all things to the better in the twinkling of an eye.

Then, there is the memory of the chronic kicker.

It readily forgets any good which people do; but the many little foibles and faults and shortcomings are never to be forgotten. He is ready to prove that you and the world in general are going from bad to worse.

The will, too, of the chronic kicker is perverted.

If his will were directed toward right and truth, that would interfere with his hobby and conceit. As he is blind and deaf to truth, it does not suit him. His will is not directed to right and reason.

And then there is the "nerve" of the chronic kicker.

He has enough "nerve" to last a dozen normal men throughout their lives. Nothing is beyond him. The weather, politics, his foreman at the shop, his parents at home, all come in for his censure. Nothing can be said or done but he knows better. Since the world has blundered along for so many thousands of years, it is just about time for him to come to the rescue and save the world in spite of itself. Had

124

he lived at the time God created the world, he might have given even God valuable advice. But God did not have the chronic kicker with Him when He created the world and so we must be content with what it is. Whatever you may say or do, the chronic kicker will imagine something better, or, failing in his imagination, he will point out to you the many faults of your way of doing things and tell you that you are wrong anyhow. You are not entitled to achieve anything. The reformation of this wicked world belongs to the chronic kicker.

He mistakes nerve for brains, but no power on earth can convince the chronic kicker of his folly.

Boys full of ardor and ambition oftentimes swell the ranks of the chronic kickers unknowingly and unintentionally.

It may be some abuse at home, perhaps, some injustice at world, some little thing that went wrong due to some misunderstanding, and the youth feels himself misjudged and underrated. In mistaken zeal, such a boy comes to think the whole world will go to perdition unless he sets things right. As a result we have another chronic kicker.

At fifteen, a boy usually sees so much injustice and wrong in this world, he cannot understand how the world gets along as well as it does. He is fully determined, so far as he is able, to straighten out things. At twenty, he finds he knows all that can be known. He cannot explain the indifference and lethargy of the many floating with the tide; and resolves to make a heroic stand against the tide. At thirty, he begins to think that there are a few things that have escaped his observation. Gradually he begins to modify some of his radical opinions and he sees a good point here and there that he has not noticed before. At forty, he understands that instead of realities he has been

125

fighting shadows all along. Human nature appears to him vastly different from what he had imagined. In making allowance for the weakness of human nature he sees much that is good. And then, as his horizon widens, he begins to see lofty ideals, noble characters, self-sacrificing souls where formerly his narrow vision saw nothing. At fifty, the world is not half as bad as he thought it was. At sixty, he thinks the world is plenty good enough for anybody and quietly laughs over his folly of former years.

One can hardly expect that the judgment and experience of a boy of fifteen would be as ripe as that of a man of fifty or sixty years. That is why you should let yourselves be governed by patience and prudence. To reinforce your faulty judgment with conceit will only make matters worse for yourself. Our judgment is imperfect and we are all too prone to judge things by outward appearances. Appearances are oftentimes misleading. To judge properly the good or bad in people we would have to consider many circumstances, motive or intention, degree or lack of knowledge, the bringing up, the environment, the passions, human frailty and a thousand and one conditions that go toward making an act good or evil. And since we are unable to know all of these conditions, our dear Lord wisely told us: "Judge not lest you be judged." Only God, the searcher of our hearts, is able to fully know us and to judge us fairly and honestly. To avoid being classified with the chronic kicker always bear in mind that you and your fellow-men are human, that we are at best little bundles of inconsistencies, and that things will go wrong sometimes in spite of best intentions. Look at the dark side of human nature if you must, but don't forget to look also at the bright side. It will often be bright enough to make you forget the other side. Be generous enough to have a kind word even for those who have fallen. Where others may rejoice with the devil over the downfall of a soul, where the uncharitable view with suspicion all the rest of mankind, you should have a word of pity for the man who fell and a prayer for his soul that it may find its way to the Divine Throne of Mercy.

CHAPTER XXI. THE GENTLE BOY

No doubt you have often heard the word "gentleman." Two distinct words are united to form this one word. The idea we derive from the word "man" is that of something strong and powerful. The word "gentle" conveys the idea of kindness and of restraint. And so, by placing these two words together, we express our idea what a man should be--a gentleman.

If a man were to make his way purely by his brute force he would not be unlike the proverbial bull in the china shop. But God wants us not only to be men, but gentlemen. We must use our force and strength not as brutes having no higher law to guide them, but as men guided by a spiritual law. We must be possessed of a still greater power or force controlling our animal power. The exercise of this higher, spiritual force, that of itself should be stronger than our bodily, physical forces, enables us to curb and check ourselves.

We are not losing any strength, but, on the contrary, are conscious of a still greater strength of a higher order when able to restrain ourselves, when able to check the force of our passion. And in governing, directing, and curbing our animal strength by the nobler strength of the soul we become what God wants us to be, gentlemen.

To arrive at a proper understanding of this important word, it will be advisable to explain in the first place what the word does not stand for, and so do away with any false notions we may have about it.

To be a gentleman, it is not necessary to follow the latest styles, wear patent leather shoes, rainbow-colored socks, and all the other trimmings. Such things may be good enough for a dummy in a clothing store, or a brainless dude. Some think that to be a gentleman one must be a sissy. But an overgrown baby is a poor apology for a man. Others have the mistaken idea that a gentleman must have no more backbone than a dishrag, tolerating and permitting wrong, for fear he might injure the feeling of some brute.

Such conduct, however, is cowardice, and a thing most heartily despised by a true gentleman. If our passions and animal strength are stronger than the powers of our soul, we will be either bullies or cowards, according to the advantages from either standpoint. Hence neither expensive clothes, nor polished manners, nor the strength of a Sampson, nor money, are necessary conditions for being a gentleman.

To be gentlemen, we must have a soul stronger and nobler than our body. The body must not be master of the soul; the soul must govern the body. Only then, when the soul is able to govern and direct the forces of the body, when it can check and control our animal passions, are we entitled to receive the highest title under the sun--the title of gentleman.

And you, boys, to become gentlemen, in later years you must be "gentleboys" at the present time. There is an old saying: "You cannot make a silk purse out of a sow's ear." I know every one of you will want to be a gentleman in later years. To become a true gentleman, you cannot begin training any too soon.

How are you to go about in this training?

From day to day, you grow in size and strength of body. From day to day, you realize that you can do more,

129

and do better, than a few months ago. Now this very growth and increasing strength of body is not without its dangers. Because you realize your strength, you may be easily made to think that all things are in your power and at your mercy. Because you realize your strength, you may think you can handle things and people as you like, or crush them when you will.

Although your growth in strength and power has its dangers, it would be folly to check or dwarf it. You cannot remain children forever. You must grow. You must also use all reasonable means to promote your strength and health and growth. But while you are doing this, you must not overlook the development of the soul. The reason why the quality and number of gentlemen is low at the present time is that we have so many men with giant bodies and dwarfed souls.

In developing bodily strength, do not overlook the soul. Bear in mind that, as your bodily strength grows from day to day, your soul must not only keep pace but even be stronger than the body. You may know from your own experience how hard it is to keep two boys from trying to beat each other. They will wrestle and tumble, and jump and box, and race, to see who of them is the stronger and more skillful. Each one will try his best to show that he is the superior in one or more sports.

The same is to be said of body and soul. Our body will want to be the stronger of the two and make the soul do its bidding. The soul will want to have its own way. The body will put up the claim that it is stronger and that might is right. The soul will object and the stronger of the two will win.

I know you have, in the past, been mixed up in these fights of body against spirit. Who came out ahead? If your soul has lost in every count something is wrong. You must never permit your soul to be weaker than your body.

But, some will say, how can we ever train our souls? How can we get at the soul? Let me explain.

We must develop and strengthen the faculties of our soul by exercising them just as we develop the muscles of our arms or legs by exercise. There is mental culture as well as physical culture.

The soul has three faculties, memory, understanding and will.

These three faculties must be trained by mental exercise, as muscles are trained and developed by physical exercise. When you went to school, you began to train particularly your memory and understanding. The will is equally as important as the other two faculties, but oftentimes receives the very least training. For that very reason, the brightest people are very often the saddest of failures. The most brilliant minds at times go astray because, by lacking will power they lack the proper balance of their mental equipment. You may have a memory so retentive that you can memorize Webster's Unabridged Dictionary, your understanding may be so vast that you can master every art and science and language, and yet, if you have no will power, you will be a rank failure.

There was never a wiser man than Solomon. He had a saintly father, was brought up as good children should be. He was a model young man, and the first years of his reign gave promise of years of blessing and prosperity for the land. But he neglected the training of his will. He became fickle, gradually turned away from God, erected temples to pagan gods to please his friends, offered sacrifices to idols of stone, and even dragged his people down with him.

You see, then, how necessary it is to train our will.

It will be natural for bodily strength to dwindle with age. But the soul, being immortal, must be kept in training up to the last moment of our life. If we permit the will to grow weak it will never be able to check and restrain and control the passions of our body.

The question now is: How to train the will. I may be able to better explain this by an example. When you go to the grocery to buy sugar you do not hold up your hat and say fill this hat. You ask for sugar by the pound. When you ask the distance of one city from another you are not satisfied when told it's far, or very far; you want to know how many miles. And so we have measures and weights for all things.

And these measures and weights are regulated and determined by standard measures and weights kept by the Government. From time to time officers of the Government will go and inspect the shops and stores to see that the measures and weights by which they sell agree with the standard weights and measures kept at Washington. And so it happens that the inch, yard, mile, ounce, and pound, and pint, and bushel are exactly the same from New York to San Francisco.

In a similar manner, we have an official rule or measure for our will. If our will agrees with that measure we know it is correct. And the rule by which we measure our will is nothing else than the holy Will of God. This holy Will is the standard by which we learn whether we are right or not.

The holy Will of God stands for purity, for piety, for obedience and every other virtue. If our will is correct, it will stand for the very same virtues. The holy Will of God forbids every sin, even the very least, and so our will must measure up to the holy Will of God by being opposed to every sin.

Knowing thus the measure by which you must gauge your will, it remains for you to train the will. The opportunities will not be lacking.

Your body will want to have this or that pleasure; it will want to have an amount of ease and of self-love. Your passions, the animal nature of man, will want to have their desires gratified. They may crave revenge for some slight, real or imaginary, some evil thought will demand acceptance, pride or envy may want to possess your mind. Then, with the grace of God, comes the right will. The body will fight against the spirit. The will, however, measures up the demands of the animal passions and learns that they do not agree with the requirements of the holy Will of God. The will knows that God forbids sin and commands holiness.

Again, there are numberless opportunities for practicing virtues.

There are times when the virtue of piety, of purity, of obedience, of humility or of patience, can be exercised. They may not please or favor the inclination of bodily ease. Our will, in measuring up to the holy Will of God, learns that these very virtues are pleasing and right in His sight. There remains nothing else for our will to do than abide by the standard rule of the holy Will of God. Our animal passion may fight against being compelled by the will; they will not want to submit, for our body will want to govern the soul as the soul is determined to govern the body. Which should win this struggle? The soul, of course.

Grow strong and healthy in your body, by all means. But do not forget that bodily strength is not noble unless guided by a higher and righteous strength, the strength of soul. The noblest strength is restraint.

133

Be "gentleboys" by properly controlling your passions and your animal strength, so that in later years you may be true gentlemen.

CHAPTER XXII. THE TOUGH KID

There is a certain class of boys who seem to have but one object in life, and that is to lean up against the walls of the bar at the corner and thereby keep them from toppling over. Of course, this is hard work and must yield some reward. And so these boys watch for "easy marks" at whose expense they can get free drinks. While waiting and watching for them, these tough kids keep the sidewalk in a filthy condition by flooding it with tobacco juice and ashes and molest girls and young women with impertinent remarks and foul jests.

So long as these boys have their parents to fall back on for board and lodging they are more or less harmless. But if this source of supplies ceases for one reason or another, and as they are too lazy to work and too proud to beg, they often have recourse to stealing and all kinds of dirty work to make a living. From that time on, they begin to gather experience, and they are soon able to state which jail is the easiest and which prison the most severe. A few weeks or a few months of liberty are generally followed by as many months or years in prison.

And to replace the older tough kids who have become burglars and crooks, there is always a fresh supply of would-be toughs, ready to walk the same road. The walls of the bar are safe from falling, for as soon as one shift is promoted to jail, another takes its place. Another set of loafers courts the same disgraceful fate for the sake of a few free drinks.

The tough kid does not like work. If by some chance he does take a job, he either quickly gives it up again or he is sent away because he is too careless and lazy to be of any use. In the meantime, the tough boy grows up to the years of manhood. In these years he will lose his parents and find himself without a roof to shelter him. It may be that he inherits a few hundred dollars that his thrifty parents have saved by denying themselves many a pleasure. But the fool and his money are soon parted. It took the parents years of labor to save that little fortune; they deprived themselves of many good things, even of ease and of comfort, that their children might have a start in life. The unfortunate tough, however, squanders this hard-earned money in a short time and he finds himself worse off than before. The money has wetted his hunger for more. He has discovered new wants and likes and is bound to satisfy them at any cost. Then the tough becomes a thief.

Running water is not a breeding place of germs that breed disease. It is in stagnant swamps where the germs that spread malaria, typhoid and yellow fever are produced.

In a similar way, vice has little chance of finding shelter in those who are busy with work. Industrious people find little time to pay attention to the lure of sin. Their mind is too much occupied with the work before them.

To keep the mind occupied with our work is the best means of keeping the devil at a distance. Not a single one of the countless thousands of our Saints was an idler. All of them were hard and faithful workers in their various vocations.

In still and stagnant waters, however, one poisonous insect may deposit thousands of eggs. The sloth of the water favors their development, and these pests will gradually infect the whole place. The evil suggestion which the devil deposits in an idle mind finds a fine breeding

136

place. It will thrive and spread. Evil thoughts will create evil desires, the desires will lead to actions. The devil, indeed, loves nothing more than idleness, though he himself is anything but idle.

From this example, you will understand that the tough is more exposed to temptations of all sorts than the boy who is a faithful worker. His love of idleness makes the tough unfit for the struggle with temptations. His mind and heart will become a breeding place for sin. As a swamp contains countless varieties of vicious insects and poisonous germs, so will the mind of the tough contain the germs of every vice.

Hence we find the tough foul-mouthed. His words will not only be coarse or vulgar, they will be sinful. He has no regard for purity; he has no respect for anyone; no respect for authority of any kind. There is no bit of sentiment or feeling in him. Nothing but the club of a policeman will be able to stop him from casting insults and indecent remarks at those passing by. He will curse and abuse that most holy Name at whose sound all knees should bend. If the mouth speaks of the abundance of the heart, the heart of a tough must indeed be vile.

The tough becomes a victim of intemperance. He begins taking the first steps towards that vice by hanging around bars when he should have been working. This vice begets others. The craving for drink will become so irresistible that, if he cannot get it by fair means, he will get it by foul means. It has happened that toughs killed a man for a few pennies with which to buy a drink.

Homeless, friendless and moneyless, but still craving for drink, and for the gratification of other passions that drink has bred in him, he finds himself compelled to steal to satisfy his craving. Little thefts will not satisfy him, and he will try to make bigger hauls, even at the risk of

137

taking the life of his victim. And, as the moth hovers around the flame regardless of singed wings until it pays with its life for its heedlessness, so will the tough not learn by his sad experiences, until a life sentence or the gallows make an end of his vicious career.

A short time ago, a young man was lynched in one of our western cities. He was one of those who did not want to work. Wherever there was easy money in sight he was on the spot. So it happened that he was hired by the Anti-Saloon League as a private detective, although his past record was by no means favorable. In his eagerness to gather evidence he killed a man. The murdered man was so well thought of that the indignation of the people of that town knew no bounds. The jail was broken open and the unfortunate young man was taken out and hanged. When the lynchers had placed the rope around his neck, he asked permission to say a few words. The request was granted. "Let me warn the young men," he said, "from following my example. Don't be afraid of earning your living in an honest way." These were his last words.

The life of this unhappy young fellow was cut short in his early twenties. Had he grown up to be an honest and industrious young man, he would now be alive and respected by all those that knew him. As it is, he had been a failure. He heaped disgrace upon the heads of a good father and a loving mother. What did it profit that boy to shirk work and become a tough? He paid the penalty of death.

The tough can never be happy.

Though the life of a tough may be ever so sad and repelling, there is still the temptation for all of you-to follow just this kind of a life. Consequences will be disregarded, as they have been in the past. The very brightest of you is as much exposed to the danger of becoming a tough as the rest of you. One will find even university graduates among burglars and crooks. I was greatly surprised the other day to hear a most disreputable-looking tramp address me in well-chosen words: "My dear sir," he said, "I am in financial difficulties and any assistance from you would be gratefully appreciated. "

Nor is only the bright boy exposed to the temptations of a tough life; you, working in your shops and factories, are exposed as much as the rest. The very fellow working at your elbow may be a tough. For some reason or other he may be working with you. He will have a story to pour into your ears about the ease and luxury of idleness, the drudgery of work, and the injustice of the foreman, the dishonesty of the rich, and a thousand and one other woes and ills--mainly imaginary--intending thereby to make you waver in your love of work. The very next week this tough may be dismissed and another of his ilk may be working at your side. And hearing the same story from many, you, too, may be misled to think there is some hidden or secret charm about being an idle loafer. Bear in mind, therefore, once for all, that there cannot be any happiness in idleness and sin.

So far, I have mentioned idleness as the great factor in the make-up of the tough. But to idleness we must add recklessness. The tough has absolutely no regard for anybody or anything. He snaps his fingers at the laws of God and of the land. He pays no attention to the voice of conscience. He fears neither God nor the devil, and cares not for heaven or hell. An idle boy may be of harm only to himself; he may ruin all his prospects of success and happiness. But if, together with his idle habits, he has a reckless disposition, he is a danger not to himself only but to all others about him.

The reckless boy betrays his evil disposition early by his contempt for the wishes and commands of his parents. And soon he will show the same contempt for the commands of all other authority. You have, then, reason to be on your guard. Avoid even contact with the tough. Go your way and let the tough go his way. The very fact of coming in contact with a tough may cast a blight upon your life. A vile snail crawling over a leaf may not destroy it, but it leaves a slimy track across the leaf marring its former beauty.

As for your own conduct, never give way to idleness. Your ambitions may not be realized as quickly as you may desire; disappointment and failure may make your work seem useless and bitter. But others have overcome these difficulties and they merited a well-earned reward. If others could persevere, why not you? Keep up your courage, and your faith in yourselves, and you are bound to win at the end.

And, finally, never become reckless. If you wish others to respect your rights, you must respect the rights of others.

Ships at times run upon hidden rocks. If they do not free themselves the winds and the waves will batter them to pieces.

So, too, many a man runs upon the rocks of adversity. If he ceases his efforts he will go to pieces. Such an unfortunate man is a menace to himself and to others. He shatters his own welfare and the welfare of others, and, in the final crash, he will blame and curse God and man for the misfortune that is entirely of his own making.

CHAPTER XXIII. TRUE FRIENDSHIP

My dear boys: Do you remember how glad other children were to come and play with you when you had some new toys? For a while, at least, they would be able to enjoy your playthings as though they belonged to them. The time when other boys saw your new glove, or wagon, or bat and ball, and asked that they might play with them was the dawn of friendship. Friendship does not cease when we put aside the toys of childhood. As years pass on, the necessity of friendship appeals to us all the more forcibly. It is our ambition to become equipped with all the good qualities that go to make a good, a perfect man. And, since we discover that we lack a number of good qualities in our make-up, it is the most natural thing for us to look around and find them in someone else. If we are fortunate enough to discover such a person we feel ourselves drawn to him in friendship, since through the means of that sympathetic bond we share--at least indirectly--the qualities we lack and would like to call our own.

Glittering toys brought you together when you were children. And, as children, you liked other children for the pleasure they offered you by letting you share their joys. Now you have noticed that life is not all play, that it means real hard work. And, while you feel the need of friendship all the more, you also learn to understand that it rests upon other foundations than mere enjoyment.

You begin to know yourself and, if you are candid, you will admit that there are good qualities missing in you

141

that you see in others. At times, you will be in need of advice; at other times, of help. Times will come when a kind word of encouragement will mean a great deal to you. You understand that you are far from having all the sources of strength you should have to be independent. You look around and study other boys to discover the good qualities that you need to perfect yourself. You find one boy who is a good, willing soul. Him you make your friend, that, if you should ever be in need of help, he may stand by you. You find another who is prudent and reliable and you make him your friend so that, when you are in any difficulty, he may advise you as to what you should do. You find another who is at all times cheerful and happy. No troubles seem able to cloud his smile, his cheerful disposition overcomes all obstacles. There are times, when you are discouraged and downhearted; times, when a kind word will mean a great deal to you. You make this happy boy your friend. When you are feeling blue and discouraged you desire to see him smile at you and make you forget your trouble.

You see how prudent a boy is who knows himself and, knowing his shortcomings, selects friends whose good qualities make up for those he lacks. A locomotive is a great machine; but of what use is it if it lacks steam and coal, and a fireman and an engineer? It is of no use at all. The very moon would be a dark, unknown body if it were not for the sun casting its light upon it.

In like manner, a man without friends is often helpless, useless and, at times, dangerous. For that reason, take care to steer clear of the boy who is without friends, unless his lack of friends is due to a cause for which he is not to blame. Such a boy may be a stranger to most or all of you, because his parents have come here from some other city. This boy shows a good will by the fact that he joins the church. He may be slow to seek new friends because he cannot forget the old ones. Give such a boy a fair deal. But you will find boys who are friendless though they may have grown up in the very block in which they live. Usually, the friendless boy will be the lad no one can get along with. He will be so conceited about himself, that he feels no need of friendship. He will take the advice of no man, and consequently makes blunders right and left. He thinks he knows it all, and only succeeds in making a fool of himself. He confides in no one, and suspects everybody.

The friendless boy is not the only one against whom you must be on your guard. There is another about whom you must be careful. That is the boy who is the friend of everybody. You may hear people praising a man saying of him that he did not have an enemy in the whole wide world. That compliment is often a very doubtful one. We cannot serve two masters. If you have enough backbone to call a foul-mouthed boy to task for his vulgar talk he will not call you a friend of his. If another boy, whom you know well, is getting the habit of missing holy Mass on Sunday and you talk to him kindly, asking him to come to church with you, he may tell you to mind your own business. He will hardly think of calling you his friend. Still, you may be able to convert both of them and make them feel ever grateful to you for your acts of kindness. For this reason you should be manly enough to speak up whenever prudence tells you that your words are in place. Where they will be of benefit in one case, they may not be heeded in ten other cases, and these boys and their followers will consider you as anything but a friend. You see, then, that the saying of being the friend of everybody must be taken with caution. It is often a pretty sure sign that the poor lad who is called the friend of everybody is a weak character. We cannot remain neutral when it is a question of right or wrong. A weak character may be the friend of everybody, but he has the making of a poor friend, indeed.

Besides being aware of the boy who wants no friends and of the boy who is the friend of everybody, you must avoid counterfeit friendship as you avoid counterfeit money. With a little care you can tell both. You can recognize the counterfeit from true friendship by its improper motive.

Just watch the boys! Did you notice that a small boy is allowed to play with much bigger boys if he has a bat and ball? They make a fuss over him for the sake of that bat and ball. But, as soon as they can get along without the bat and ball of the little fellow, he is left out of any further games. They will find fault with him, they will tell him to go and play marbles. As long as they needed his bat and ball they were his friends. Here you see counterfeit friendship.

Years roll on and these boys, who are friends only if they can profit by friendship, have grown to the age of manhood and seek other victims. The victim will be a jolly, good fellow, till his money is gone. Then the friendship comes to a sudden end.

It stands to reason, then, that, in the choice of friends you should exercise care and judgment. Never listen to or confide in a flatterer. His only object is to deceive you and to further his own plans and benefits.

Never make a shiftless and lazy boy your friend. If his own parents cannot reform him, it will be a hopeless and thankless task for you. Far from reforming him, he may exert a harmful influence over you.

Never make the disobedient boy your friend. If he disregards his duty to his parents, how can you expect him to respect your rights! If he has no love for his own people, how can he have regard for you?

True friendship, you must bear in mind, is not one-sided. It has its mutual obligations. It is not enough to pick out some one in whom you see a good quality, one that is lacking in your own character, but you must be able to show him that you are not without your good points which you are willing to share with him for his benefit.

True friendship must be more willing to give than to take. True friendship will create a rivalry of generosity. In this spirit of generosity we begin to learn that giving is a greater pleasure than taking. And so, while our lives are made happy by giving and receiving, we make less of the troubles and sorrows of this world.

Regarding friends, two chief points should guide your choice. In the first place, select your friends--other things being equal from among those of our own faith. Though we should never lack in charity and kindness towards all men regardless of faith, of classes or color, or even of merit, the bond with which our holy Faith links us together should never be lost sight of. The Communion of Saints binds us together for time and eternity. It is plain, then, that, in the choice of friends, we should look to those of our own household first. Faith best teaches us our own short comings. At the same time it directs our attention to others in whom a truly Christian life is manifest. This alone gives us countless good lessons and inspirations. Faith makes us brothers of Christ, children of the heavenly Father. What, then, should be more natural than that all should be of one mind and heart! Hence true friendship, like charity, rests best upon the foundation of our holy Faith. Friendship is a flower that may grow anywhere. But it will bloom to best advantage, and bring forth richest fruits, if planted in the soil of our holy Faith.

It may not be out of place to say even at this time, that, by seeking your friends from among our own fold, you

145

avoid the danger of forming friendships that lead to a mixed marriage, and to the misfortunes that go with most of them.

The other suggestion regarding the choice of friends is this; Next to your parents, your own parish priest should be your dearest friend. The number of boys that know absolutely nothing of their priest except his name, and never speak to him except in the confessional, never see him except at the altar, is surprisingly great. It is a sad revelation of the lack of confidence and of trust that many boys have for the priest. The priest, however, is only too anxious to win the confidence of the boys; too glad to be of any help. That the priest can be of great help in many different ways goes without saying. His very position gives him prestige and influence the power of which is seldom fully appreciated.

The claim of Columbus that the world is a globe was looked upon by most people of his time as too silly to be worthy of serious thought. He went from country to country seeking support. After countless humiliations he came to Spain. Here he won the friendship of a priest, and humble son of St. Francis. This same priest vouched for him at the royal court, the palace was opened to him and he was enabled to lay his plans and proofs before king and queen. They were favorably impressed with him, and he was given boats, provisions and men to set out upon the journey that ended with the discovery of a new world. Now if Columbus had despised the friendship of the priest as most people unfortunately do, the probabilities are, he would not have been given the means to carry out his plans and discoveries.

With the parish priest as his friend, a boy is bound to win success in his affairs, temporal and spiritual.

CHAPTER XXIV. BAD COMPANY

No doubt you have heard that, years ago, when someone was sick with smallpox a sign was put upon the door stating that the whole family was quarantined. No member of that family was allowed to leave the home, nor was anybody except doctor and priest allowed to enter that house, until the quarantine was removed. The reason that such precaution was enforced was to prevent the spreading of that disease into other homes.

What a blessing it would be to have such a danger sign on the doors of houses where bad company is met! People are mortally afraid of diseases like small pox or yellow fever; in an epidemic they will flee from the city in which the disease is prevalent; people will flee from their friends and relatives endeavoring to save their own lives. But no such precaution is taken against places and people that spread a more malicious disease-the disease of the soul. And yet bad company has caused more sorrow and suffering than all the epidemics put together. Hospitals, asylums for the insane, poorhouses and prisons, all give testimony to the ravages of bad company.

Some few years ago, I knew a boy who had the misfortune of falling in with bad company. His father was a righteous man, his mother a model mother. Yet it seemed as though the peace and virtue of his home were not to the liking of this boy. He wanted to be free of every restraint, and, especially, did not like to work. One day, the boy instead of going to work, joined the idle crowd of other boys as fond of loafing as he was. They fell in with a couple of tramps, who talked so interestingly about their wanderings and about their free and easy life, that this boy proposed to join their crowd, since he was only too glad to find a way of living without having to work. Without saying a word at home, he left that very same forenoon. A passing freight train carried the crowd away.

You may imagine how his parents felt that evening waiting for him. The parents asked the neighbors but could get no information. The next day the father went to the police station to have the police help him find out what happened to his son. But the boy could not be found. A week passed without news of the lost boy. It seemed as though the earth had swallowed him alive. His father had been in poor health, and all this worry hastened his end.

In the meantime, the boy was loafing through the country. But, never having been away from home, and, also, because he found tramps and hoboes very different from the company to which he had been accustomed, he found the new life anything but a happy one. Homesickness and disappointment brought about the desire to return home and ask forgiveness. On the one hand, however, he was ashamed to write home telling his parents of his predicament; on the other hand, he realized that the money needed to go home meant a little fortune. Finally, he found an opportunity to board a freight train with a crowd of three others, somewhere en route, however, the four tramps were discovered by the train crew, and it was also discovered that some of the freight had been opened. The four were at once arrested, and, after a speedy trial, all four were sent to the state prison. The boy, because it was his first offence, was given two or three years; the others got a longer sentence.

About this time I was called to this boy's home. His father was very low. After I had administered the last

Sacraments, he drew a letter from beneath his pillow, asking me to read it. It was a letter from his boy written from the state prison. I could see in the poor man's eyes his anguish about the boy's condition, and also his longing to see the boy once more before death came. I tried to console the poor man as best I could and asked to borrow the letter. I took it at once to a friendly judge, explaining to him all the circumstances. He then wrote to the authorities under whose jurisdiction the boy was, explaining the conditions, and the outcome was that the boy was pardoned. But he came home too late to find his father alive.

I can still see before me the dying man calling for his son. He died with a prayer upon his lips for his lost boy. And now I want you to imagine yourselves in the place of that boy. Think of how he must have felt when thrown in with disreputable tramps of every sort of degradation. Think of how he felt when he was arrested and convicted. Think of how he must have felt in prison in the constant company of thieves and murderers; how he must have suffered under the severe discipline of the prison; how he felt when he wrote home telling about his shame, and finally, what a shock it must have been to find his father dead when at last he did come home.

The family sold what little property they had and moved to another place, where the boy did not have to hide his head in shame. But he profited by his severe lesson, and now, I am happy to say it, he is a model young man.

All this may sound to you like a story one may read in a story book, yet every word of it is true. You yourselves may have heard of similar examples. Possibly you may know of instances like the one I have told you. Still, very few people are willing to learn from the lessons and experiences of others. There is a certain spirit of gambling in every man. Though we know the odds are

149

against us, we take the risk, hoping to be the lucky one in a hundred, in a thousand, to escape the evil consequences of our folly.

Go to any prison and ask the inmates what brought them to their life of crime, and, if they will tell you the truth, they will say that it was bad company. Go to any hospital and ask to be taken to the ward where most loathsome sicknesses are treated. There you will find young people paying the death penalty for their sins against purity. Go to the asylums of the insane and you will find many who must trace their condition to the excesses of their shameful lives. Go to the poorhouses, ask some of the old men there why in their old age they must depend upon charity, and, if they want to be truthful, they will have to admit that it is the final result of bad company. In their days, they were young and foolish, found jolly good friends, went out with the boys to have a good time. Finally they were out of money and out of friends. Then they grew old and helpless, were unable to work and hence must end their days at the poorhouse. If they had led decent lives, they might now enjoy a happy home and grateful children would be their joy and consolation. If it were not for bad company, we might close up most of our prisons, asylums and poorhouses.

Hence, my dear boys, since you know where bad company leads to beware of it. At times, parents place too much confidence in your judgment. Thinking you know all the harm bad company can inflict, they give you a great deal of freedom. Never betray that confidence of your parents.

Bad company is a temptation to which every boy is exposed.

The boy staying at home will be exposed to the wiles of it. The shop or factory in which you work will have

150

plenty of bad company. You will hear all kinds of talk about, or rather against, religion, against the authority of parents. These lads will tell you what a pleasure it is to be dishonest, untruthful, how much more profitable it is to sleep or go fishing on a Sunday instead of going to Holy Mass, and, not content with so much harm they will pour the most deadly poison into your ear, telling you to forget the instructions you have received regarding holy purity. Still the boy

living at home has some support. The example of his parents, brothers and sisters, his going to church, his Holy Communions will counteract the snares of the devil, provided he is sincere.

Great though such temptations are, the boy away from home has to meet even greater temptations. He has not the pious example of his dear ones to look up to, and he must depend upon himself. For that reason I always admire the boy who, when coming to stay in a strange place, makes it a point to look up the priest at his earliest opportunity. I have had several such boys come to the priest's house, introducing themselves to me, telling me where they are from and that they wish to come to church as they were accustomed to do at home. These boys may have their faults, as we all have: but I consider them as honest and manly fellows of whom God and His angels are proud.

If, owing to circumstances, you must go from home to work elsewhere, let your first care be to look up the parish priest in whose locality you find work. He may be of great help to you in more ways than one. Possibly he may know of better paying work than you could find for yourself.

From what has been said, you should take the warning to stay away from bad company. Either you are a little saint, or you are weak. In either case, bad company is out of the question. For, granting you are a little saint, bad companions will have nothing to do with you. They do not stand for any kind of preaching. To mix with them, even for the object of bringing them around, will be useless. They will give you to understand that they will not listen to your talk. One never sees a white dove among black crows. If you are weak, you have all the more reason to keep away from bad company. Your very weakness should be a warning to you. You should, and you do, know beforehand that you will not be able to resist temptation. Why, then, enter temptation? You pray every day, "Lead us not into temptation." Why, then, should you seek temptations? One day we all hope for the bliss of being in the company of angels. We cannot prepare ourselves for this bliss by now seeking the company of devils. Hence, avoid bad company!

CHAPTER XXV. FIRST COMMANDMENT, OR DUTIES TOWARDS THE HOLY FAITH

We shall now begin to treat of the Ten Commandments, and we will endeavor to see what special bearing each one of them has for you at your time of life. You have seen, before this, how duties grow with age, how responsibilities grow greater and heavier the older you grow. As children, you had few and easy obligations. Your minds were not fully developed, your strength was not fully ripened, and the trials and sufferings of the more mature age were unknown to you. Now, however, since you have advanced in years, you face new duties and responsibilities which in ten years from now will seem trifling in comparison with others you will have to answer to at that time. And so our duties grow. It must not be forgotten that graces grow, too, in proportion to the duties. No matter how heavy duties may seem, with the help of God we shall always feel that the yoke of Christ is sweet and His burden light.

The benefits you should derive from these instructions are twofold. In the first place, your attention will be directed to the dangers and pitfalls which, at your age, are fatal to so many. And, finally, by discussing these topics in a new light, you are given additional suggestions, you will know the meaning of the Ten Commandments better, and will be able to examine yourselves more carefully when going to Confession.

When speaking of the duties of a member of the Church, I mentioned daily prayer as one of them. The instructions you received on this same subject before and since your first Holy Communion will, I hope, never be forgotten. Better still, I hope you will never lose sight of the resolution you made never to forget your daily prayers. Remain faithful to that rule! Daily prayer, however, is not the only obligation imposed upon us in the First Commandment. There is one regarding which you may hardly ever examine your conscience and that is the duty we owe to God on account of holy Faith.

The most precious gift God has bestowed upon us is holy Faith. To teach us this holy Faith, our Divine Savior had to come down upon earth. He had to walk from place to place teaching it, and for all His efforts and sufferings He drew upon Himself the implacable hatred of the Jews. He was persecuted until He was made to die upon a cross like the worst of criminals.

If it were possible to trace our ancestry up to the Reformation and beyond, most of us, if not all, might discover that we are the offspring of martyrs. In Germany, England, and Ireland, thousands upon thousands suffered persecution for the sake of Christ. They were robbed of house and home, were banished, put in prisons, or executed as criminals. Blood was shed in the Middle Ages in a manner more cruel and revolting than even in the early persecutions when the tormentors were misguided pagans who knew not God. All this suffering has been undergone for the sake of the same Faith which now, through the grace of God, is our blessed inheritance.

These two considerations show us what a priceless gift our holy Faith is and how willing we should be at all times to defend our holy Faith, if need be, even with

154

our blood. Countless others have given their life for this Faith. Should we think less of it than they?

To summarize our obligations towards our holy Faith let me say: we should know it, and show it.

It is true, you learned your catechism from cover to cover; a pious mother taught you the very first lessons. A faithful parish priest spent years and years in preparing himself to teach you the way to Heaven. Then, in the course of time, a final and thorough explanation of our holy Faith was given you when you were preparing to receive Holy Communion for the first time. Since then you received special instructions by way of conferences, and general instructions in sermons. All the instructions and sermons ever given are nothing else but an explanation of some one of the solemn and holy truths God has deigned to reveal to us. But, let me ask you, what do you remember of all the instructions you have received up to date? Possibly, you may be able to recall some little story that was given by way of example. The very application of it, however, has escaped your memory. To learn in order to forget, means that all your efforts to stock your mind with knowledge has been a hopeless and thankless task.

Are you still able to answer the ordinary questions that are asked of us by Protestants? If you are told that you adore the Virgin Mary, are you able to explain the difference between adoration and veneration? If you are asked about indulgences, the Sacrament of Penance, holy Mass, and the like, are you able to give an intelligent answer? There was a time when you did know these answers. If now you do not know what to say, you cannot look these questions up any too soon. Who knows but you might be asked any of these questions this very day. We should at all times be ready to give a reason for the Faith that is in us.

155

Ask a man why he is a Republican or a Democrat, and he will give you one reason after another why he belongs to this party or that. Nor will he be satisfied without an effort to convince you that his party is the only party to which a man should belong. He will try to make you join his party. Now ask a man why he is a Catholic! What will he have to say! Will he be able to give his proofs, showing that there can be but one true Church, and that the Catholic Church is that one Church? Will he make any effort at all to make one single convert? "Why," he will say, "That is the business of the priest." Too many Catholics, if asked why they are Catholics, will have a puzzled look, and say they were brought up that way. And that is about all they will be able to say.

It is a mistaken idea to think that only the priest is to know the Faith. It is not necessary for you to have the extensive knowledge of religious matters that is demanded of the priest; yet the elementary knowledge of religion should be possessed by all.

If the plain people knew and showed their holy Faith to better advantage there would be more conversions. You boys, in your offices and factories and stores, reach the very people that will steer clear of a priest whenever they see one a block away. Everyone of you should be a little missionary in his own way. But how can you be one, though, unless you know your holy Faith?

There is no need of beating around a bush. We must admit a widespread ignorance about holy Faith. Every Sunday some part of our holy religion is explained to the people: and how little they worry over missing a whole series of sermons! At everyone of your conferences some part of your religious duties is explained to you, and how easily a conference is missed. "He who is of God will hear the word of God." As to reading some book of instruction,

156

like "The Faith of our Fathers," "The Following of Christ" Or other books explaining the holy Faith in an able manner--that is nowadays a scarcity. It is no longer fashionable to read such books. In the meantime, however, some cheap and trashy novel is more fascinating. Yellow papers, cheap magazines, the stage, movies--all make one great, united effort to undermine Faith. Through their agencies, people are given a wrong idea about religious matters. Sin is made to look like virtue, and virtue like foolishness. And, because a Catholic, owing to his ignorance in matters of Faith, is unable to point out the mistakes of popular notions regarding our Faith, he begins to feel ashamed of his holy Faith. It is true, he still goes to church on Sundays, he receives the Sacraments from time to time, and he says his prayers, but all is done in a half-hearted way. He begins to think that sin is not so dreadful after all, and that all he ever learnt about God, Heaven and hell may be explained in more ways than one. He sins against holy Faith every day, hardly realizing the danger of his position. Some of his forefathers suffered imprisonment, banishment and even death rather than betray their Faith; and he--he is as ready to exchange it as one would a coat.

Ignorance in matters of Faith, so far as it is due to neglect or indifference, is sinful. A sensible boy who must admit his knowledge has grown a trifle rusty, should by all means try to regain the knowledge he had of his holy Faith when he left school. With a little care and diligence he can easily regain it, and even widen his knowledge. But instead of adding to their knowledge of holy Faith, what will most of them do? They will destroy it by reading papers and books that make religion a mockery.

From what has been said, you will easily understand that you are bound in conscience to have a practical knowledge of your holy Faith. The better you understand it, the better will you like it, and the more will

157

you strive to live according to its rules. The less you know of your holy Faith, the greater is the danger of losing it.

To know our holy Faith is only half our duty. We must also show it. Our everyday life must be the outward sign of the inward Faith. Nor is it enough to simply live up to our holy Faith; we must confess our holy Faith in public whenever the glory of God or the salvation of our souls demand it.

The world hates nothing more than a coward. In most cases it will be useless to hide our Faith. Our very conduct will reveal what we are. In many instances, our very name will indicate our religion.

This reminds me of a conversation I overheard some time ago at a hotel. It happened that during a convention of Freemasons I sat next to a table that was reserved for Masons. A party of five sat down, when one of the number saw another friend, and beckoned him to come to them. He was introduced to the other four as a fellow mason. The new party had a very pronounced Irish accent, we will call him Sullivan, though that was not his real name. After the introduction, one of the party said in a joking way: "You must have been a Catholic at some time, judging from your name!" "No, I never was," Sullivan replied. "But your name gives you away." Poor Sullivan had a hard time trying to convince his new friends that it was his father who had fallen away from the Church. Still he blushed and became embarrassed. I doubt very much whether his new friends believed him at all. The manner in which he was teased for being an ex-Catholic must have been anything but agreeable to him.

The mistrust that even well-meaning Protestants have towards persons who are disloyal to their faith is easily explained. How can any man be true to his fellowman when he cannot be true to his God?

Never be ashamed of showing your colors. You will be thought more of for that very reason. Your neighbors, your friends, your fellow workers and people you deal with, all know what you are. It would be the height of folly, then, to try to hide your religion. And, after all, a religious conviction that is not worth showing is not worth having.

Let me repeat, in conclusion, that you should know your holy Faith and be willing to live up to it, and should show it, so that, in time, Christ may not feel ashamed of introducing you to His heavenly Father.

CHAPTER XXVI. SUPERSTITION

Man is by no means an independent being. He is bound to depend upon other beings for his very life. As an infant, as a child, a boy, a man--up to his very last breath--he must depend upon other beings for the food he needs and for the clothing to keep him warm. And in spite of all the help other created beings can offer him, he feels the need of the help of a still higher being to supply wants no other being has the power to satisfy. And this help can only come from God.

By our faith, we know that God is almighty, infinitely wise, loving, just and merciful, true and holy. Holy Faith teaches us to call Him our Father. As a father guides and directs his children, so our Heavenly Father guides and directs us in His own sweet way. It is the object of holy Faith to bring God and man closer together. On the one hand, holy Faith teaches us our destiny and our position towards our Heavenly Father: on the other hand, we learn what God is and what He expects of us. In other words, Faith shows us our relation to God, and His to us.

Faith teaches that without God we are as helpless as infants. And, in their eagerness to find help somewhere, people without Faith will have recourse to some senseless being and sign, from which they expect to receive the help that necessarily can only come from God. This, then, is the excuse for superstition. It means the transferring of the trust we should have in God to some senseless being or sign that is unable to be of any help even to itself.

A man of a firm and living Faith will never be abeliever in any superstitious sign. For how could the God Who clothes the lilies of the fields and feeds the birds of the air forget those whom He created to His own image and likeness? If He loved us so as to send His only begotten Son to suffer and die for us, in order to save our immortal souls, could He do less for us than He does for flowers and birds? If He does so much for flowers and animals what, then, will He do for His children?

A famous writer remarked: "The weaker we find Faith, the stronger will be superstition." Superstition, then, is not to be looked upon as a part, or result, of Faith. It is rather a result of the lack of Faith. As such it is both an insult to God and an insult to intelligence.

The very fact, my dear boys, that we may look up to God for our safekeeping should fill our hearts with assurance and consolation. We have His sacred word that He will watch over us and, in His own way, guide us towards our eternal home, Heaven. He has given us a most solemn pledge that He will grant us all the graces, and more than we need, to gain our salvation. Why not, then, trust this almighty God, our Father! But rather than place confidence in the fatherly care of God, some people will place their trust in a rusty old horseshoe! And that piece of junk they consider more helpful than the providence of God Himself! Such is the insult hurled at the Omnipotence and Mercy of God. Is it a wonder the Catholic Church takes such a firm stand against all kinds of superstitious practices?

Superstition is, likewise, an insult to intelligence. How can any man in his right mind claim that a horseshoe, a rabbit foot, or any other such silly thing, can do as much, or even more, than God Himself!

161

We know, for instance, that a magnet has the power of drawing iron to itself, if both are brought near enough to each other. Now, if a person would wish to claim that the same magnet can attract paper, or wool, or wood, we would consider him as very ignorant. A horseshoe is useful in its way, but it has no more power of attracting good luck than a magnet can draw wool or paper.

It would, indeed, be an unprofitable task were I to discuss all the many kinds of superstition. I will point out two of the more common abuses: the one is to attribute peculiar powers to articles blessed by our holy Church, the other, fortune telling in its various phases, including the seeing of so-called ghosts at spiritualistic meetings.

It is, indeed, unfortunate that people will misuse even sacred things, ascribing to them certain powers not understood or implied in the blessings attached to them. Although God has wrought miracles in favor of pious souls who used these blessed articles with devout intentions, yet it cannot be argued that, because God has miraculously saved the life of a person for the sake of the holy scapular, anyone may jump into deep water and expect the scapular to act as a life preserver. We know of instances where God saved the lives of people through a rosary or medal of the Blessed Virgin Mary; that, however, does not mean that everybody having such a medal or rosary in his keeping will be safe from sunstroke, lightning or drowning, or that he will be fire and bullet-proof. Our holy Church blesses many articles, like candles, medals, rosaries, crosses, palms, holy water, ashes, and so forth. By using them with a devout disposition we may, and do, receive certain favors, blessings and graces. It must, however, be understood that we receive only such that are indicated by the words of the blessing that our holy Mother Church puts upon them. In His infinite bounty and love, God may, at times, grant extraordinary graces, may even permit miracles to happen through the pious use of sacramentals. But to claim that the blessed articles are possessed of such power is absolutely wrong and sinful.

Always make it a rule to handle blessed articles, as rosaries, holy water, medals, and so forth, with due respect and devotion. Be content to use and apply them according to the wishes and the intention of holy Church. The graces, spiritual favors and indulgences you receive through them are surely to be prized, yet there is absolutely no necessity of assigning more powers to them than the wording of the blessings will permit. Hence do not attribute powers to holy things you know they cannot have. It is bad enough to attach supernatural powers to things, like a horseshoe. But to be superstitious about things blessed by the Church, and to use them otherwise than the Church wants them to be used, is a still greater wrong.

In connection with what has been said about the abuse of holy things for superstitious purposes, a few remarks must be made regarding fake prayers and charms, with which at times the mails are flooded. I mean the endless chain-prayer fad. That so many people are fooled by the endless chain-prayer is amazing. A certain prayer, supposed to have been written by Christ, or to have fallen down from heaven upon the holy grave at Jerusalem, must be copied a number of times and sent to as many people, who in their turn must copy it as often and send it to as many more, and so on! And the poor individual who gets that prayer and does not copy it and send it to as many, will be punished. His house will catch fire all by itself, he will be struck by lightning or by an automobile, and a thousand other evils will befall him. On the face of it, you must see that such things are false. To protect the faithful, the Church has made a law that all prayer-books and all prayers must have the approval of some bishop. The bishop of the city in which a pious book or prayer is printed must give his permission for publishing it. And, before he gives his consent, he has some learned priest go through the whole book, word for word, to see that the book or prayer contains nothing contrary to our holy Faith. Only after this priest renders a favorable report will the bishop give his consent to have the book or prayer printed and given to the people. So whenever you come across a Bible, prayer book or prayer, that does not contain the permission of some bishop, you will know the Church has nothing to do with it. When the Church does not indorse a prayer book or prayer, you know there is a reason. Hence you need not worry about such prayers. They can neither help nor hurt you.

As to fortune telling, let me say this: For very good reasons, God has withheld the future from us. Still, there are some persons who want to know the future. They go to a fortune teller who knows less about them than they do themselves. Once at a world's fair, I was approached by a fortune teller. He said: "Sir, I would like to tell you your fortune." I turned to him and said: "Sir, do you know my name?" He said, "No." "Do you know what I am?" I asked him again. And again he had to say "no." "Well," I said, "if you know neither my name nor my business how could you tell my past or my future ? You might take me for Mr. Brown, or Jones, or Smith, and tell me theirs, but not mine."

If these fortune tellers could really tell the future for only half a day ahead, they would not have to wait for foolish dupes at twenty-five or fifty cents a head. If they knew only one hour ahead what horse would win a race, what copper or railway stock would go up, which baseball team would win, why, they could make a fortune in one day. They could live without worry ever after. They know absolutely nothing more, even less, than the person going to them for information. You may hear that so-and-so went to a fortune teller and that he or she did hit the truth. But such is within the reach of all.

A fortune teller may tell you that one of your family will die. I can tell you the same without laying the cards. For, in the course of time, some one of your relatives will have to die. I cannot tell you who it will be, or what day and hour, but neither can the fortune teller tell you that. He may say, you will go traveling. Who does not go traveling nowadays? But I could not say when you will go, where you will go, or what train you will take, and the fortune teller does not know it either. Hence, fortune tellers, to be on the safe side, will confine themselves to things that are as much applicable to you as to Smith and Brown or anybody else.

Some people never feel well unless they are humbugged.

The same may be said of fortune tellers who claim to bring the dead back. They are frauds. God will, at times, permit the dead to speak, as the lives of the saints inform us. When such events take place there is no charge for admission, as with spiritualistic deceivers.

A poor woman, mourning the loss of her husband, went in her uncontrollable grief to a spiritualistic medium to be able to speak to her husband, for two dollars each time. She imagined that the white robed figure was really her husband. After a few weeks, her conscience not giving her any rest, she went to her parish priest to find out whether these meetings with the ghost of her husband were proper.

"How much did it cost you to see your late husband?" the priest asked. "Two dollars each time," the woman replied. "And how often have you seen him?" the priest asked again. "About ten times," she replied. "Well, now," the priest said, "your husband was a hardworking man; you must work hard to earn your living. Supposing your husband had any important message for you, do you not think he could come and speak to you directly without forcing you to give twenty dollars of your hard earned money to another person who has no interest in your meetings with him?"

The poor woman saw the force of the argument and had no more meetings with that "ghost."

There may be times when circumstances point to the help of the devil in bringing about apparitions. In such cases, there is all the more reason for us to stay away. But usually the success of spiritualists depends upon dark rooms, clever tricks and a wholesale fraud. Some of the most startling apparitions have been explained as very clever tricks.

The Church, whenever her priests give any blessings, puts these words upon their lips: "Our help is in the name of the Lord, Who hath made heaven and earth."

We have all reason to feel happy, secure and grateful, because we have God to take care of us. Our trust is not placed in some helpless thing or empty sign, but in the Almighty and infinitely merciful God.

CHAPTER XXVII. CURSING

It is often the hardest thing in the world to keep from the knowledge of others our private thoughts, desires, or inclinations. Our very walk, our way of dressing will reveal whether we are slouchy or neat, lazy or active. Some little detail in our general bearing and appearance will reveal whether we are well balanced or not. Nothing, however, will betray us more quickly than our tongue. Other indications may, at times, be misleading: our tongue never. People will not take our measure only by what we say, but how we say it. If we express our thoughts in poor English, they know our education has been neglected. If our talk is slang, they conclude that our upbringing and our company are anything but refined. If every other word you say is a curse, they will keep you at a distance if they have any regard for their own reputation.

Happily, in these times, it is no longer considered good form to be blustering and cursing and swearing like a madman. Even those who care nothing for God or devil, for heaven or hell, will refrain from vulgar talk because they forfeit by such talk the esteem and goodwill of people of refinement. What, then, should be said of a Catholic boy who is guilty of cursing? There are no words strong enough in our language to condemn the practice of cursing as it deserves to be condemned. All that can be said, so far as a boy is concerned who is guilty of cursing, is that it is very, very deplorable, and that such a fellow is not a fit companion for any decent boy.

There are some who make light of cursing by saying: "Oh, what's the difference! One little word cannot do any harm." The littleness of it does not make a word good or bad. It is the meaning that counts. A word need not be a yard long to become a mortal sin. To bring this thought home to you, bear in mind what cursing really means. There is the infinitely loving, just and merciful God, whom you, a little sinful mite, ask to damn someone for whom our dear Savior bled and died. You appeal to God to do something that is unjust, simply because in your fit of anger you wish to bring more harm upon another than you yourself are able to do him. The holiness, justice and mercy of God, however, forbid Him to damn people, or things, simply because it would suit your whim or fancy. The insult we offer God in asking Him to do such a wrong is so base and horrible that there are no words with which to express it. To curse is an insult to the holiness, the justice, and the mercy of God. Nor is cursing a meaningless trifle when considered in the light of fraternal charity. We are bound to love our neighbor as ourselves. To wish him temporal or eternal harm, and even ask God to inflict it, is certainly anything but charity.

An old adage says: "There is a place for everything." And there is a proper place for cursing. When we hear a man talk French we have reason to think that he is a Frenchman. Another who talks Russian, will probably be a Russian. Our language, maybe even our very dialect, will betray us. People of Boston, or of the West or South, have each their own accent. We can tell by the way people talk whether they are of the West or East, North or South, and cursing is the language of hell. The damned curse themselves and their fellow sufferers without ceasing. The souls of the damned curse the devil for having misled them, and he, in turn, curses them for having been such fools as to believe him more than God. Between those that gave, and those that followed, the bad example fierce curses are exchanged, and nothing but curses. Not a kind word is ever spoken there: not a word of pity or of sympathy; nothing but angry curses are shouted in that bottomless pit.

Is it not a disgrace to speak the language of hell? Is it to be wondered at that the boy who curses loses the esteem and respect of every decent man?

One would hardly think it possible that there can be malice worse than even the devil's malice. The boy who in his profane talk abuses the most holy name of Jesus does so with the greatest irreverence. But even the devils guard their tongue. They, at least, never abuse the most holy Name of our Savior. At the sound of that most holy Name, even the devils bend their knees in fear and trembling. He, then, who is guilty of pronouncing the most holy Name of Jesus Christ irreverently, is guilty of a crime that not even Satan would dare to commit.

From this, then, you may judge whether cursing is a meaningless trifle. He who would make little of it either does not know what he is talking about, or he tries to mislead you purposely.

As to the effect of curses, suffice it to say that, like stones thrown up in the air, they come back again. Usually they hurt him who utters them. It happened some time ago that a hot-headed farmer was scolding his hired help for not working as fast as he wished them to work. He found fault with the men who were pitching hay and said: "I will be damned if I can't pitch hay faster than you lazy dogs." He got up on the wagon, but in swinging his pitchfork he lost his balance, fell over backwards and broke his neck. He was dead when picked up. Let us hope that his last wish did not come true.

What would you say of a boy who claims he cannot tell the truth because he got so used to lying he can no longer keep from it? Would you excuse his lies because he has developed the habit of lying? You would say, there is no excuse for forming such a habit. In like manner, there is no excuse for saying, "I got into the habit of cursing and cannot stop it." You can stop it and you must stop it. That is all there is to it. You had no business to form such a bad habit and now you must break yourself of that habit. The sooner you do it, the better it will be for you. To contract a bad habit is a great wrong; to keep this habit is another great wrong. And, since, with the grace of God, we can break ourselves of any bad habit, it is foolish to say we cannot. It would, in that case, be more correct if you would say you will not. There is no reason or excuse for us to fly into a rage and passion whenever something goes wrong. A little pot will boil over much faster than a big kettle. In like manner, a little, narrow mind will become hot over things that a big, broad mind passes off with a smile. Learn to control your feelings, your temper, and your tongue. You will make your life miserable by letting them get the better of you.

The saddest feature about the habitual curser is that, usually, a curse is the last word he says in this life.

When I was a boy, I knew a man who had been brought up as a Catholic, although, so far as I knew, he never lived up to his holy religion. I can still remember how we boys used to stand around that man whenever he had been drinking, to hear him curse and swear. In his impotent rage he was a strange sight to behold. On his deathbed, he refused to have a priest called. Having foolishly wasted his health and earnings, he had few that stood by him at the end. His tongue was dying; he was hardly able to speak; but still he cursed. When finally unable to speak his lips still moved. What he said could not

170

be understood. Let us hope that these last words were an act of contrition. And God grant that our last words on earth will be a prayer. The chances, however, are that, if guilty of cursing habitually, your last words will be a curse.

No well-disposed boy will wish to be guilty of cursing, or of abusing the most holy Name of our Redeemer. Yet there are any number of boys who, while they would not think of irreverently using the name of Jesus, make use of some other words that sound very much like a genuine blasphemy. You sometimes hear men and boys saying, "Judas priest." The expression they place upon the word is, to say the least, not very edifying. It is always advisable to refrain from words that have a striking similarity with some holy name or thing. In some unguarded moment there may be a slip of the tongue and you say a word you do not mean to say. Eventually, you may no longer mind if your tongue slips; and from that stage to a bad habit is not very far.

There is no denying the fact that we all are at times provoked beyond endurance, and many men find relief in saying something forcible. It is human nature. So when such a time comes for you, follow my advice and you will not go wrong. Take a full breath of air and say real loud and as forcibly as possible: "Jumping fishhooks!" or "Great Guns," and "Happy Hooligan" may be used for sake of variety. By saying any, or all, of these words you avoid the dreadful calamity of an explosion, the rupture of a blood-vessel will be averted, and, after you have had your harmless say, you may come to again and have a quiet laugh all to yourself for having come out of that great crisis with so little effort.

Try to acquire an even temper. Never be overjoyed one day and depressed the next. Let no day pass by without making an effort to be more patient, and forbearing, and meek, than the day before.

Our dear Savior gave us a beautiful lesson of patience and meekness on one of His journeys to Jerusalem. He desired to stop at one of the cities in Samaria, and sent two Apostles ahead to find lodging for the night. Instead of receiving Him with open arms, the people started a riot and actually forbade our dear Lord to enter the city. The insults that were hurled at their divine Master made the Apostles so indignant that they asked Him whether they should not call down fire from heaven to destroy that godless city.

And what did Christ say? Did He say, "Yes, you are right, these people are an ungrateful lot and fire is even too good for them"? He said nothing of the sort. He even called the Apostles to task for having such a revengeful disposition. Without the least sign of impatience or of ill-will He said : "You know not of what spirit you are. The Son of Man is not come to destroy souls but to save."

Tired though He was, Christ walked on with His little group of faithful Apostles until the next little town was reached. There they found shelter for the night. Our dear Lord would have been perfectly justified in punishing these ungrateful people, but He took their insults in good part. "Learn of me," He says, "for I am meek and humble of heart." And let us raise our hands up to Him, praying: Oh, Jesus, meek and humble of heart, make our hearts like unto Thine.

CHAPTER XXVIII. SUNDAY

Even at your age you must have seen many of the ways in which the world spends Sunday. In summer, the people attend picnics, take in excursions, or go fishing and camping. In winter, hunting, skating and indoor games take the place of some mere amusements. And then there are often theatres and shows that attract people. You will find this class of people going to church on Christmas day, or on the feast of Easter, you may find them there attending some fashionable wedding or funeral. And these people go to church on such occasions not because they desire to comply with a duty, but to show to the rest of mankind that they can dress more handsomely than others may think them able to afford. But as for going to church Sunday after Sunday that is more than they are willing to do. Their amusements and social obligations give them no time for regular churchgoing.

Still, we may, to a great extent, excuse many of these worldly people. After all, what inducement can the bare walls of a Protestant church give to people? They can easily find better speakers than their ministers, and better singers are heard in most theatres. They have indeed no obligation to attend their church Sunday after Sunday, nor can they see a good reason for attending even at a sacrifice or discomfort.

These excuses do not, however, apply to Catholics. We have a strict Commandment to attend holy Mass every Sunday, under pain of mortal sin. We know, too, what the holy sacrifice of Mass means for us, what graces it holds in store for us, and we know, furthermore, that there is reward for the observers and punishment for the violators of the Third Commandment. And yet there are Catholics who think little or nothing of missing Mass on Sunday. The most foolish excuses are offered. I have known a man who would not go to Mass because he was not allowed to join the choir. Who does not know of people who do not go to church because they are unable to show off fine clothes. Women have stayed away from church for no other reason but that their hat does not look as handsome as the hat of another woman. Men stay away from church because they claim they have no Sunday suit. Unfortunately, it is true that people will judge one another by their clothes and by the size of the bank account. But

God does not mind these little things. He looks at our hearts. We may have no bank book to our name; no property at our disposal; our clothes may be two or ten years old; and yet, if our heart is free from mortal sin, we will be a pleasing sight to God. He will be glad to see us Sunday after Sunday as we come to pay Him the homage due to Him. A sin stained conscience, however, is hideous to God no matter how costly the clothes and jewels.

But there are also Catholics whose only reason for breaking the Third Commandment of God is their entertainments. This class simply does not care for the Church, and far from feeling ashamed they even boast of their indifference and ridicule others for going to church.

It is harder, still, to explain how a Catholic boy can stay away from holy Mass on Sundays after he has left school only a year or two. This boy has been well instructed by the school sisters, and by the priest. This boy had grown accustomed to come to Mass every Sunday. Those who were his schoolmates remained faithful to their duty. He has grown indifferent.

Some boys have the mistaken notion that religious duties are a matter of compulsion. They think they must comply with them when they are watched, and that they may evade them when not watched. They look upon the rules of the parish school as some sort of tyranny, and once beyond the influence of the priest and the school, they feel as though they were free to do as they like. But if there is one fact that you should take to heart more than another when you leave school it is this: God desires your willing service in obeying the Commandments. It is left to your conscience. You have received all the instructions necessary to give you a good knowledge of your holy religion. You know well what God forbids, and what He commands you to do. God does not intend to deprive us of the liberty of our will. God wants to be obeyed freely, willingly and cheerfully. Even your guardian angel may only urge you, but cannot compel you, to obey God.

What made your parents help to build this church and school?

No one compelled them to make so many sacrifices! What makes people come to the Masses on Sunday, crowding the church for every Divine service? What makes Catholics abstain from meat on Fridays and fast days? What makes a sister of charity lock herself up in a convent and devote her life to charitable work? What makes the priest say Mass every morning, preach the word of God, spend hours and hours in a narrow confessional, and hurry to the sick and dying even though he endanger his own life? The answer to all these questions is Faith. We must be led by Faith, and should live according to it.

Let this lesson teach you, then, to live according to the instructions you have received. Keep the

Commandments of God, as Faith tells you and because Faith tells you. Likewise keep this Third Commandment as God wants you to keep it, and because He wants you to keep it.

Your Faith bids you to come to holy Mass on Sundays and feast days unless some important reason excuses you. In case you have any doubt as to whether there is sufficient reason for staying away from holy Mass, ask your confessor. Faith tells you what holy Mass is; tells you what an honor it is even to be allowed to be present at it; it tells you what graces you receive from it, and how perfectly God is honored in this great sacrifice. Faith tells you why you should keep holy the Lord's Day. Faith commands you to honor God and rest your body. After God gives you SIX days to work for yourself, it is no more than right and just that you should set one day aside for His glory and honor. He might ask more of us. The very fact that He asks so little of us ought to dispose us to give Him the entire day. To begrudge Him the short time of a holy Mass makes us look dreadfully small. Faith tells you that God rewards those who observe His day and punishes those that desecrate it. Faith tells you who it is that is present upon our altars. The Third Commandment is so exact and plain that we cannot help but understand it. We know exactly what it stands for, know what it commands and what it forbids, know the why and wherefore of it, and the consequences of our actions regarding it. This certainly ought to be enough for us.

God leaves everything to our good will. We may comply with His wishes and reap eternal reward, or we may oppose His Commandments and, in that case, face the consequences. It is ours to choose between life and death; Heaven and hell. Now if we want to show good sense, we will see that we promote the honor and glory of God and the salvation of our soul.

The meaning of attending holy Mass and of avoiding servile work has been explained so that I may pass it over this time. But there are two other things I would like to impress upon you.

The first is this: Never permit yourself to be misled by the bad example of others. If you live long enough you will see plenty of people who never go to church. I met one of these kind a few days ago and asked him to come to church. I got little satisfaction. He told me how good he was because he had not killed anyone and had not stolen anything. "'Those are only two Commandments you keep. How about the other eight?" I asked. To this question I got no answer. To come to Heaven, it is not enough to dodge the jail in this life. The fact that a man has not been locked up for a crime does by no means give him an admission ticket to Heaven. The one reason, in fact, why some people will not kill or steal is that they are afraid of being locked up for it. If it were not for jail and gallows our life would not be as secure as it is. Because others will not go to church can never be a reason for you to stay away from church. The time will come when some will laugh at you for being pious. People will say you are not up-to-date, that there is no God, and all such talk. But he laughs best who laughs last. It may even be that a brother of yours, or a dear friend of yours, will for some foolish reason stay from church. And they will try to make you think as they do, will put or try to put all kinds of silly notions into your head. Let them talk as much as they have a mind to. Remember that we must mind God above all other things. The devil was not satisfied when he was sent to hell. He wanted others to do as he did. He tried all he could to turn our first parents 'away from God, in order to drag the whole human race to hell with him. The bad example you see round about you is only another trick of the devil. It has been good bait with many other people, and the devil sees no reason why you should not be caught with it as easily as others have been caught.

If you must follow an example, take the example of pious and saintly people. If the world only took to heart the example of saintly people instead of the example of the wicked, this world would be a far better place to live in. There would be less greed, selfishness and vice of all kinds, and more charity instead.

The other thought I want you to bear in mind is this: Never, excepting in the greatest necessity, take work that prevents you from going to holy Mass every Sunday.

I understand perfectly well that some work must be done on Sundays. Some people must be found to do that kind of work. But, on the other hand, there are employers and foremen that demand work done on a Sunday without reason or necessity.

In looking for work, bear in mind you have not only a body to feed but a soul to save. What would it profit you to gain all the money in the world for the benefit of your body, if thereby you would lose your soul. The bargain would be a very poor one, indeed. Hence, in looking for work, always make sure that you can take care of the welfare of your soul. If for some reason or other you take night work, you will have to spend some part of the Sunday in work. But in most cities you will find excellent arrangements for such workers. You can hear a holy Mass either as you come from work or you may go home, take a little rest and go to a late Mass. It is only a question of good will with these workers whether they want to go to church.

Many people can make no headway. They work in vain. They work seven days each week. At the end of the year they are exactly where they were the year before. If you want God to bless you and your work, keep His day holy. Possibly God's help is not with them, because they refused to be with God.

CHAPTER XXIX. OBEDIENCE

A few days ago, I met a man of nearly sixty years of age, as he was leaving the cemetery. He had planted some flowers on the grave of his father who had died the week before. When he met me, he had tears in his eyes. "Father," the man said, "now I only feel how much I depended on the sound advice of my father. I never undertook anything in business or in other matters without asking Father first. And his advice was always wise and prudent. Now I feel that I am alone. I must depend upon myself." And this very man who spoke thus, my dear boys, had grown-up sons and daughters. Still, he always looked up to his father and never undertook anything without his advice or against his will.

Nowadays when boys reach the age of seventeen years--even before that--they yearn for freedom, for liberty. They will not hear of restraint, of obedience or of advice. They want to do as they please, what they please, and when they please. The obedience that a conscientious father or mother exacted in former times grates upon their up-to-date mind. The old folks may demand obedience of younger sisters and brothers, but are too far behind the times to tell the boy of fourteen what to do or what not to do. He thinks he knows everything. He has left school, and possibly earns the magnificent sum of seventy-five or a hundred dollars a week. Therefore, he argues, he is his own master. Not even a suggestion, or a hint, or a counsel, is taken in good part. The yoke of obedience that proved so galling and irksome is cast aside and the boy thinks he breathes more freely. He may think so.That is all. He labors under a dreadful illusion.

Well, some may say, how long must we practice obedience? Will we be bound to obey after we are of age? The fact is, my dear boys, that the obligation of obedience never ceases. It binds us always. Unless we learn well how to obey when we are children, the obligation to obey will prove harder from day to day. No man is excused from obedience. The higher he ranks in society or office, the more exacting will be the obligation of obedience. The President of our country cannot do as he likes. He has to obey the Constitution and the laws of the land. Practically, he can do nothing without the will or against the wishes of Congress. Congress, in turn, cannot enact laws opposed to the Constitution. The priest of a parish, though he must be obeyed by the people of the parish in all things lawful, is responsible to his bishop and must obey the instructions he receives. The bishop, in turn, although the priests of the diocese obey him, cannot go beyond the orders and instructions given him by the Holy Father, the Pope. The Holy Father, in turn, although all Christendom obeys him as the representative of Christ, is bound to obey the laws of God as rigidly as his humblest subject.

Man, no matter how high he may climb upon the ladder of authority, will always find another just a trifle higher than himself, to whom he must be obedient in all lawful things.

You see, then, that there is no end to obedience in this life. It is binding upon all, the rich and the poor, the wise and the unlearned, the high and the low. You cannot find a single being, outside of God, that is not bound to obey.

Nor does obedience end with our last breath of life in this world. Even in the world to come we will be bound by this law. There is obedience in Heaven as well as in hell. The source of authority, God, is the same in both places. There is this difference, however, that, while in hell obedience only adds to the greater humiliation and suffering of the damned, in Heaven it proves to be a source of greater happiness and love of God.

It is true that there are people who claim they are their own masters, that they can do as they please, that no man has any right to make laws for them. They claim that, since they have been given a will and understanding of their own, they can use it as they think best. You will find people who disregard and break the laws of God if by so doing they derive any temporal benefit. For the sake of gaining another dollar, or for the sake of pleasure, they will miss holy Mass on Sunday or feast day. The support they should give the Church is spent in some other way. These people even boast of their disobedience and make fun of those who are faithful to the holy Will of God. Not content with doing wrong themselves they try to induce others to do as they do. The very fact that God does not punish them on the spot, and that they may possibly prosper for some reason only known to Divine Providence, is used as an argument in their favor.

But let these people boast of their independence as much as they like. Let them do as they like. The time will come when they will have to obey the call and voice of God. They may be deaf to His voice now, but the time will come when there will not be a doubt about the meaning of that call. In life they may have done just what they pleased. But the time will come when the boast will die upon their lips. That time comes with the parting from this life. These independent people will not be able to wait one minute or even a second to do as they please when God calls them from this world. They will die in obedience to the holy Will of God. They will render an account of every thought and

181

word and deed and omission in obedience to the holy Will of God. They will obediently submit to the judgment of God, not for a short space of time, but for all eternity.

You see, then, that, even when people fail toobey God in this world, they will obey God in the next. You understand, too, how silly it is of us to think that, after a certain number of years, we are our own masters, to do as we please, what we please, how we please. That time will never come, whether we will spend eternity in Heaven or in hell.

Obedience is a part of the Providence of God in our behalf.

Since our first parents sinned by disobedience, God ordained that salvation can be obtained only by obedience. To put stress upon obedience, at the sign of atonement on our part, He has so organized the entire plan of our social order that one person must be obedient to another, without exempting a single being from the necessity of obeying. Hence, all authority comes from God. To humble our proud minds and to bend our stiff necks in obedience is, at times, a hard task. And yet you will learn in later years, when you will have responsibilities of your own, when you will have to command others to obey you, that it is far more easy to obey than to command. In fact, no one should command who has not learned to obey.

Now that you understand that obedience is binding upon us for time and eternity, you will see the reason for being obedient to parents. In the first place, it is the holy Will of God. God wants us to obey, to help us gain Heaven.

Parents do not command or forbid something just to show their power, but to help us. Remember how helpless a little child is. When you were little tots you may have wanted to eat some poison you saw, just because it looked tempting. Your parents had to forbid it; perhaps you cried and yelled and you had to be punished even. Your parents wanted to save your life, and if you had not obeyed you would have died.

Now you may be a boy of fourteen and have your little head crowded with all kinds of wisdom. You may know more history or botany than your father. But do not think for a moment that to get along in this world your book knowledge will be enough. There is a certain knowledge called experience that you have not. And if you want to get lessons in that science you will have to go to your father and mother and take their advice.

Obedience should be its own reward, for I do not like the idea of children asking to be bribed to obey. When a child must be given a penny to behave it is not an obedient child. In course of time, it will gain the impression that money is the only thing on earth to work for. If it pays more to be bad than good that child will be bad. In later years, it will do and be whatever pays best. It will have no idea of another motive or reason for obedience.

Since you understand that we must obey for time and eternity, the obedience we owe to our parents is a training for the obedience we will have to practice in time to come.

The degree of obedience exacted of you at present grows in proportion as the years pass on. The older you get, the higher you advance in honors and responsibilities, the harder obedience becomes. Now, your obedience demands few and light sacrifices. In later years, obedience will ask for many and great sacrifices. If you cannot be obedient in little matters now, will you be more able to be obedient in matters of importance in after years? We must begin by

183

being faithful in little things before we can be faithful in things of importance.

It is necessary, therefore, to learn how to be obedient. The sooner we can master that lesson the better for us. You have noticed how the examples of your arithmetic become harder for each grade. You will not be able to master the examples of the tenth grade if you do not know how to solve the examples of the first grade. Unless you learn to obey whilst you are a boy, your life as a man will be a failure. Learn, then, my dear boys, to be obedient, in order to promote the honor and glory of God as well as your own temporal and eternal welfare.

CHAPTER XXX. SCANDAL

A great many boys do not know what scandal really means. They give scandal and they take it and yet they do not know, and sometimes will not want to know, the real meaning of the word. Most people understand by scandal the spreading of tales injurious to reputations. To discover some hidden or imaginary fault of a neighbor, to spread as widely as possible, and, thereby, to cause all sorts of mischief, is only one of the ways of giving scandal.

It is a mistake, however, to take a part for a whole. Scandal means more than that. Scandal means the force of bad example. And bad example finds its force of doing harm in our inclination towards evil. Inclination towards evil is one of the wounds that original sin has inflicted upon mankind. This evil inclination induces us to discern and to follow the evil example of others. We may see just as much, and even more, good example. But there is greater attraction and more plausibility in evil example. If we see So-and-so doing something wrong, we at once ask: if he can do so why should we do otherwise? Do we ever draw a similar conclusion when we see others giving a good and noble example? We even suspect and question the good motive of those who give a good example. Now, if our good inclination was as strong as our evil inclination we would find it easier to be uplifted and inspired by good example than to be dragged down and tempted by bad example. Keeping this idea in mind, the true meaning of scandal will be more readily understood.

Any sin in word, action or omission, committed in the presence of others and causing them, or giving them, the occasion of spiritual harm is scandal. The sin of scandal will be venial or mortal, depending upon the sin thus committed. If the sin committed in the presence of others is a mortal sin, the scandal resulting therefrom will likewise be a mortal sin. To give you some examples of scandal I might, for instance, mention filthy talk, passing around bad books or pictures, missing holy Mass on a Sunday and boasting of it, making fun of others who are faithful to their religious duties. For, as I explained to you before, the bad example given by word or action tempts others to act in a like manner.

Some people make light of scandal by saying: "Well, no one need do as I do unless he wants to. They know well enough." It is true that we know well enough. But, owing to evil inclination, knowing and doing are two different things. The fact remains that by doing wrong in the presence of others we give scandal.

The kind of scandal to which you are most exposed at your age is bad company.

There is no need of telling you that the devil is aware of your good will, of the instructions you have received and are still receiving, and of the means of grace you have at your disposal. If he were to appear to you in his horrible person, dread and fear might kill you on the spot. You would never think of committing even a venial sin. But he wants your soul and he will try to destroy all the good that has been done for you. He wants to pluck from your heart all the good instructions you have received; he wants to rob you of all your merits; he wants to keep you away from the means of grace, for he knows only too well that the more use you make of them, particularly of Holy Communion, the harder It is for him to get a hold upon you.

To bring this about, he will send bad company to do the dirty work for him. And bad company does that kind of work with a vengeance. Bad companions will tell you how foolish it is to pray, how silly to receive the Sacraments; they will tell you that life is short and that we cheat ourselves if we do not enjoy its few pleasures. For many boys these and similar ideas of their bad companions are like sweet music. That is exactly the talk they like to listen to. With bad company showing them how, they learn only too gladly. So you can see the devil has some mighty good and able workers in this world

In your factories and shops, you will be exposed more than anywhere else to bad company. It is there you will hear the foulest talk, the dirtiest stories, and the most blasphemous remarks about God and religion. If a complaint to the foreman or the managers will be of no help, but will rather tend to make matters worse, and if you cannot get work at another place, all you can do will be to take it in quietly and say nothing. Pray silently that the temptation may not harm you and that God may forgive the wicked things that are said. Of course, it is understood that you must never pick any such boys to be your friends. Let them be ever so funny and entertaining otherwise, it makes them so much the more dangerous. Treat such fellow-workers with kindness and consideration, but at the same time keep them at a distance. One of them may speak to you about going to see some show. From what you are being told, it is one of the kind you would not dare to take your mother or sister to see. Your common sense will tell you that if it is not fit to be seen by them, neither is it right for you to see it. Keep away from the class of boys that frequent places of doubtful character. Bad company may want to poison your mind by speaking of the faults of parents or priests, and in this manner endeavor to undermine respect and love and obedience towards your

187

superiors. Do not listen to such talk. It is nothing but a bait of the devil.

So far, it has been taken for granted that you are the innocent and suffering party. However, it will not be amiss to examine yourself and see whether you have not been guilty of giving scandal to others. And here it will be well to call your attention to your responsibility towards younger brothers and sisters. The older children of a family are the assistants and helpers of the parents in bringing up the younger children. By their example, they either help their parents or they frustrate all their efforts. The good example of an older brother will be a great help for the parents and an inspiration for the younger children. Likewise, the bad example of an older brother will be imitated by the younger children.

Do you ever speak of the faults of your parents to your younger brothers or sisters? Do you ever talk back to your parents when they want you to do or leave something? As the younger children begin to understand that you no longer obey your parents they will soon want to know why they should obey. Are you guilty of using unbecoming language in the presence of younger brothers or sisters? Do you brag about any of your sins to them, as, for instance, cursing, foul talk and the like? Have you ever spoken to them of worse things than this? If you are guilty of any scandal towards your own flesh and blood, your younger brothers and sisters, the malice of it is all the greater, because your brothers and sisters are the ones you should love most dearly, next to your parents.

"It is impossible that scandals should not come: but woe to him through whom they come." "It is better for him that a millstone should be hanged about his neck and that he should be drowned in the depth of the sea." These words of our dear Savior give us to understand in the plainest words what He thinks of scandal. Our Divine Savior was all kindness and mercy and charity. He had a kindly smile and a gentle word for the greatest sinners if they were but repentant. Yet He would rather see a man mercilessly drowned than have him give scandal.

For your guidance, it will be best to lay down the following rules of conduct, that you may never be guilty of this terrible sin:

In the first place, avoid every mortal sin. You know how readily bad example is taken. If in the past you have been guilty of scandal, all you can do is to make up for it as best you can. You must try and bring those you have scandalized back to virtue. You will have to give good example by your life so as to make up for the bad example; and, finally, pray much and pray earnestly that no evil results may follow from your wicked actions.

Some years ago, a Catholic young lawyer opened an office in one of our large cities. He was of a good and pious family. One of his first callers was another lawyer, who welcomed him to the city, wished him success and gave him some advice. "Above all things," he said, "if you want to make headway in this town you will have to give up going to church. I was brought up a Catholic, too, but I got over it. It's all right to pass off as a Catholic sometimes--to get Catholic votes if you run for some office--but otherwise I don't bother about it and get along fine." The young lawyer answered that if he had to throw his religion overboard to make a success in law he would give up the profession and would make his living in some way in which he would not have to deny his God. Here was one instance where bad example was given but not taken. But God only knows how many others that have in contact with this apostate lawyer have heeded that bad example.

To avoid scandal, we should refrain from doing things that are perfectly lawful, if for some reason or other they will likely be misunderstood. For instance, an invalid person has received permission to eat meat on fast days. If others, not knowing that he has been dispensed, would take scandal by seeing him eat meat it is advisable for him not to eat the meat before them unless they can be informed that a dispensation has been obtained.

Finally, there is another kind of taking scandal, the pharisaical way. If the keeping of a law of God will cause some to be shocked and scandalized we are still to keep that law, taking care not to offend God to please such people. All that remains for us to do is to make our position clear and obey God rather than man. Christ knew that by healing the sick on the Sabbath He would scandalize the Pharisees. This could not induce Him to omit His works of mercy. He simply explained the, law of the Sabbath and left the Pharisees to say what they pleased.

Now, since you understand what a great sin scandal is, it will be well for you to examine your conscience and see whether you have ever given or taken scandal. If you have given it, try by all means to right the wrong. If you have taken it in the past, avoid it in the future. Let the good example you see about you inspire and guide you to a better and holier life.

·

CHAPTER XXXI. FURTHER THOUGHTS UPON THE FIFTH COMMANDMENT

There are two other matters we must touch upon in treating this commandment, although people are little inclined to give them the consideration they require. It is remarkable how this commandment is neglected in the examination of conscience. Boys will say to themselves: "Fifth Commandment-- Well, I have not killed anyone." But even though you are not guilty of murder you may be guilty of sins against this commandment.

The first question I want to propose to you is this: Do you ever expose your life or health without necessity?

Boys consider it a badge of honor and bravery to risk life or health for some foolish prank. A poor swimmer will strike out beyond his depth. Some reckless fellow will try and skate upon ice no thicker than the blade of a penknife. Another will look into a loaded gun that always goes off when it shouldn't. Others drive their bicycles or automobiles at breakneck speed, or get reckless with machinery. One can hardly pick up a paper without reading of accidents and loss of lives that could have been prevented with a little care and prudence. The fact that some persons have had fortunate escapes is no guarantee that they will always have such luck in future. It gives them no right to trifle with death and call cowards those who have more regard for their life.

There are, indeed, times when we must expose our life to danger. A priest and a doctor often expose themselves to danger in attending the sick. Firemen, nurses, policemen, soldiers and sailors must risk their lives when duty calls. But all these cases are of men who devote their lives to the welfare of others, and who are ready to make the sacrifice of their lives to save the lives of others. These people, too, are under the special protection of God. If, by chance, they should lose their lives in their calling they are martyrs of duty, and God will reward them.

But where there is no obligation arising from either duty or charity, we are by no means allowed to risk our life.

You understand that only He has a right to life Who gave it. We have not placed ourselves into this world. It is God who gave us life. He has placed us into this world giving us a certain length of time, and graces wherewith to gain eternal life in Heaven. God can and will take this temporal life from us, when and where and in what manner He sees fit. Hence, any act on our part, whereby we place our life in danger, is nothing else than disputing this right of God, or taking it out of His hands. It stands to reason that if, by our actions, we interfere with the plans of God in this most sacred right of His, He cannot be indifferent in the matter. And we shall be the losers if we trifle with the rights of God.

Realizing that your life belongs to God, you will understand why you are not allowed to expose your life to danger by any unnecessary risk or carelessness or recklessness. If duty or charity urge you to expose your life to save the life of another, you may depend upon the help of God, because then the risk is taken for the love of His commandment.

It is unlawful for us to risk our lives unnecessarily, and it is equally wrong to shorten our lives by any act of indiscretion, or by sin.

Under this heading I must place the use of tobacco by smoking and chewing.

I know you want to be men, and you can hardly wait the time when you can feel the first little hairs on your upper lip. But let me tell you, your troubles will begin soon enough without trying to hurry them along. Stay boys as long as you can. A pipe or cigarette in your mouth will not make a man of you. You cannot call a snowman a man though he has a corncob pipe in his face. A man may look well with pipe or cigar; a boy looks foolish.

It is not to begrudge you a little pleasure, if you are told to abstain from the use of tobacco. It is for your own good. Doctors will tell you that, while the use of tobacco is comparatively harmless to people who are fully grown unless some organic trouble makes the use of tobacco harmful, its use is surely dangerous for boys. For a healthy growth, it is necessary that all the organs of your body grow uniformly, If most organs grow uniformly, but one, the heart, is retarded and does not grow in proportion to the other parts, you will, in all likelihood, be one of the number that die young. If the heart is too weak to do the work for the overgrown body it will naturally give out. With boys who use tobacco whilst in the state of growing it often happens that some part of the body stays behind. To grow up in such a manner, with an organ like the heart remaining weak, will mean physical collapse when sickness overtakes you. You, with your natural craving for long life, will you try to undermine it? Do not think of smoking until you are fully grown, when you can smoke in public without fear of being laughed at. You will then enjoy a pipe or cigar all the more.

193

You must observe the same precautions, for a similar reason, regarding all alcoholic drinks. The use of such drinks must not be allowed except in accordance with the instructions of a doctor. The effect of alcoholic drinks upon the undeveloped body is similar to that of tobacco.

Even in later years, never allow yourself to hanker after drink. Check, at once, all such tendency. When you see that drink is getting the better of you, abstain from it altogether.

There is no need of going into further details, about this matter since in school you have been informed about the principal rules of health. Remember the various rules of health that have been explained to you, and act accordingly.

It will be well, therefore, to examine your conscience from time to time, to see whether you recklessly expose your life to dangers of any kind, or whether you have contracted habits that tend to shorten your life.

The other matter to which I wish to call your attention is cruelty to animals. It is true, this subject is not directly within the scope of this commandment; yet it is of particular importance at your stage of life to realize that cruelty to animals helps more than anything else to destroy the nobility of character.

God has made us masters over the lives of animals. To be cruel to animals, to hurt them wantonly, to make them work excessively is an abuse of the trust and authority God gave us, and it betrays a mean and low disposition.

If it is necessary to kill an animal, it should be killed as quickly and painlessly as possible. To make it suffer unnecessary pains implies an act of faithlessness to the trust God confided to us and an act of barbarity to a creature that is unable to help itself. People who are cruel to animals are also cruel and heartless to human beings over whom they have power.

That you may understand what influence cruelty to animals has upon the formation of character it will be enough to ask you towards which animals a boy will be cruel. A boy will never try to be cruel to an animal that is able to resent the cruelty by doing injury to the boy. He will pick out some small animal, an insect, a butterfly, or the cat, and tantalize them. Does this not show cowardice in the boy? As a fact, cowardice and cruelty go hand in hand. A coward will always be cruel to those weaker than himself. Upon them he practices the spite and malice that he dare not show towards those stronger than he. He makes the weaker ones suffer innocently for the wrongs, real or imaginary, that he suffers from those stronger than himself.

You know how the world hates a coward, how unhappy he is, and what a poor likeness of God is his mean, little and shriveled up soul. Avoid, then, cruelty to animals. Never permit yourself or others to be cruel to animals, but be at all times ready to defend the weak against the strong. By so doing, you will build up a noble character, a character that will be the pride of God and His angels and your consolation in life and death.

CHAPTER XXXII. THE WAGES OF SIN

There is no subject upon which a priest will talk more reluctantly than upon the subject of impurity. Yet, the times in which we live, the many temptations to which you are exposed in your tender years, make such instruction a most solemn duty to the priest. Were I to remain silent upon this subject, I should be guilty of gross neglect of duty. Let us first say a Hail Mary to implore the most pure Mother that she may, through her Divine Son, grant us the grace to derive profit from the consideration of this difficult subject.

There are poisons so dangerous and deadly that even their very fumes and smell kill. In like manner the sins of impurity, even the slightest impure thought, if entertained knowingly and willingly, destroy the spiritual life of the soul. There is nothing small or trivial in sins against holy purity. You have been told that these sins may be committed in thoughts and desires, words and actions. This should put us all the more on our guard. Most other sins are committed because of a temptation presented by some one of our senses or faculties. But regarding holy purity, the devil assails us from all sides at the same time. Temptation may be caused through the eyes, the ears, the tongue, even the sense of touch. Our mind, our imagination, our memory, our will, they are all equally exposed to the same temptations. If we bear in mind that this sin of impurity can attack any and all of our bodily senses, any and all of our mental faculties, then we begin to understand the dreadful hold this sin can gain upon people.

It may not be so difficult to defend ourselves against the attacks of one foe: but when we are attacked from all sides, when all our senses and mental faculties are attacked at the same time, the fight is a dreadful one. But even then we need not despair, for the greater the temptation the greater will be the amount of graces to overcome them.

A special reason, then, why we should be upon our guard against impurity, is that we can be attacked at any time and from all sides. Another reason why we must be on our guard is the way of the world. Outside of our holy faith, there is little knowledge and apprehension about this vice. The world admits it in a general way, not as a vice or crime, but, as a passing and harmless inclination. And the world finds all kinds of excuses for it. Hence we must be on our guard and not let the mistaken notion of the world take hold of us. Of sins, too vile to be mentioned, the world thinks little; indeed, it passes them off as a joke. The world calls our view an old-fashioned idea about the right way of living. The world will say that you are behind the times. You may even hear indifferent Catholics making such remarks. Therefore, unless you are on your guard, you will begin to doubt and then to question the teaching of our holy religion upon this subject.

But if sins against holy purity are harmless, if they are nothing but a joke, what about the physical ruin, the dreadful diseases induced by this loathsome sin?

The world may make little of the sins against holy purity, but the fact remains that the world enforces secrecy concerning them. The foul-mouthed boy or man will be careful not to unload his foul talk at the wrong time or place. The boy given to dirty talk will never use an improper word in the presence of his mother or of his sisters. Were there no harm in them, why could not these remarks be made in their presence? The boy or man guilty of improper

197

actions will look for the cover of night and privacy for their indulgence. If these actions were harmless, why is he so careful in hiding them? The fact is that these sins are so shocking and so humiliating that a boy will, in truth, be ashamed of himself. In his heart he knows he does wrong, and so much does he dread the evil that may and must follow that he tries to have these sins kept under cover. But, no matter with what secrecy and privacy the sinner may surround himself, the sins will not remain a secret forever. And, what makes matters worse, the guilty party will be his own accuser. The sins he tried to hide from all the world he himself will reveal to the whole world.

You may ask, how does a sinner reveal his sins? Who causes him to betray himself? God, who has set a reward for every good deed, has also set a punishment for each and every evil action. The worse the crime the greater the punishment must be. And the most humiliating punishment for sins against holy purity in this life is inevitable acknowledgment of these sins. You inquire how the sinners reveal these sins ? You may know that every characteristic trait of a person is imprinted upon his face. You can tell without much experience whether a man is jolly or severe, whether he is a miser or a cheerful spender, whether he has an ugly temper or whether he has a gentle disposition, whether he is frank and candid or cunning and deceiving. The face will have certain lines, the mouth and eyes will have a certain expression that point to the character of the person.

And so does impurity place a stamp upon the face, and marks it with a sign of warning. A person may have a homely face. Yet, if that homely face bears the stamp of kindness and charity, it will possess attraction and charm. Such was the face of Lincoln. But the most beautiful face will be repulsive if it bears the mark of impurity. We reveal our character, our virtues, and faults in our faces.

198

Our faces are open books to all that can read. We may hide our hands, we may disguise the body; but the face remains the open book for all.

Nor is this all the punishment God meets out to the impure. He sends the sinner various forms of sickness as part of the punishment. The sinner will be ashamed to reveal his condition even to a doctor. Often there is nothing that can stop the ravages of the dreadful sickness. The sinner, aware of his fate, is grasped by despair. He suffers for the rest of his days the pains of hell in his miserable decaying body, and, unless he truly repents, faces eternal damnation in the life to come. And the world looks upon this sin as a joke, a harmless human trait. Is it not plain that the world is greatly mistaken if we consider the consequences of this sin? You can hardly pick up a paper these days without reading of a young man or young woman having committed suicide. To spare relatives, the papers will state that the unfortunate person had been in poor health for some time, and was at the time momentarily insane. You will probably find it stated that the deceased had a large circle of friends, that the news is a shock and surprise to all, and no reason can be imagined to explain the rash act.

All of which is well enough to tell the public, but it does not state an explanation of the act. When the impure see ahead of them sure death and disgrace, then, if they have lost all faith, which is usually the case, the next thing they think of is suicide. It seems to them the lesser evil.

That the sins of impurity must be horrible beyond the power of words to express must be taken from the fact that all this physical misery is only a small part of the punishment. The just God adds to it in many cases the loss of faith. Loss of faith leads to eternal damnation. From

199

the greatness of the punishment we may judge how much God abhors this sin.

Great as the allurements may be, great as the dangers are, still greater are the graces to overcome the temptations to this sin.

To avoid these dreadful sins, we must take proper precautions. Hence let me lay down three rules for your conduct:

In the first place, you must keep away from bad company. Bad company, bad books, bad theatres, are all alike in their consequence. Immoral companions may be ever so polished, entertaining and full of fun, you must shun them altogether. Countless thousands have gone the way of perdition through bad company; do not try to swell their ranks by becoming one of their number.

In the second place, you must frequently receive the holy Sacraments. In many cases, impurity will be the reason why boys stay away from Confession and Communion. If you have had the misfortune of committing such a sin, do not make a bad Confession by not revealing it. And then there may be no more chance you have to reveal it. And then, there may be no more chance for pardon. It may be out of the question for most of you to go to Holy Communion every morning. But with real good-will you will be able to receive Holy Communion every Sunday. That weekly Communion will be your greatest protection in preserving the purity of body and soul.

In the third place, practice a childlike devotion to our Blessed Mother, the most pure Virgin. Not one of your daily prayers should be ended without a prayer to the Queen of Virgins. We can do our Blessed Mother no greater favor, nor cause her more pleasure, than by asking her to pray for us that we may remain pure in heart and mind, for love of her and of her Divine Son.

CHAPTER XXXIII. THE BEAUTY OF PURITY

As there is no vice more loathsome and horrible than impurity, so purity is of all virtues the most charming and beautiful. Not without good reason has the spotless and fragrant lily been chosen as the emblem of that angelic virtue. And if you wish to know what God thinks of this great virtue, pay attention to what I am going to say.

In the first place, no virtue demands greater sacrifice and more care than this virtue. St. Jerome calls this virtue a living martyrdom. The sufferings of the blessed martyrs were generally of comparatively short duration. The martyrdom which this virtue exacts of us lasts for one's entire life. We must guard not only one of our senses or faculties, but all of them. All senses and faculties are exposed to temptations against holy purity, and so we must keep all of our senses and mental faculties under careful control. We must guard our eyes like a St. Aloysius, our ears like a St. Stanislaus, our lips like a St. John. The self-denial demanded by this constant watchfulness is severe enough to be regarded by the Fathers of the Church as a martyrdom.

Another reason why God values this virtue so highly is because purity is the crown of all other virtues. It presupposes the presence of many, if not all other, virtues. They that are pure of heart love prayer. They have the virtue of piety. They must be firm, and pray for grace and strength. Needless to say, God will never be deaf to the prayers of the humble. Again, the pure of heart love the virtues of penance, of self-denial, of charity. They must have the virtues of meekness, of patience, and of zeal for the glory of God. They must practice the three divine virtues of Faith, Hope and Charity, in such a perfect manner that the other virtues find their support and strength in them.

Another reason that makes us understand why God thinks so much of the virtue of purity is that the pure live the life of angels. For that reason this virtue is often called the angelic virtue. The saints that have shone preeminently in it, like a St. Aloysius, have been called "Angels in the Flesh." The reward, then, will be the reward of the angels. Indeed, the virtue of purity in the human soul is even of a higher order than the purity of the angels, and hence will be given a reward far above that of the angels. The reason of this will be apparent to you if you reflect that the angels preserve their purity without any of the temptations to which the flesh is heir. The angels have not to guard the senses, the eyes, the ears and the tongue. They have no idea of what it means to resist inclinations towards evil. For these reasons the reward will be greater for the human soul that remains pure, than for the angels.

If, from what has been said, you gain the impression that, owing to the many sacrifices which purity demands, the life of the pure is a sad and gloomy existence, you are mistaken. With all its constant martyrdom it is the happiest life on earth.

You know from Bible History that Paradise contained many trees, only one of which was forbidden to our first parents. The fruit they were allowed to eat was far more choice than that of the one forbidden tree. In a similar manner, the pure at heart know of many pleasures, consolations and joys that are withheld from those who give themselves up to impurity.

Purity gives a peculiar expression to your bearing and character. It may, perhaps, be too subtle to analyze or explain, but you are convinced that it is there. A pure boy and young man will be of a happy mind. His cheerfulness does not depend upon the weather. His eyes sparkle with a fire not of this world. Trees and flowers, lawful pleasures, labor, and rest, they all give him a gratification of which the worldly minded have no idea. The pure at heart see beauty and charm where the sinful see only the commonplace. How much better is it to enjoy such tranquility, such peace of mind, than to live in fear and gloom, than to be suffering tortures of conscience that the hidden sins will become known. Is it not worth a great deal to be able to look every man straight in the eye, without having to fear that he might read the meaning of a secret line in our face that would tell of a sinful life?

The peace of mind that purity gives would indeed be reward enough for this life. But God in His high regard for this virtue offers many more rewards for a life of purity.

As impurity undermines health and causes loathsome disease, the virtue of purity is the surest means of promoting health and strength of body. A strong constitution and undefiled blood are the best protection against most sicknesses. Nothing in all Creation is grander than the sight of a pure boy or young man growing up in all his strength and beauty of health, and with an innocent and honest look in his eye. Purity ennobles and elevates even our body, giving it a charm that is the delight of God and His angels. Even the wicked are both awed and inspired at the sight of a pure young man. They may be unwilling to be pure themselves, but, nevertheless, they are compelled to admire and respect purity in others.

God in His infinite generosity adorns the soul as well as the body of the pure. But He beautifies the soul of the pure far more than the body.

To the pure of heart, God will grant more graces, and more valuable graces, than to those that must go to heaven by way of penance. They that go to heaven upon the path of innocence, receive the choicest blessings and graces. Purity gives them a more complete insight into the plans of God. Through special graces they receive warning beforehand of impending temptations and dangers. Purity gives them a greater and more pure love of God, thus preparing them to undergo any sacrifice, to suffer even death, rather than to forfeit the priceless charm of purity.

As most people that lose their salvation lose it through impurity, so is the virtue of purity one of the safest marks of belonging to the elect. About the joys and rewards of the world to come our dear Savior has told us very little. But He did reveal that the pure will receive there a special reward. They are to stand nearest to His Throne, and are to chant a song of praise that no one else will be able to sing.

Now, my dear boys, when we consider all these advantages and all the bodily and spiritual, temporal and eternal rewards, should we not be induced to preserve the virtue of purity? In no other way can we gain the consolations, the peace of mind, the manifold blessings for body and soul for time and eternity. Surely, the prize is worth every effort we can put forth.

The question that now remains to be answered is what must we do to preserve this virtue of purity? And in answering this question I can advise you to do what the saints have done to preserve that priceless jewel.

First of all, the saints constantly lived in the presence of God. One thought was at all times uppermost in their minds. They realized that, no matter where they were, no matter what they did, God was at their side. That thought gave them strength to fight against the temptations, to suffer anything for the love of God. By constantly keeping God before their mind, the saints turned suffering into joy and trials into victories. Where others were overwhelmed with temptations because they lost sight of God, the saints accepted and conquered temptations as a matter of course. In the fiercest assaults of the devil they had but one thought, God. And, like Joseph in Egypt, they asked themselves: "How can I do this sin in the presence of my God?" The thought of God's presence was at once the consolation, the strength, the hope, and the happiness of the saints.

And how did the saints manage always to think of God? They lived in a spirit of prayer. Unfortunately, we have an idea that prayer is a formal affair--a few minutes each day--and that we spend the rest of the time in an entirely different atmosphere, as it were. Now this is a sad mistake. Even when our lips do not move in prayer, we can and we should keep alive the spirit of prayer. Excepting only sin, is there anything in this world that does not remind us of God? The sky with the handwriting of God upon it, the trees and flowers, the hills and the waters, the fields laden with the gifts of God, our senses and mental faculties, the very work we do. Everything can and should keep the thought of God constantly in our mind. True piety does not consist in the few short prayers we utter with our lips, but in a constant disposition to connect everything we see and do with God. This is the meaning of the spirit of prayer. The saints made a prayer of their every act. Every act of penance, every act of self-denial, every act of charity was simply nothing else than a prayer. Their entire life was one constant prayer.

This spirit of prayer implies regular Confessions and frequent Holy Communion. Do you know why our Holy Father is so anxious in insisting upon frequent Holy Communions, even daily where possible? It is for no other reason than to keep mankind pure.

If sinners would begin to go to Confession and Holy Communion as frequently as the saints and with the same zeal, they, too, would become saints. As a rule, however, those that need penance most will be the last to do it; those that need the Sacraments most are the most negligent in receiving them. They are compelled to receive the Sacraments at Easter time, but then many receive them not because they love God and their soul, but because of the law. It stands to reason that these people lack the spirit of prayer and, hence, endanger their purity of heart.

Besides the spirit of prayer, the saints shine forth as models of a childlike devotion to our Blessed Mother. Sincere devotion to our Blessed Mother is taken as a guarantee of eternal happiness. The favors and blessings she secures are in proportion to the honor given to her. Hence we need not be surprised that her special admirers and clients receive special benefits. We learn this from the lives of the saints. The greatest of favors she can obtain for the children that love her most is the jewel and crown of all virtues--*purity*.

The virtue of purity is, therefore, worth our every effort. Even the loss of life would be small in comparison with the loss of this angelic virtue. In order to preserve and develop this virtue we must follow the example set us by the saints. Let us, then, live in a spirit of piety and practice a childlike devotion to our Blessed Mother. Let us live a life of angels so that we may share in their glory.

CHAPTER XXXIV. DISHONESTY

A boy or young man starting out in life must bear in mind that he owes it to himself and to his family to establish a reputation for himself. His honesty or dishonesty will be the standard whereby this reputation shall be measured.

You will easily understand that the boy who is a plain thief will not long be found in the ranks of society. His place will be found for him in some reformatory. But there are many other ways of being dishonest, which, though at the start they may be overlooked and pardoned as boyish pranks, are nevertheless fatal in their consequences. Apart from the fact that nothing is ever gained by dishonesty, owing to the obligation of restoring things that were taken unlawfully, and of replacing the equivalent of things that were injured or destroyed, there is another disadvantage in being dishonest. It is the forfeit of the esteem and good will of our fellow man. And the loss of reputation or of character is a loss that no amount of ill-gotten gain can outweigh.

A boy who shows a disposition towards dishonesty will reveal this bad trait without being aware of it. People will not be long in guessing about a dishonest boy. Nor will they be slow in showing their distrust.

The dishonest boy usually shows a liking for pranks that do harm. He is ready to wantonly injure and destroy the property of others. Windows of vacant houses, young trees, fences and gates, flowers and shrubs are the

208

special objects of his fancy. Never for a moment does he seem to realize that all the damage he inflicts will have to be made good. He destroys for the sake of destroying. His pranks may be looked upon by some as thoughtless pranks. The dishonest boy enjoys it if the owner of the injured things gets vexed and scolds.

The dishonest boy is great at finding articles. At least he says he is. He finds pocket knives, playthings, small change and other things that may look a great deal like the knife or playthings that disappeared from your possession. But he will claim that finding means keeping. Later on, when he goes to work, the employer or foreman soon notices that things are disappearing. He will not know how to explain the loss till he begins to suspect the boy. Whatever the boy works at, he at once considers it his right to take things home if it can be done without exposing himself to the risk of being caught. The things he will take will be small articles that can easily be hidden and the loss of which will not amount to much. When he works by the piece, he will find a means of charging up more work than he has done. In his opinion that is not stealing. That is only a matter of cleverness. It is a calamity of the present time that any amount of dishonesty, even plain stealing, goes under the name of business. Only a small percentage of the thieves are put in jail. Many crooks are too clever to fall into the clutches of the law. Their ill-gotten means enable them to have able lawyers, and justice is often hoodwinked. But God, the Supreme Judge, has said in plain words: "Thou shalt not steal." There are no exceptions to this law.

Eventually, the dishonest boy will be caught and he loses his place. He looks elsewhere for work. In a new place he may succeed for a while, but the reputation he made for himself will follow him. It means looking for another job. He may find work in another town, but his evil reputation will be like his shadow. It will not leave him.

209

A man does not become either saint or criminal in one day. The process in either direction takes years. When, therefore, you read of a man having been convicted of some great theft, you may be sure that he has been a thief for many years before. It is probable that he began with stealing pennies and pencils. His vice grew with the number of times it was committed. So it is with vice; it rows and keeps step with the reputation it deserves. Bad reputation and vice go hand in hand. When you see a tree branching out you know that the roots of that tree are spread in proportion to its branches and twigs. And the more a vice spreads at the root, the more will its bad reputation spread out in all directions.

For that reason, then, a boy makes a fatal mistake when he thinks he can confine his dishonesty to things of little importance. He cannot be dishonest even in little matters without at the same time losing his reputation for honesty.

Unless a tree is cut down or destroyed in some way, its roots will continue to spread, and so will its branches spread in proportion. In like manner, vice will grow from bad to worse, and one's reputation with it, unless the vice is torn up root and all. Hence, though the dishonest boy will not intend to commit mortal sin, he will drift into it and, to save himself the reproach of conscience, he will excuse his sins under the title of cleverness or good business. The big thieves in jail will tell you they never intended stealing as much as they did. But they saw the chance, and could not help themselves. As a rule, they will feel more sorry for having been caught than for the wrong they committed. Whether, if they get another chance of stealing, they will remain honest, remains to be seen. As a rule, a cat will not quit catching mice. That is its instinct. And it is a hard matter for a thief not to steal when he sees the chance. Stealing has become a habit with him. He may

210

possibly have looked upon the whole matter as a joke at first. But it is anything but a joke for him when he finds himself behind iron bars. His photograph and measurements are sent all over the country, and henceforth he will be a marked man. Wherever he may go, he will find himself the object of the detectives' attention. Every movement he makes is carefully watched. Such, then, is the life of a thief. The world shows him no mercy. It may seem pitiable in some particular instances; yet one cannot blame people for guarding their own interests. When a boy or young man abuses the confidence people placed in him, when he can no longer be trusted, it is little wonder that he finds himself watched and distrusted. What other treatment does he deserve? It means nothing else but reaping what he has sown.

Of course, if a repentant thief returns his ill-gotten gains, and tries to redeem himself, he deserves our pity and our good will. When he tries to turn over a new leaf, to start a new life, we should give him every encouragement that discretion will suggest. But these instances happen so rarely that it will not only be advisable but necessary to be on our guard in dealing with those who have lost their reputation.

Seeing to what dire results dishonesty leads, you should certainly be resolved to be scrupulously honest in all matters large and small. In honesty, as in everything else, it is the small things that tell. It is the little things to which you may attach little importance, which others go by in sizing you up. We must never overlook trifles. Our dear Savior Himself lays stress upon them, since He says: "Because thou hast been faithful in little things I will place thee over many."

You may have many things from home, a certain influence, means, a good name, a certain rank or position

211

in life and business. But all things you may inherit amount to little in making your success permanent. The reputation that is yours must be made by yourselves. The good name of your father or grandfather will help very little if you fail in keeping up your reputation. The good name and reputation of your father or grandfather, that took them years to establish, may be lost in the time of a few hours by your own foolish or malicious conduct. Their good name will no longer be a protection or help to you. Hence, bear in mind that you yourselves must establish your reputation for honest. No one will take your word for your reputation. It must be proved by your actions. People are only too readily inclined to think evil. The least suspicion against your honesty will often be passed around from one to another, and it may even happen, as it has happened more than once, that your reputation will suffer even when you are entirely innocent of any wrongdoing. Therefore, be honest in the smallest things, even though they are of no greater value than a pin. Let people feel that you can be trusted, that you are reliable, that you are honest, that you never abuse their trust or confidence, and thus you will build up a reputation for yourselves which will be a greater asset in life than either money or power.

CHAPTER XXXV. VARIOUS KINDS OF LIES

Speaking of lies, it may be well to bear in mind that not all lies are begotten by the tongue. We can lie also by our actions. A sincere Protestant told me that if he were a minister, he would use but one text of the Bible for all of his sermons, and that text is: "Thou shalt not bear false witness." No doubt, if people would or could fully realize what injury they inflict upon themselves and others by lying, there would probably be an end to lying. Instead of that, however, the majority of people think little of lies. If, by a lie, people can avoid some little inconvenience, then they see no harm whatever in lying. Still St. Augustine says: "They that lie are children of the devil, because he is the father of lies."

The reason why God despises lying lips is because He is the God of Truth. Christ says of Himself: "I am the way, the truth and the life." Hence to be guilty of lying is to offer an insult to the truth that God so much loves. No matter how harmless a lie may appear at the surface, still, as a lie, it is opposed to the truth of God, and because it is opposed to truth, God must despise it.

Lies range from venial sins to mortal sins. If the injury or loss suffered by others on account of our lie is a great one, the lie is a mortal sin. Where injury or loss are slight, or if there is no loss or injury, the lie is only a venial sin. It is at times very difficult to say where venial sin stops and mortal sin begins. Therefore, if our conscience causes us any misgivings as to the gravity of a lie, it will be for the advantage of our peace of mind to confess the lie, whether it may be mortal or venial, and abide by the decision of the Confessor.

Lies are sometimes classified as jocose lies; lies said in a spirit of levity to pass off an untruth as the truth. Such lies, though intended for jokes, may not always end as jokes. Some years ago, a farmer, at work in the field, was told on April Fool's Day to hurry home, as his house had burnt to the ground. The news was such a shock to him that he dropped dead. The joker had not meant any harm. It had been intended as an April Fool joke, but that did not bring the dead man back to life. When a jocose remark is obviously not true, it is not a lie since there is no intention to deceive. A lie includes the intention of deceiving, of making someone believe an untruth as though it were the truth.

Then there are officious lies. We are often asked about private, personal or business affairs by people who have not the right or privilege to ask; people to whom we are not responsible for our actions. And sometimes we think that by telling them a lie we will avoid giving them information we do not desire to give. Even though this may not injure them in the least, it is still a lie and as such displeasing to God, the lover of truth. To tell such people abruptly that their questions are impertinent might cause hard feeling, even enmity. To tell them the truth may, at times, be imprudent. So the only lawful way out of the difficulty is to give evasive answers to such questions. St. Thomas of Canterbury gives us an example of this kind. Some of the nobles at the king's court discovered that St. Thomas, the Archbishop of Canterbury, was disliked by the king, and they made up their minds that he must die. St. Thomas heard of this and, disguising himself, mounted a horse and fled. Some of the soldiers that were to kill him met him on the road. They asked him whether he was the archbishop. He could not say "no," for that would have been a lie; if he said "yes," they would kill him on the spot. So he said: "Do I look like an archbishop traveling?" The soldiers, knowing that bishops and archbishops traveled with a large body of servants and guards, then went their way without molesting him. Sometime later, St. Thomas gladly gave up his life so that the lives of others might be spared. St. Thomas loved truth and hated iniquity, and for that reason he made a bitter enemy of his king. It was for truth that the Saint finally suffered and died.

Then there are the so-called lies of necessity. To save little or great annoyances to ourselves or others, people do not hesitate to tell lies. Also, in such cases, an evasive answer is advisable and allowed. For instance, you may be asked by some boy for the loan of a dollar. You may in the past have loaned him money that he has never given back. And you know beforehand that if you lend him more you will never see the money again. Now, a correct answer would be that you have no money to lend, meaning--not to him.

Then there are lies said with the object of shifting blame we have deserved upon others who are innocent of the charge. Such lies are a sure sign of a cruel and cowardly character. You may have broken a windowpane or some furniture at home. There was neither malice nor forethought in your act. It was an accident. But you know that your parents think a great deal of the article that has been broken and you fear your parents will be very angry. You are asked about it and you blame your smaller brother or sister for it, and even say you saw them break it. Though they say they did not do it, they are unable to prove their innocence and must take the punishment that should be yours. You will only understand how mean such conduct is when you yourself will some time suffer for the faults of another. The guilty party may consider it a joke to make

215

another get the scolding. But it is a very poor sort of a joke; a joke that has a sharp sting. Others may join in the laugh at the expense of the innocent party, but the guilty party reveals a treacherous, mean and ugly character, and that joke will be a danger signal for others. They will, thereafter, keep on the safe side of you. They will take good care that such a joke shall never be played at their expense.

Such so-called lies of necessity are not much of a joke. If the injury or loss inflicted upon an innocent party is a serious matter, the lie becomes a mortal sin. Nor is it enough to simply confess such a sin. The injury or loss resulting from that sin must be compensated. Unless we repair the loss or injury that we thus cause, the sin will not be forgiven. We are allowed to repair injury caused by dishonesty without exposing ourselves as thieves. But the restitution caused by our falsehood forces us to expose ourselves. We must admit that we have told a lie.

Therefore, if we do not like to pose before the world as liars, we must avoid lies that cause harm to others. If we have done wrong, let us be manly enough to admit it. Most of our little faults and many of our greater faults will be overlooked and pardoned if we are manly enough to admit them. No one is above mistakes. People will overlook many things for the good reason that others may overlook their shortcomings. But they demand that we be upright and manly. Our reputation may suffer by other faults, yet we may be able to redeem ourselves. But if, by lying, we cause suffering or loss to an innocent party, we tear our reputation into shreds. You see, then, that, by shifting blame and responsibilities upon others, we are the losers, even though, for the time being, we may escape blame or punishment for our bad actions.

As I said in the beginning of this conference, there are other lies besides those told by the tongue. These lies are characterized by the word deceit. You may know some people that are nice and kind to your face. They flatter you, encourage you, have all kinds of pleasant things to tell you. Yet their purpose and aim are to harm you. They pose as friends, and at the same time they are your worst enemies. Their advice will try to make you act in a way to injure yourself. You may be sure of another thing. These deceitful people will be cunning enough to profit out of the mistakes you make by their advice. They will be around you as long as they see some benefit coming to themselves. The moment you are no longer useful to them, they will cast you aside as one would throwaway a squeezed lemon.

There is another kind of deceit to which I must call your attention. It is sanctimoniousness. A certain class of people, like the Pharisees of old, will try to convey the impression that they are extremely pious and God-fearing, although they are secretly rather the opposite. You will usually see them making a big sign of the Cross when they bless themselves, you will hear them tell how much they pray, but they will be most severe judges of their fellow beings. They will never miss a chance to enlarge the faults of others and they lament about the wickedness of mankind. They will also, behind your back, rip up your reputation--if they can safely do so.

Deceit is as low and disgraceful as any lie spoken by the lips. Oftentimes its evil consequences are more far-reaching than those of a spoken lie.

Learn, then, to train both your tongue and your actions, to speak never an untruth, to abhor lying and deceit, and to avoid those who practice these vices.

217

CHAPTER XXXVI. DEFAMATION OF CHARACTER

When you wear your Sunday clothes you are very careful not to soil or tear them. When you have your everyday clothes on, you care little what you do. You run, jump, roll on the ground, and play ball, not caring whether you soil or tear your clothes by sliding to a base. If you do soil or tear them you think, "Well, there is not much lost," but, when you have your Sunday clothes on, you act with great caution. Your Sunday suit has considerable influence upon your actions and general bearing. Now, the consideration the Sunday suit requires of our outward actions, the consideration of character, or good reputation, requires of our interior life.

People without a good reputation are like boys without Sunday clothes. Neither cares very much what is done, since there is nothing much to lose or spoil. People, however, that have a reputation to live up to, are careful in what they say or do. Like the boy with his Sunday suit, they have something to look out for.

A good reputation, then, is one of the most valuable possessions of a man. He may have money in the bank, he may have all kinds of precious stones and jewels, may own shares in railways, he may be proud of his health, his strength, his family, his home, his talents. But all these possessions are as nothing in comparison to his good name. Ask him which he would rather lose, his wealth or his good name, and he will answer: "I would rather lose all I have than forfeit my good name." It may be easy for him to make another fortune, but to regain a good name or reputation that has once been lost is extremely difficult. If he were asked whether he preferred his good reputation or his health, he will tell you he would sooner lose his health. For with care and the skill of a doctor he may regain his health, but to regain a lost reputation is next to impossible. If he were asked whether he would not rather lose his good name than his life, he would say: "I will rather sacrifice my life, for without a fair reputation life itself is worthless." You know, boys, as well as I, that many boys have no good reputation. Their faults and vices are by no means hidden. They commit them openly, even boast of them. But can you call them happy? Does anybody who is respectable say a kind word for them? Are they not mistrusted and watched? Do you not know, as well as the rest, that the future of these boys will in all probability be spent in jails and prisons, that even their graves may proclaim their unfortunate lives? You see, then, that a life without a good name is a useless and unhappy life. Man has nothing in this whole, wide world that he appreciates more than his good reputation. With this thought in mind, you will be able to understand, at least to some extent, what a cruel wrong it is to injure or take away the good name of another. By taking his money you obtain something. By taking away his good name you are not richer by a single penny, yet you take from him the best he has, the thing worth more to him than all his money, and health, and life itself.

Now the question arises: How can one injure or take away the good reputation of another?

In the first place, we injure the reputation of another by exposing his hidden faults. You are well aware of the fact that all of us have faults. We are ashamed of them, try to keep them hidden, try to overcome them. Such is the endeavor of all that are well disposed. The hidden faults that Tom, Dick and Harry have are theirs. No one else has

219

any business exposing them, because everyone else has faults of his own. And, if he thinks anything of his good name, he will try to keep his own faults hidden and try to avoid them. But here we have to take account of poor, weak human nature which is tempted to hide its own faults by calling attention to faults of others. It is likewise easy to increase the number of our hidden faults, instead of lessening them from year to year. And so it happens that, while trying to save our good name, we are inclined to harm the good name of another. To expose the hidden faults of others means making them public or open faults. Again it is a weakness of human nature to spread rather the faults of others than their good qualities. No matter what good a man may accomplish, his motives will be questioned. The work itself will be belittled. The more it shines forth as a work of living faith, the more it will be hushed up and ignored. But let a good man make the least false step and it will be made public fast enough. The evil tongues will wag and wag and say: "Why, so-and-so always pretended to be so good--and just listen to what he said, what he did." And even this will not satisfy the wicked tongue. The next remark will be something like this: "If so-and-so has done this, you may be sure it was not the first time. He did worse than that, only it was not found out." This brings suspicions upon suspicions. Thereafter, if it is at all possible to connect his name with evil, even when there is no probability or even possibility his reputation will be assailed and gossip grows to calumny.

As an excuse for gossip, it will sometimes be said that the fault exposed was a real fault. "It is nothing but the truth." Granting the fault to be a real fault, that does not entitle us to publish it. We too, have some real faults, yet we will scarcely feel inclined to give anybody permission to spread the news all over the town. If we are not, by our office or relation, responsible for the behavior of others, their faults need not worry us. The less we speak and even think of them, the better for us. It may, however, be well to remark at this time that there are two instances when we are allowed to talk of the hidden faults of others. If you know of a boy who is addicted to a particular sin, especially if it be some mortal sin, either of two ways are open to you. If you think you have influence over him or that he would take it in good part, you may call him aside at a suitable time and give him a kindly talk about the fault of which he is guilty. Then argue and reason with him, try and convince him that he is doing grave injustice to himself, and that you are actuated only by a motive of charity in talking to him about it. If you, however, have reason to fear that your kind advice will not be taken in good part, it will be advisable to report his conduct to the teacher, if he still goes to school, or to his parents if he has left school. But if you know that his parents are lax and that they approve of everything their boy does, it may not be prudent to inform them. Very likely they know the shortcomings of their boy. In that case all you can do is to pray for him and keep silent.

If you have been guilty of exposing the hidden faults of others, you are bound to make restitution by speaking to those who heard you about the good qualities of those injured. Even then, you have reason to fear that the injury your talk caused will not be entirely remedied. Some of your listeners certainly spread your remarks or even added to them. Your talk may have had a far greater reach than you ever expected. Therefore make it a rule never to talk about the faults of others.

The injury that may result from exposing the hidden faults of others is certainly bad enough. But a still greater injustice and injury is committed when, instead of exposing true faults, we invent faults of which they are entirely innocent. This is called calumny.

221

When people suffer by having their secret faults exposed, the partial loss of their good reputation may be looked upon by them as a temporal punishment of their sin. By calumny, however, we cause another to suffer innocently a partial loss of his good name or his entire good reputation. The victim has done nothing to deserve such a loss. A case of this kind was called to my attention some time ago. A poor man had found work as night watchman in a factory. The wages were small, but they fed the man's family of six. One day, the manager heard it said that this man had been seen drunk. Without giving him a chance to explain or defend himself, he was discharged and his family starved for nearly two months before he could find other work. He applied at several places, but was told he could not get work on account of his bad reputation. He never found out his accusers and he was entirely innocent of the charge of drunkenness. The injury the innocent man and his family had to suffer was extreme. From this one example, you may see what it means to make good an injury of this kind. In this case, the guilty party would be bound to get the work back for the poor man, and also pay him the loss of wages. The guilty party owes an apology to the innocent sufferer, and must retract his lies with all those to whom he passed the lie. The full restoration of a reputation is almost impossible for two reasons. In the first place no man likes to confess that he is a liar. It is extremely hard for any man to say : "I have said this, but I must say I have told you a lie. The man is innocent of the charges I made." The other reason is the unwillingness of the people to believe the truth in such cases and their readiness to spread evil reports. Behold how the wind scatters the leaves of a tree. Yet it would be far easier to collect the scattered leaves of the tree than to trace the course of a calumny. People may know many good points of a man, but they will never be talked about. But give a hint of his wrongdoing, whether true, or false, and the news will be spread rapidly. Yet, unless we repair the injury, as far as

222

it lies in our power to do so, we cannot expect to have the sin of calumny forgiven. The fact that it is humiliating to expose ourselves as liars does not excuse us from retracting a calumny.

Hence, my dear boys, just as you wish no one to question your good name, be very careful never to injure the fair name of another. Whenever you hear companions talk against an absent one, take his part even though you may have some suspicion that what is being said is true. Even though what they say is true, they have no right to speak against him. And if their charges are without foundation, are groundless suspicions or downright lies, you have all the more reason to take his part. That will free you from responsibility, and help to avoid the many evils resulting from calumny. If you have common sense, your judgment will tell you to steer clear of a crowd of slanderers. When you have turned your back, they will probably attack your fair name. Hence, the less you have to do with such people, the better off you are.

CHAPTER XXXVII. ST. AGAPITUS

There are a great many people laboring under the mistaken idea that saintliness is a mode of life proper for a person who has reached old age. A great many others have the equally misleading idea, that a young man must lead a frivolous life for some years before there can be any thought of "settling down." Owing to this mistaken idea, people will pardon many things at twenty which they will not forgive at forty. Still sin remains sin, whether committed at ten or seventy years of age.

Since we belong completely to God, it stands to reason that He has a valid claim upon not only the last few years of our lives, but the entire life. From the cradle to the grave we are God's. Hence we are bound to serve Him not only for a few years, but during our whole life. Saintliness, then, must be looked upon as a duty that begins to devolve upon us with the use of reason. Indeed, the probabilities of ever becoming saints will be far removed, if, as boys, we lead sinful lives. It is true, that many have become saints who as boys gave no indications of future holiness. But we must not forget that a great many more have continued to walk upon the road of sin up to their last breath. As boys, they were bad. As men they grew worse.

When our dear Savior asked us to be just and holy, He did not refer merely to our last few years on earth, but to our entire life. A good start means a great deal in play and business. It means a great deal, too, in holiness.

To show us the profit of an early start in holiness, the Church has countless saints who were models of many virtues even as boys. We can do nothing better than call to mind some of these heroes of virtue in order to learn from them how you too may be saints even as boys.

In the first three centuries after Christ, there lived some of the noblest models of boys. A few of their names have come down to us in history. Forest and meadows contain many more flowers than we notice by passing through them. So, too, the first ages of the Church have a great number of saints, known only to God and their guardian angels. The writing of a history of the martyrs was not thought of at that time. Later, when men began to record the names and deeds of saints, it was natural to overlook countless names, and no attempt was made to give a full list of all those who gave their life and their all for the sake of Jesus. But, although the records are by no means complete, we have many examples of boys who sacrificed their lives for the same holy faith, that now by the grace of God is ours. Such a boy was St. Agapitus.

During the time of the Emperor Aurelian, there lived a boy who, by his saintly conduct, attracted the attention and admiration of even the pagans. To the pagans, purity in a boy was a curiosity, to say the least. It was something strange. And as they became convinced of the purity of this boy, they could not help but admire and reverence him. The name of this boy was Agapitus. Finally the emperor heard of this saintly boy and expressed a wish to have him at the palace.

Such was the confidence in God of this saintly boy that he went fearlessly to the palace of the emperor, although he realized the danger to which he exposed himself. The emperor was favorably impressed with him and promised him honors and wealth. He could have had any

225

position of honor as he grew older, he could have had everything in the world that heart and mind can desire upon one condition: that he give up his holy faith and become, again, a pagan. But the little saint would rather share the poverty of his parents, and all the sufferings poverty brings with it, than indulge his body for a time and have his soul lost forever. Many other young men or boys would have jumped at the tempting offers the emperor made! The emperor found himself begging a boy to accept his favors, a mere boy who had the heart to refuse all his gifts! The mighty Aurelian was not accustomed to be refused. When he found that he did not have enough of honors or money to bribe this boy, he changed his tactics. Since it was the object of the emperor to turn the boy back to paganism, he tried to frighten him with the severe punishment inflicted upon Christians for their faith. In those times, it was considered a crime to be a Christian. No torture was too revolting if it added to the suffering of the martyrs. The emperor had the boy sent to the torture chamber. Not only was the boy a Christian; by rejecting the offers of the emperor, he was guilty of most outrageous insult. The emperor commanded that the boy be placed upon the rack, an instrument of torture by which every bone of the body was drawn out of joint. You know how painful it is to sprain an ankle or even a finger. Imagine, then, what a pain it must be to have every bone drawn out of joint; the shoulders, the elbows, the wrists, the fingers, hips, knees and ankles and feet out of joint at the same time. Thus, with every bone of his body tortured, the boy was asked again whether he still would remain a Christian. He answered: yes. He was then thrown into a prison, where he found no gentle hands to give his distorted body the least care. No food was given him; not a drop of water. After four days he was again dragged before his judge. The same question and the same answer. He was willing to die rather than deny his holy faith. Then he was stretched out upon an iron frame and burning coals were placed all over his

226

body. Even then he gave the same answer. The judge was resolved to break his spirit and ordered that he be hung up by his feet. A smoldering fire was started beneath his head. When they asked him again, he answered by praying in loud voice. The judge then ordered boiling water to be poured own his sides. Even pagans who witnessed the scalded flesh severed from the body of the boy felt sorry for him. At the moment, however, when the boiling water was poured over the boy, the cruel judge dropped dead. The emperor, hearing what had happened, ordered the boy beheaded. This is in short the story of the suffering and death of St. Agapitus. He died at the age of fourteen years.

Does the life of this saint teach us any lesson? Let us see.

Is your life saintly and blameless, as that of St. Agapitus, so that people will find cause to admire it? Have you ever caused anyone to be edified by your good example? Do you lead such a saintly life to make people declare you certainly are a Catholic boy for none other could be as pure and gentle? Do you not rather try to hide the fact of your being a Catholic for fear you might be asked about it, or that you might lose your position? Do you not, by vulgar talk and actions, create the impression as though you were anything but a Catholic? Often boys are working side by side in factories, and neither suspects the other of being a Catholic, though both of them are. When God and Religion are mocked they stand there laughing with the rest. If the early Christians had had no greater courage, Christianity would, to speak from the human standpoint, have been wiped from the face of the earth, and paganism would still rule the world.

Imagine yourself in the place of this saintly boy, Agapitus, Had you been called to the palace of the emperor would you know the catechism well enough to answer the

227

questions of the emperor? Had you been given promises of money and honors, what would your choice have been? Too many people at the present time will readily sell their souls for money or honors. Men are told that if they remain Catholics they can never get ahead and make a mark in this world. Some prefer their holy faith to all the world may offer them: but, alas, many take what the world offers and give their souls in payment for it. Think of the suffering St. Agapitus underwent for our holy faith. Life was as dear to him as it is to you. He felt the pain as you do. He was no older than most of you. And yet, you are afraid to show your colors for fear that some may laugh at you for being a Catholic. You are afraid of losing a few pennies, and you hide your holy faith for fear of missing a chance of getting on in this world! And it is the very same faith for which martyrs, like St. Agapitus, gave up their lives!

Yes, boys, let us admit it: We are often cowards, when it is a question of showing our holy faith. "He who will confess me before men, him will I confess before my Father who is in heaven," our dear Savior told us. If we are ashamed of Christ, He, in turn, will feel ashamed of us. If we pretend not to know Him, not to belong to His Church, the time will come when He will ignore us and not know us.

Remember St. Agapitus and his suffering the very next time there is occasion for confessing or defending your holy faith. Know your holy faith thoroughly, so that whenever you are asked regarding any point of it you may explain it clearly. Never give consent to anyone to speak disrespectfully of God or Religion. People may not at all times agree with you, but they will admire you, nevertheless, for not being afraid. Suppose you do lose your position on account of it. Do you think that God will let you fight the battle alone? He will be at your side. You may lose in things temporal, but you will be the gainer in spiritual and eternal blessings. With temporal things we must part someday. Death parts us from all of them. But the rewards we gather for the life to come are ours for ever and ever.

And last, but not least, let your conduct be the real proof of your faith. Lead a virtuous life, so that people are compelled to say that you cannot be anything but a model, saintly, Catholic boy.

CHAPTER XXXVIII. ST. GEORGE

Nothing calls forth our admiration more than true manliness and courage. Other good traits may cause us to say words of praise here and there, but manliness most compels our admiration. True courage and manliness are all the more admirable when we find them linked to a steadfast Faith.

Such an example of true manliness we find in St. George.

His father died when the saint was a child. His saintly mother took him with her to the Holy Land. This was, of itself, a great grace for the boy, for the lessons he had learned about our dear Savior were brought home to him all the more forcibly by visiting the sacred places where our dear Savior was born, where He lived, suffered, and died for us. His mother being of a wealthy and influential family, George had all the benefits that pleasant surroundings, able teachers and social rank could bestow. Still, his head was not turned. He was always obedient and a model of purity. His wealth did not prevent him from being pious, nor his social standing from kindness towards those less favored than he. It was remarked that, as a young man, he was not frivolous and pleasure loving, such as young men of means and leisure often are. As he advanced in years, his heart remained innocent and pure, like that of a child. When this saintly young man joined the Roman army, people thought that, in the army, where he was surrounded by all classes of men, he would lose that childlike innocence. They were mistaken. An officer in the army has a hard task to gain the good will of both his superior officers and of those under him. An officer will often lose the one by trying to gain the other. St. George, however, knew how to gain the respect of those above him by strict obedience and valor, while he was loved for his kindness and consideration by those beneath him in rank.

Needless to say, this remarkable conduct of George did not escape the attention of the emperor, Diocletian. The bravery of the young warrior, his gentleness and strict attention to discipline were reported for recognition. The emperor was desirous of rewarding St. George in a fitting manner. In due time, an order reached him from his imperial master informing him that he was made a general in recognition of his valuable services, and that he was to wage war against certain Christian people. That promotion was to be the beginning of still greater honors. If this campaign would be a successful one, he might in time hold the highest command of the army. Before his youthful mind all these possibilities must have arisen. Ambition, the joy of victory, the imperial rewards, all beckoned to him. But how the world was disappointed! St. George resigned his commission in the army, stating that, since he was a Christian himself, he could not wage war against his brethren. No one was more surprised and dismayed than the emperor himself. Immediately he forgot the heroism of the young warrior, had him court-martialed, and beheaded for being a Christian. St. George gave his life for his holy Faith on April the 23rd, in the year 303. He died in the very flower of his youth.

St. George basked in the favor of an emperor. A grand career was before him. History might have recorded him as the greatest general. But all this was as nothing in comparison to his good conscience. He knew well that, if he resigned his commission for the reason he gave, it meant death for him. Nevertheless, rather than do wrong he would die.

This short sketch of St. George teaches us three lessons we might well take to heart:

The first lesson we should learn is not to depend upon the esteem of the world. The world makes its idols and crushes them.

How willing the emperor Diocletian was to reward St. George. He had heard of the bravery of the young officer, hardly more, than a boy, yet more brilliant and successful than many a seasoned warrior. The emperor was willing to give him an important commission; ready to overwhelm him with greater honors and responsibilities, should he prove equal to the trust placed in his ability. The emperor considered him as a man upon whom he could depend, in whose care he could place the safety of the empire. But no sooner did he learn that St. George was a Christian than he forgot all this and his friendship turned into bitter hatred.

Take the baseball team of a big city. One of the pitchers wins nearly all the games of the season. You will find his picture in the paper every day. The papers will print all kinds of fine stories about him, and praise him to the sky. The next season opens and the fans want to see this same pitcher again winning every game. He loses some games. What do they say then? They have no word of praise for him. The papers will demand that this pitcher be discharged. In the meantime, another pitcher is successful, and he gets all the praise. He becomes popular. But how long will his popularity last? Till another is found to do even better. Then he, too, will be criticized and forgotten.

Therefore, never depend upon the world to praise you, or to give you favors. As soon as the world finds that it

232

can use you no longer, it will have enough of you. You may have served the world ever so faithfully, even to the detriment of your soul. But the moment another will serve it better than you, your past services will no longer be considered. You will be pushed aside and another idol will be set up in your place.

The second lesson follows from the first. It is wiser to serve God. What an amount of good we could do if we served God half as well as others serve the world. We must obey God rather than the world, but some boys seem to forget that they have a conscience and that it has been given to them to follow it.

Let us suppose that your employer tells you: "I know tomorrow is Sunday, but I want you to be in the shop all day and to attend to any work that may come along." How many, or how few, of you would tell that man: "I am a Christian and I must go to church. I must obey God who tells me to keep that day holy."

I know that there is some work that must be done. Still, I need hardly tell you that employers often demand work of Catholics that is not necessary. And the work is sometimes given them with no other object but to undermine their faith. You may know of some people who are idling all through the week, but on Sunday they work like slaves to catch up. Or, let us suppose you work in a factory. The young man at your elbow openly brags that he does not believe in a God. He tells you all kinds of stories to make you think less of your holy Faith. Have you the courage to tell him that his talk is disagreeable to you? Are you able to tell him where he is wrong?

Again, let us suppose that the people for whom you work are much opposed to religion. You fear that if they learn that you are a Catholic you will lose your place. Which would you rather lose, a few dollars or your soul? There are

233

Catholics who will not go to Mass on Sunday for fear that they might lose customers! Too many people of the present time do not know what it means to make sacrifices for the sake of religion. They have invented so many "ifs" and "outs" that they feel fully justified in hiding their Faith beneath a bushel when there is question of worldly success. Sacrifices, such as the martyrs made, are no longer fashionable.

It is true, at the present time Catholics are not, on account of their faith, exposed to capital punishment as in times gone by. But, since the kingdom of Christ is not of this world, and since the world and Christ will never be at peace, because the teaching of Christ goes contrary to that of the world, you may easily understand that the world will see to it that Catholics will have to suffer in some way for a Faith that is so much hated and persecuted. A Catholic who lives up to his convictions will be looked upon as a citizen of the second or third rate, never as the very best. Certain offices and places of trust and honor will be denied him owing to his Faith. If a Catholic were to run for president a howl would go up from North to South and from East to West. Now and then societies are organized, and flourish for a time, with the special object of keeping Catholics out of office. Another way in which Catholics are made to suffer for the sake of their Faith is their taxation for schools to which they cannot in conscience send their own children. Our holy Faith is worth any and every sacrifice we can give. Our very life is none too much to give up for it. To spread this holy Faith even our Redeemer had to suffer and die. Are we better than He that we expect to be treated with more consideration? To suffer for the cause that He has suffered for makes us all the more like to Him.

The third lesson we derive from the life of St. George is this: The saint was willing rather to die himself than to inflict suffering upon his fellow Christians. How do

234

we treat members of our holy Faith? By the wish and command of Christ we are to love our neighbor as ourselves. We must practice charity even towards those least deserving of it. We are not permitted to bar even our worst enemy from the obligation that charity imposes upon us. True, it is impossible to have the same desire of kindly feeling towards all men. Without injuring the rights of any of them we may show more regard for some than for others. Being human, we are tied more closely to those of our own blood. But, apart from this greater duty towards those of our own kindred, we have reason to ask ourselves how do we treat the members of our great spiritual household? How do we act towards our fellow Catholics ? What rivalry and envy exist among Catholic families! While they call God their Father and the Blessed Virgin their Mother, they act like enemies rather than like brethren. What rivalry is sometimes found in parish societies? Those that are least fitted even for the lowest office are constantly aspiring for the highest. And if they cannot get it, they mischievously scheme until they ruin the society. Even a Sodality is not always free from such disturbers.

As Catholics we should help one another. Are we doing this? You may know of a poor Catholic boy out of work. He is a good fellow, hardworking, honest and willing. You may know of a place open for a boy. Do you think of putting in a word for your Catholic friend, or don't you rather say: "Let him look out for himself. I had to look out for myself, too." Take another case. A Catholic boy is accused of something of which you know that he is entirely innocent. Do you take his part? Do you stand by him, defending him, or do you let matters take their course, feeling that the trouble does not concern you?

Manliness and courage are a great adornment for the boy, and Catholic boys and men have special reasons as well as many special opportunities to practice them. Let St.

George be your example, and your reward will not fail, as it did not fail him.

CHAPTER XXXIX. ST. STANISLAUS

In the year 1564, two brothers entered the University of Vienna, in Austria. The name of the older boy was Paul Kostka, the younger one's name was Stanislaus. They were the sons of an illustrious Polish family, and their means and noble rank opened to them the fashionable and exclusive circles. In their ways, the two boys were as far apart as the North Pole is from the South Pole. Paul was worldly, Stanislaus, a saint.

Paul made the best of the opportunities which money and influential connections offered. Life to him meant nothing but tasting all the pleasures that youth and means may procure. His stay at the university was merely a means of getting an amount of pleasure he was not able to enjoy at home. It is to be expected that a pleasure-loving youth like Paul Kostka could have little thought for anything so serious as the saving of his soul. If religion interfered with his pleasures, religion was bound to suffer. And so Paul drifted with the tide of the easy-going and pleasure-loving society. In name, Paul was a Catholic. And that was about all that can be said of his religion. Needless to say, he was a most popular young man. He was the example of good fellowship, full of fun, witty, and brilliant.

The younger brother was quiet, unassuming, and nicknamed "the saint" by the frivolous companions of Paul. While he was not liked by the friends of Paul, they could not help admiring and respecting him. No one dared to make an improper remark in his presence. He was bold enough to let the friends of his brother know that he did not approve of frivolity. He was as much a friend of piety and purity as Paul was a friend of loose morals.

I need hardly tell you that Paul left nothing untried to make Stanislaus join his way of living. Not only Paul, but also his companions, made it hard for him to walk the narrow and straight path. The saint was surrounded by wickedness. There was no one to give him a kind word of encouragement. When Paul found that the united efforts of himself and his companions were of no avail, he went so far as to misrepresent his brother at home. He informed his parents that Stanislaus was a good-for-nothing, a hypocrite, an idle dreamer, too silly to take the world as it is. The saint bore all the ridicule he received from his own people and said nothing. What kept him up in these severe trials was his childlike devotion to the Blessed Virgin. He knew that, though his earthly mother might question his motives of piety, his heavenly mother would not only understand him, but be of more help and consolation to him than the best of earthly mothers could ever be.

As a last effort, Paul took lodgings with a Protestant family, and his brother had to accompany him. This family was bitterly opposed to everything Catholic. Stanislaus had to suffer countless insults. His Faith, however, could not be shaken. During his stay at this place, he became very sick. He begged his brother to call a priest, but his brother only laughed at him. When the saint saw not a single soul in the house ready to do him this favor, he had recourse to the Blessed Virgin to help him. His prayers were answered. Angels entered his room and brought him the Holy Communion, which human beings refused him. After receiving Holy Communion from the hands of the angels he had a vision of the Mother of God with the Infant Savior. The Christ child left the arms of His Mother, and came to embrace him. It repaid him for all the trials and

238

suffering he had to endure. It was in this vision that he was told to join the Society of Jesus. Long and earnestly had he prayed to know his vocation! He realized that he was on earth not to seek pleasure but to do the holy Will of God. In this happy vision, God Himself told him what to do. While there had been doubt whether he would ever recover from his sickness, he got well immediately after the vision. It was not an easy matter for him to leave Vienna and join the Society of Jesus, but where there is a will there is a way. St. Stanislaus had no other means open to him but flight. He, therefore, resolved to walk the entire distance from Vienna to Rome. It takes a railroad train about a day and a night to make this trip, so you may imagine what a task it was for a sixteen-year-old boy to travel this distance on foot. He had to pass through parts unknown to him, with not a penny in his pockets, and depended upon charity for the bread he ate and the shelter he needed. It was a long and tiresome journey, but finally he reached Rome. He had the great good fortune of receiving the religious habit from the hands of St. Francis Borgia.

St. Stanislaus was by no means a strong boy. He was in delicate health. Nevertheless, he was severe with himself in doing penance. The journey from Vienna to Rome was a great task for him. However, he had been accustomed to fasting three days each week, and so he knew no fear of hunger. Even while living with his brother in Vienna he had secretly scourged his tender body to keep passion and senses under perfect control. It was no wonder, then, that during the novitiate, instead of being a pupil in the practice of penance and mortification, he became the model for others. From the time he entered the order, he was a model and source of edification for all. He died young. In his eighteenth year he contracted a fever and succumbed.

Such is briefly the life of St. Stanislaus. Some of you, in listening to this story, may have wondered that so much was said of the life of his brother, Paul. It was done with a purpose. The life of Paul adds, by its contrast, to the beauty of the life of his brother, the saint.

The life of the older boy, Paul, shows that, no matter how good one's parents may be, no matter how well children may be instructed and trained, they must labor for their own salvation. No one else can save your soul for you. You may receive all kinds of advice, all kinds of help, but the real work is your own. I dare say there are many boys who imagine that, since they have attended a parish school, and have pious parents, they can do much as they like without danger of going very wrong. The life of Paul Kostka is a lesson to the contrary.

Paul had the same bringing up as his saintly brother. He had the same pious and careful parents, the same training, the same opportunities. He might have become a saint like him. But all the training, all the good example, did not avail Paul. He was completely taken up with the things of this world.

You may say the two boys had different dispositions. Paul was lively, full of fun, while the saint was of a quiet disposition. This argument is misleading. Disposition is not sinful, nor does it follow that a quiet disposition is necessarily an indication of saintliness. Neither is a cheerful disposition a sign of wickedness. Most saints, indeed, of whose lives we have knowledge, were cheerful and happy. The constant union with God can scarcely have any other effect upon character than cheerfulness and happiness. Disposition, then, has nothing to do with saintliness.

When we read of the great deeds the saints have performed, we are inclined to think that they were made of different clay than we are. Nothing is more erroneous. The saints were human, and they had trials and temptations, as we have. Their inclination towards evil was as much of a hindrance to them as ours is to us, and they had feelings like we have. Fasting was not a pleasure for them. They felt the pangs of hunger as well as we do. The mortifications to which they subjected themselves hurt them as much as they would hurt us, if we were brave enough to inflict such suffering upon ourselves for the expiation of our sins. When laughed at and made fun of, when called hypocrites, and made to suffer untold insults, they were very conscious of the injury. When St. Stanislaus was laughed at for being pious, when he was called a hypocrite, when he fasted and performed other severe works of penance, if caused him physical and mental suffering. Indeed, if it had not, he would have had little merit. The way to heaven is a painful and difficult way. We must be ready to suffer, both in our body and in our mind, if we want to ever get to heaven. Since heaven is a place of reward, we must earn and deserve heaven, or we will never reach it.

Both St. Stanislaus and his brother, Paul, are dead for nearly four hundred years. Whether Paul ever got to heaven after his careless life on earth, we have no reason to know. Let us hope that, through the prayers of his saintly brother, he may have had the grace of repentance. However that may be, who, today, has a kind word for Paul? Anyone who reads the life of the saint reads also how cruel Paul was to his saintly brother. Several hundred years have passed, and even now he may be asking himself what good his life on earth was to him? His pleasures, his dissipation are gone. He lived for the world. What did the world do for him? Nothing. Four hundred years gone, and, behold, the name of Stanislaus is revered and honored throughout the whole Catholic world. Countless societies, altars, and churches are erected in his honor. His is a glorious name. His life has been preached to thousands and thousands of boys and young men, as an example worthy of imitation. And when we have passed away, the life of St. Stanislaus

241

will be told to countless others. His name will live to the end of time.

His life on earth comprised only eighteen years. How little and trifling his good works must seem in comparison to the reward he now enjoys for nearly four hundred years! And these four hundred years are but the beginning of his never-ending rewards.

Now, then, which example will you follow, Paul's, or the example of Stanislaus? Let us say a prayer to St. Stanislaus that he may assist in obtaining the grace for us to follow in his footsteps, so that we may after this short life, be permitted to be in his blessed company for ever and ever.

CHAPTER XL. ST. PANCRATIUS

St. Pancratius was a boy of twelve years when he was sentenced to death for his holy faith. He had been found guilty of being a Christian. In those pagan times, it was considered one of the greatest crimes not to bow down to idols of wood and stone. To those pagans their many vices were no crimes at all. But to be a Christian was a crime so great that only death was fit punishment for it. Young as the saint was, he was dragged to court and tried and found guilty. He might have saved his life; indeed, he was told to consider his tender years and all that life would hold in store for him. But the condition of safety was such that he could not accept it. To save his young life, he would have had to break the very first Commandment of God. He would have had to offer sacrifice to an idol of stone and pay to it the honor and homage that belongs to the true God only. There was the alternative of breaking the Commandment of God or of dying. St. Pancratius preferred death to sin.

Nearly every large city in those days had an open-air theatre. Imagine an oval-shaped field large enough for a baseball diamond. All around it rows of seats are built, so that thousands can see the performances. In this arena all kinds of contests, such as gladiatorial fights, races and the like, took place. By some arrangement the arena could be flooded, permitting the performance of naval battles. Beneath the seats of the people there were the dens for prisoners and animals. During the first three hundred years after Christ, one of the most popular forms of pastime

243

consisted in witnessing the public executions of Christians. At times, as many as a hundred and more Christians were led out into the middle of the arena to be devoured by wild beasts.

When we bear in mind that these executions were sometimes of daily occurrence, we can comprehend to some extent how many martyrs gave their lives for their faith. The Christians, half-starved in their miserable prisons, and scarcely half clad, huddled together in the arena to await their death. They could hear the roaring of the wild beasts, and the boisterous jeering of the crowds that had come to see them suffer. Mothers would hold their infants close to their bosoms; little children, not realizing what was to happen, would cry and cling to their parents, the men and women would encourage one another for that last and hard struggle, and would pray aloud. Upon a signal the gatekeeper would draw the iron doors to free the wild animals that had been starved so as to make them more ferocious at sight of their human prey. Lions, tigers, leopards would rush from their cages and the final cries of agony would be drowned in the heartless cheering of an audience more cruel and bloodthirsty than even the beasts of the jungle.

In their frenzy and hatred against the Church those pagans knew no mercy. They spared neither age nor sex.

Among these victims we behold a boy of twelve-St. Pancratius. A leopard is crawling toward him noiselessly like a cat, its eyes burning with a cruel fire. The boy saw it come, but he stood erect, his arms expanded, so that he looked like a living cross. In another instant the leopard buried its teeth in the throat of the young martyr.

Such was the death of St. Pancratius.

244

The pagan world, in gloating over the death of Christians, never stopped to think of the meaning of these deaths. Each death meant that another soul was lost to their cause. Paganism had neither charm nor terror to induce the Christian to leave his God and turn to their many idols. The death of a boy, like St. Pancratius, meant that even this boy could not be induced to leave the Church of the true God and accept what paganism could give in her place. What did paganism offer? It offered honors, money, safety of life. For How long could it promise to give them? Ah, there is the difference. The time during which a pagan might enjoy the things of this world was very uncertain. And, then, death. And though the world may make great strides in all sciences and arts, it is unable to defeat death. You see, then, that paganism offered something it really did not have in its power to bestow. In course of time, our dear Savior came down upon this world and made us a better offer. He offered us a life that shall never end. Thoughtful people who heard the message did not need much time to decide whether they wanted such benefit for a short and uncertain time, or forever. They preferred the happiness of another world that shall never end, to a passing semblance of happiness that must end with death. All the countless, blessed martyrs of holy Church proved, by their death, that they preferred eternal life at any cost to a doubtful earthly happiness, that can last for a few years at the most.

We, too, have made this choice.

After our first Holy Communion, when we renewed our baptismal vows, we solemnly swore to renounce the devil, all his pomps, and all his works. It was then that we resolved to choose the eternal life in preference to the doubtful and uncertain glamor of this world.

But it is not enough to simply say: "Yes. I want to go heaven." Therefore, our dear Savior says, "Not he who

245

says Lord, Lord, will enter the kingdom of heaven, but he who does the will of My Father." We must live in conformance with the will of God. If heaven were not a reward, there would be no necessity of faith, no need to comply with the duties it imposes.

Since you, boys of the Sodality, have made your choice to be on the side of God, remember that you stand shoulder to shoulder with the angels and the saints. The fight will be bitter, but we are sure, beforehand, that the side of God cannot lose. The reward, too, is worth every effort and every sacrifice we can make.

You are so often told about making sacrifices, what do we mean by sacrifices?

Owing to our inclination towards evil, and the dictates of a sinful world entirely governed by it, we are prone to sin. It is as easy for us to sin as for a stone to fall downward. Of our own efforts, we can never curb or conquer this evil inclination, we need the grace of God that is obtained by us in receiving the holy Sacraments and in saying our prayers. By cooperating with these graces, we wage warfare against our flesh. We strive to live our lives not according to the dictates of our flesh, but in compliance with the holy will of God. We deny ourselves the gratification of our desires, and these acts of self-denial are sacrifices. We may, for instance, be laughed at for being Catholics, and our feeling of pride and self-respect is ruffled. We may desire to avoid this ridicule, yet faith tells us we must be ready to suffer anything for the sake of God. And, with the help of His grace, we conquer our inclination and feel happy in the thought of being considered worthy to suffer together with Christ and His martyrs. It may be a question of losing work on account of our holy faith and our evil inclination may tell us that we have to live, that everybody has a right to get along in this world and to earn money. But faith asks us what will it profit us if we win the whole world and in the end lose our soul. With the help of the grace of God we will be able to bear the loss, if God so wills it, feeling sure that we will gain more than the loss has been worth.

The world holds out many pleasures. Your passions will whisper in your ear that you live but once. You are young only a short time, and if you don't enjoy the pleasures of the world right here and now, you will never get a chance. But faith tells you that just because you live but once, and have only one soul, you must save it by all means now and at the present time. The present time is all you have in which you can save your soul. The future is not within our disposal. With the grace of God, you will be able to make sacrifices of all the pleasures the world might tempt you with, and forsake them for the Cross of Christ.

Remember the great sacrifice St. Pancratius made. He gave his life for his holy faith, which, by the grace of God, is also your faith. He died a cruel death. Do you think that he could have made this great sacrifice without making many smaller sacrifices before? God and His angels only know the number of the other sacrifices he rendered. Each sacrifice made him more capable to make a greater one, and so on, until he was called upon to render the greatest sacrifice in his power of giving--his life.

The time may come when God may demand a great sacrifice from you. How will you be able to offer it unless you accustom yourself right now to make smaller sacrifices readily and cheerfully? If it is too hard for you to deny yourself some little lawful pleasures, will it be easy for you to deny yourself some greater, unlawful pleasure? You will never be able to come up to the expectations of God and His Angels unless you perform the little voluntary or necessary sacrifices for which occasion offers itself at the present time. There are countless opportunities every day. And when, at times, a certain sacrifice seems harder than usual think of St. Pancratius giving his life. Pray to him that he may intercede for you to make your sacrifices perfect and of merit for the eternal life.

CHAPTER XLI. BLESSED HERMANN JOSEPH

About the year 1150, a child was born to certain poor parents. They gave to the little boy the name of Hermann. When he subsequently entered the monastery, he was given the name of Joseph. The parents of the boy had at one time been very rich; but, owing to some misfortune, they were compelled to begin at the bottom of the ladder a second time. Their change of fortune, however, had no evil effects upon their faith.

How often do we not see people turning away from God after their fortune has turned either for the better or worse? People who were leading a pious and God-fearing life when poor, will forget all about God as soon as they become rich. Then they have no longer time to go to church or to say their prayers. Money makes them so conceited that they imagine they alone have earned what they have. They have no idea of thanking God that He blessed their efforts, that He gave them health and strength of body, without which they would have never been able to work. Money makes people worldly. They firmly believe that making money is the only real business and work they have. To get more money, they will not even stop at dishonesty. They will be cruel, and know neither mercy nor charity, when it is a question of earning money. Some people you see gradually losing their grip on fortune. Money seems to glide through their fingers and in a few years they are as poor as the poorest. They may have enjoyed some pleasures and honors that only wealth can afford, and with the loss of money they forfeit all influence. These people, too, will forget God. Misfortune makes them lose all Faith and Hope in God.

They blame Him for the loss of their fortune, get sore at the whole world and distrust even their best friends, whereas if they would be sincere and candid, they might find many reasons to convince themselves that their waste and recklessness was the real cause of their ruin. But, being discouraged, disgusted with God and all mankind, they are possessed by a spirit of false pride and they too, forget to pray. They imagine that, since God permitted them to suffer, they need no longer pray to Him.

The parents of Blessed Hermann Joseph were not of this kind.

When they had fallen from the position of wealth to poverty, they looked upon it as a trial sent by Almighty God for their sanctification. With Job, they said: "The Lord hath given, the Lord hath taken; blessed be His holy name."

As a good tree brings forth good fruit, it was natural for these good parents to bring forth good children. All their children were known for their piety. God permitted, however, that one of them, Hermann Joseph, should receive an extra share of holiness. This little boy had the faith that can move mountains.

Blessed Hermann Joseph was of such angelic purity of heart and mind, and withal so simple and plain, that, what others considered great miracles, he looked upon as a matter of course.

From childhood on, as soon as he was able to walk, he felt himself drawn to one of the churches of his native city of Cologne. And there he would pray for hours at the time. He always selected a statue of the Blessed Virgin Mary as the object of his attention. In her arms she held the Infant Savior. At such visits, the Infant Savior was seen to leave the arms of His Divine Mother and play with the little saint. Very often, when his parents would be sorely distressed, he would come home with bread under his arms. When he was asked who gave him that bread he would say a beautiful lady gave it to him. His brothers and sisters were anxious to know who that beautiful and generous lady could be. They followed him to church though he was not aware of their presence. He prayed and chatted as usual with the Most Blessed Mother and the Child, and on leaving he was given his usual loaf of bread. From that time on his parents and brothers and sisters treated him with a feeling akin to awe. One day, he was given an apple. The other children ate their apples as soon as they got them. The blessed Hermann Joseph did not eat his, but took it to church. He knelt down before the statue to which he was accustomed to go, and offered the apple to the Infant Savior. The Infant again left the arms of His Divine Mother to take the apple.

For that reason, whenever Christian art portrays this saint, he is shown as a child kneeling before a statue of the Blessed Virgin and holding an apple in his hands, while the Infant in her arms is seen reaching out His tiny hands to receive it.

At another time, it was during winter, the saintly boy came to church barefooted. When Our Blessed Lady saw him shivering with cold, another miracle took place. To show how much she appreciated his visits she gave him enough money to buy a pair of shoes.

By the way, do you know of any boys that stay away from church on Sundays because they say they have no fitting suit to wear? The excuse is very often a very poor one. You will find the same boys at other places where they ought not to be. We do not come to church to advertise the clothing stores: we come to pray. If God were to form His opinion of us by the clothes we wear, it would be a hard blow for the poor. Luckily for us, He does not follow the

251

style of the world, and He judges us not by the clothes but by the heart within. The Blessed Virgin will not work the miracles for everyone that she has wrought for blessed Hermann Joseph. So you might take it upon yourselves to act in her stead. You may have clothing you can no longer wear. Be assured that if you take it upon yourself to act as the almsgiver of the Blessed Virgin, she will never forget that she owes you a debt of gratitude, and will more than repay it with countless favors andgraces that she will procure for you from her Divine Son.

When this saintly boy was twelve years old, he entered the monastery of the Premonstratensians of St. Norbert and, after he had finished his course of studies, was ordained a priest. With his added years, his piety and simplicity of heart grew in proportion. He was favored with numerous other visions, the Blessed Virgin called him her chaplain, he wrote some spiritual works, gave missions at various places, and died at the ripe age of ninety.

Though he lived to an old age seldom given to men, he is best remembered as a saint of and for boys. His humble simplicity, his unfeigned piety, his childlike purity of heart, and his filial devotion to the Most Blessed Mother of God, were those of a child throughout his entire life.

What lesson should his life teach us?

The world takes it for granted that simplicity of heart must be put aside with knee-pants. The world considers it as a matter of course that the young man must taste of the forbidden fruit and grow worldly-wise. There is, however, no reason for this presumption. With the added years we should not drift away from God, but always approach Him nearer and nearer in our efforts of becoming more like to Him. To grow in justice and holiness is, after all, our most important duty.

How often must we not hear that going to church, saying the daily prayers and receiving the Sacraments, is good enough for children, but that young men, meaning, thereby, even boys of sixteen years, are above that! When these people are asked about priests and monks and sisters praying and going to church, they will answer that it is the business of the clergy and of the religious to pray,-that is all they have to do! If that were all they have to do, I fear that convents and monasteries would soon be overcrowded and that there would be so many priests that not a tenth part of them could get parishes. God never intended that only one or two classes of people should pray. If He had, He would certainly have told us so. But when you listen to the instructions of Christ, you will find that the duty of prayer is binding upon all until death. "Oh, well," you will hear some say, "I did not mean that priests only should pray. I know many old folks that have nothing else to do, and they pray from morning to night. They have the time." According to this worldly reasoning, we should be pious in childhood, then, when we become able to work for a living, we may safely give up praying, and work, and work, and work. During that time men need care very little for the commandments of God, may break them as often as they please--provided there is no danger of being found out and locked up for so doing. There need be no worry about the hereafter till people get old. When they have outlived their usefulness, then they may again begin to pray, for there is nothing else for them to do!

If such reasoning were correct, it would mean that God must be satisfied to have you think of Him only when there is nothing better to do.

Suppose you were to make your father a present of a watch. You buy the watch and then tell your father: "Here, Father; I desire to give you a watch, but you will have to let me use it till I am ready to give it to you." You keep

253

the watch for years and years, assuring your father from time to time that he is going to get his watch. Then one day, after you have used it for a long time, something in it breaks. You take the watch to a watchmaker, he looks at it and tells you that you might buy a new watch for what it would cost to repair the old one. All the wheels are worn out, the spring is broken and the case looks like brass. So you take the watch back and then make a present of it to your father! Do you think that he will be pleased with that worthless thing? Suppose your father had even given you the money to buy the watch with. Would it not be an act of impudence on your part to make your father such a gift? Would not your father have reason to feel insulted?

Now it is the very same thing when we spend an entire life in sin, and, at the very end offer to God a decrepit body. Can we expect to get a great reward for anything like that? Could we blame God if He refused such a shabby gift? If He does take it at all it will, no doubt, condition a severe penance for all the wasted years: a penance, for which we may have to atone in purgatory, suffering there for every wasted minute and every grace that we have rejected in the time that is lost forever.

Never take the advice of the world when it is a question of doing something for God. Naturally, God knows far better than the world what He wants of us. God wants of us not only our first tender years but all that follow, up to our last breath. He wants us entirely for Himself. Whatever we have and are, all comes from Him, the Author of all good. The world can neither give nor take anything.

Consider how foolish and sinful it would be to waste the best years of our lives; the years when we can do the most good, perform the greatest sacrifices and earn the grandest rewards. How dare we forfeit the most precious part of our lives to give God the leavings?

Now, my dear boys, let us pray to blessed Hermann Joseph that we may obtain childlike humility and simplicity like his, and keep them for the remainder of our lives.

CHAPTER XLII. ST. JOHN BERCHMANS

The life of St. John Berchmans is a singular life, indeed. While it is not known that he performed a single, extraordinary work, every one of his acquaintances knew that he performed his everyday duties extraordinarily well. The constant thought uppermost in his mind was one we might profitably adopt for ourselves. This thought was: "I shall never be a saint unless I am a saint when I am a boy."

He was born at Diest, in Belgium, on March 13, 1599. He was blessed with saintly parents. Being gentle and thoughtful, bright and cheerful, he was a favorite with his playmates. Still, his parents discovered that he was not entirely without faults.. He was quick tempered and inclined to be easily led. His conscientious parents never permitted these faults to get a good start in their boy. They checked these faults as soon as they began to show.

His parish priest, a Father Emmerick, took a fancy to the boy because at the age of seven years of age he had mastered the Mass prayers, and took it upon himself to serve holy Mass. When the boy was nine years old the good priest took him, and a few other boys, of whom he thought that they might possibly have a vocation for the priesthood, into his own house. There the little company led a regular convent life, the good old priest preparing them for their college course. He laid down severe rules for them, dividing their time into hours of study, work, prayer, and rest.

Invariably the little saint asked for the hardest work,

the kind the other boys might consider beneath their dignity. He did that work most willingly. He was the first to rise in the morning. He did not feel satisfied if he could not serve Mass each day. His pious behavior at the altar was a source of edification even for the priest. Whenever he obtained permission to go to the neighboring church, at Montaigu, he recited the rosary going and returning. At play he was full of harmless fun; when studying no one could be more interested than he; in prayer he was a model for all. Whatever he did, whether work or play, he put his whole heart and soul into it.

After he had completed his preparatory training with Father Emmerick, we find him next in the Jesuit College at Mechlin. The training he had received at home and with the good, old priest, was a great advantage to him at the college. He quickly gained the good will of his fellow students and of his teachers. This, as you may know, is no small matter. You may be liked by those with whom you work, while your foreman may have little use for you. Or, if your foreman has taken a liking to you, your fellow workers may dislike you. All this may happen without your fault.

St. John Berchmans was liked principally because he always knew his place, and kept it. He was never bold. I dare say that few, if any, of his fellow students suspected his fervent piety, for the saint disliked to make much of himself. To give you an idea of his piety, let me tell you that the saint at Mechlin made the Way of the Cross every Friday night in his bare feet. He selected Friday in honor of the suffering and death of our dear Savior. To understand what this meant, I must add that these stations were shrines built some distance apart from each other. To escape notice he selected the time of night for his devotion. In stormy and cold weather it was a hard task to walk all that way barefooted. Besides his daily prayers, he recited

257

every day the office of the Blessed Virgin. Considering such acts of piety, it was not to be wondered at that God gave him a vocation to the religious life.

After he completed his college course he asked to be received as a member of the Society of Jesus, and received the habit of this order at the Mechlin novitiate. After his novitiate he was directed to Antwerp to continue his studies, and from there was sent to Rome. With his bundle over his shoulders he set out afoot from Antwerp to Rome, and reached the Eternal City the last day of 1618. In 1621 he was seized with a violent fever, and died.

It was only after his death that people found that he had been a saint. No doubt, if God had permitted him to live to a ripe old age, this saint might have accomplished a great deal of good. But in His Wisdom, God saw fit to recall the young saint when he was twenty-two years old. Yet in that brief life he did more good than most others would do during three and four times as many years.

In our times we find that many people have an entirely wrong idea about holiness. They imagine that to be holy one must perform many miracles, like a St. Anthony or a St. Francis Solanus. But we must remember that holiness of life does not consist in miracles, but in carrying out the holy Will of God in a faultless and perfect manner. As a special favor God grants to some saints the power of miracles, not to add luster to their names, but to induce the world to follow the way of God. The holy Apostles wrought great miracles, not for their own sakes or glory, but for the sake of making converts, that their faith might take deep roots, and that the faith might be accepted even by doubting pagans. Yet the Gospels do not record a single miracle of St. John the Baptist, although our Savior Himself said that not a greater saint was born of woman than he. The sacred text is, in this respect, silent even about the

Blessed Virgin Mary. For, though she is now more powerful than any angel or saint, or all of them combined, not a single miracle is placed to her credit while she was alive.

Hence we need not feel surprised that St. John Berchmans led so simple a life. He is a great saint, nevertheless, even though during his life he did not perform a single miracle. And yet we might well say that his whole life was a constant miracle. In everything he did he had but one object in view--to please God in a perfect way. Whenever he saw an opportunity of pleasing God better by a more perfect work, he would substitute for the less perfect work that which was more pleasing to God. There was no one in the community who pleased God so perfectly as St. John Berchmans. It was his profound humility that enabled him to make all his actions so inconspicuous that during his lifetime his fellow students and brothers of the Order did not discover his wonderful perfection.

An army can have but one supreme leader. The greater the number of dutiful soldiers following a good leader, the better they are equipped, the more chances will that army have of being victorious. The greatest general will be easily beaten if he has an army of indifferent or poorly trained soldiers. We cannot all be great leaders of men. God calls some men to places of prominence to perform grand works, some men to be missionaries, to others He gives vast mental powers, but the vast majority of men are to be privates in the vast army of God. The priests of the entire world make a vast number. Yet only a few of this number are selected to become bishops, and only one of all this number is elected to be the head of the Church in Rome.

What lesson does the life of St. John Berchmans teach us'? My dear boys, it teaches us a very consoling lesson, His life teaches us that even in the lowest rank of life we may become great saints, even though we do nothing else but perform our duty perfectly.

It may not be possible for you to become great apostolic missionaries, or founders of new orders in the Church. You may not be destined to become illustrious martyrs. God may not have made you great intellectual lights like a St. Thomas or St. Augustine, and, yet, you may become saints. You may never leave your work-bench, never rise any higher in the world than your fathers did before you; all that will not prevent you from becoming saints. All that is necessary is to do the work of our vocation for the love of God in a faultless manner, and we are saints. What matters whether the world is aware of it? It is enough that God knows the value of our works. And yet we find boys, as well as grown people, who grieve because their unreasonable ambition of being somebody in this world is not realized. They have set their whole heart and mind upon becoming great. They desire to see their names in the papers; they want to be talked about, to be considered and praised. And, if they fail in this effort, they give up in despair, and even neglect their everyday duties. They resemble the man to whom God gave one talent. He imagined that he should get as many talents as the most deserving had received. Because he was given only one talent, he refused to make proper use of it, and when God asked for an accounting, he came up and threw his one talent down in disgust. Do not make the mistake of that unhappy man. Never think that because God has not raised you to some place of prominence, your life is not worth the trouble. In the sight of God your life is as important as the life of the greatest man on earth. He has a soul to save, so have you. Indeed, it is easier for us little people to become saints than the ones that are up in the world. It should be far easier for us to perform little duties well than for the others to measure up to their heavy duties and responsibilities.

When you work, work faithfully. Try to do your work as well as you can, not forgetting to offer up all you do to God. When it is time to play, go and play, taking care that God is not offended in any way. When it is time to pray, pray earnestly and fervently. Finally, to tell you the last but not the least requisite for holiness, keep away from the wickedness of the world. Had St. John Berchmans been told that he would be ultimately placed side by side with two other great saints, St. Aloysius and St. Stanislaus, as a perfect model for boys and young men, he would very likely have considered the prediction as a very poor joke at his own expense. His profound humility never permitted him to entertain a single thought of self-praise, even though ever so well deserved.

Let us ask St. John Berchmans that, through his prayers, we may learn to appreciate the value of all our duties, no matter how lowly our station in life, so that by complying with them as faithfully as he, we, too, may after our death be numbered with the saints.

CHAPTER XLIII. ST. HERMENEGILD

More than a thousand years ago the fair land of Spain was peopled by Visigoths. While the Ostrogoths had conquered the eastern part of Europe, the Visigoths had extended their rule over the other part. The Goths were of Germanic origin. Their continual warfare had made them as bold as lions, but also as cruel and relentless as tigers. The Gothic people had embraced Arianism, a sect that denied the Divinity of Christ. Like all other sects, before and after, Arianism proceeded to persecute all that would not bow down before it. Fire and sword were its chief arguments. The Gothic people being barbaric and brutal, you will easily understand that when they sided with the Arians, Catholics could expect little mercy from them. For an apostate Catholic is always a worse enemy of the Church than one who never belonged to her.

The father of St. Hermenegild was King Leovigild, a stern and hard-hearted man. The saint being the older of his two sons, the king arranged that he should be brought up a strict Arian, because as the coming king of the Visigoths, he was to preserve the kingdom for that sect. But God, in His own most wonderful way, disposed otherwise. The people of the kingdom were no longer to be misled, but to be returned to the Mother Church they had forsaken. To show you how wonderfully Divine Providence works out its aim, consider that here was the son of a king, brought up in a false religion. Nevertheless, the youth was well meaning. By chance, as worldly people would say, he met St. Leander, bishop of Seville. From the time of their first

262

meeting this youth and the saintly old bishop became good friends. The prince could not help being influenced by the holiness of the aged bishop, and he was induced to pray as he never prayed before. And when the prince realized that Arianism was not the true religion, he was anxious to learn the truth. So it happened that the saintly bishop had the happiness of baptizing one that was to be a saint like himself.

The suffering of St. Hermenegild begins with the time when he was received into the Church by St. Leander. Both Leovigild and the stepmother never permitted Hermenegild to have many happy days. Both were very severe. After his conversion he found his home anything but agreeable. To avoid the continual taunting and numberless insults, he had to flee from home. Then men who imposed themselves upon him as friends betrayed him to his father, and he was brought back to the palace--in chains. The king was so enraged that he had his son put in prison. Castles in those days had a subterranean vault where prisoners were kept. Into such a prison St. Hermenegild was thrown. Heavy chains hung from the walls and were attached to his hands and feet.

It would have been an easy matter for the saint to obtain his liberty. All he had to do was to renounce the Catholic faith and declare that he wished to be an Arian. But neither starvation nor the darkness and filth of the prison, neither the rage of his royal father, nor the chains that bruised his tender flesh, were able to cause him to falter in the faith.

Imagine the son of a king brought up in a luxurious palace. Wherever he appeared, he received royal honors, servants waiting to do his   All of a sudden his life, with all its pomp and ease, is changed to a life of disgrace. Instead of getting the finest of food he is starved; instead of

263

going about and receiving the homage of a faithful people he is placed in chains; instead of the comfortable rooms of the palace he must dwell in a hideous prison where fresh air or sunshine never entered. If you realize what all this must mean, you can form an idea of what St. Hermenegild suffered during the time he was in prison.

St. Gregory the Great, in describing the suffering of this saint, relates that King Leovigild, at one time, sent an Arian bishop to the prison of St. Hermenegild. It was the day before Easter. The king was waiting for one word and he would have welcomed his son back and would have given him the crown. But that one word, the denial of the true faith, was never spoken. The king, in despair, ordered that his son should be beheaded that very night. Thus St. Hermenegild died for his holy faith, during the night before Easter in the year 585.

Leovigild died shortly after his son. In his heart, he could not help but admire his son for the steadfastness of character. While he did not return to the true faith, for fear of displeasing his people, he did manage to place his other son in the care of St. Leander. It was human respect that prevented the king from embracing the truth. Practically his entire kingdom was Arian. He feared his people, doubting whether he would keep the crown for himself and his son if he would join the true Church. Did the thought ever occur to him that God could have given him a grander crown than the one that was within the giving of his nation? Worldly people know but one fear: the fear of offending people. To offend God means nothing to them.

How idle the king's fears were we see in the conversion of Recared, the brother of St. Hermenegild, who was a mere boy when he was received in the Church. The fear of the old king did not materialize. The people, instead

264

of becoming vexed or even rebellious, showed by their actions that they were perfectly satisfied. Recared became popular and was idolized by his people. Indeed, after a few years the majority of the Visigoths came back to the true fold.

The one strong characteristic that stands out boldly in the life of St. Hermenegild is his conscientiousness in placing the obedience to God above all other considerations. His father was well aware that the Arian sect was not the true Church. He was a man advanced in years, he knew the world, and showed a ripened judgment regarding worldly matters of importance. Yet he was a slave of human respect. Leovigild feared the loss of his kingdom. Then, too, there was his pride. For many years he had persecuted members of the Church, and to admit that he had been wrong was more than his pride would permit. King Leovigild may have been brave and daring in war, morally he was a coward. He would stoop to do wrong in order to please the people.

On the other hand, St. Hermenegild knew how implacable his father was, for he had seen with his own eyes how his father had persecuted the Church. St. Hermenegild knew also that his father was likely not only to disown him, but even to imprison and kill him. Knowing the violent character of the Goths, the saint had all reason to fear it. Yet he worried little about his inheritance and even less about his safety. For him it was a question of receiving a better crown, a better life. To gain the kingdom of heaven, the saint was willing to sacrifice everything worldly. The severity of his father and the ill will of a nation were as nothing to him in comparison with the call of duty.

With this lofty example of St. Hermenegild in mind, let us consider how easily we are swayed by human respect and fear.

We know what God requires us to do. We are also conscious of the way of the world. We know that if we are punctual and faithful in our religious duties the world will call us pietists or bigots. If we are honest and upright, we may be regarded even as hypocrites, and no doubt that hurts. The result is that human respect often makes cowards of us. We may learn to fear the world more than God. We hear of a business man who says he does not go to church on Sunday for fear to lose trade if people were to learn that he is a Catholic. Some people will fail to observe days of fast or abstinence when they are among those of other creeds, and many would rather be looked upon as up to date, or even ahead of the times, than as faithful to the laws of God. They are far more eager to gain that worthless reward the world may give, and think little or nothing of the eternal reward God has in His power of giving. If we feared God half as much as we fear the world, we should all be saints.

After all, the world can neither punish nor reward to any great extent. Too often the world turns down the very men that served it most faithfully. The world likes to change its idols. The man whom the world worships today as the greatest ever, it will ridicule and abuse tomorrow. Human respect and human fear is one of the most compelling weapons of the devil--it is the trap into which we go most readily.

We have all reason, then, to pray to St. Hermenegild that, through his intercession, we may gain some of his strength of character. May he intercede for us, so that in the future we may be free from human respect, and that, like him, we may be ready and willing to die rather than to offend God grievously.

We have not been made by the world, or for the world, or of the world. We are the handwork of God. We cannot expect much good from the world, nor have we much reason to fear it. There is only one whom we have reason to fear, from whom we may expect great good, and that One is our Creator, God. Hence the Holy Ghost says: "The fear of the Lord is the beginning of wisdom."

CHAPTER XLIV. THE YOUNG TOBIAS

The story of young Tobias is known to you all, yet you may have failed to take to heart the lesson which it is intended to convey.

The father of young Tobias was taken into captivity together with thousands of Jews. At home, the Jews could observe the laws of their religion. When, however, they were made captives and compelled to live in pagan Nineveh, the observance of the Law of Moses was often found very difficult. The father of Tobias was one of the few faithful to the law. Whereas other Jews considered the Law of Moses burdensome, and found many excuses for not following it faithfully, he observed the law most conscientiously, even at the risk of his life. Had all the Jews been as faithful as he, God would very likely have averted the trials of such captivity. But because most of them had forsaken the way of God, and accepted the ways of the pagan world, they had to be brought to their senses by means of sorrow and suffering. And then, as now, the just had to suffer along with the wicked. But the just have this consolation that their suffering brings them still closer to heaven. It will not only diminish or cancel the temporal punishment they have merited for other shortcomings, but be a further source of rewards in the world to come.

For that reason we find the elder Tobias reconciled to his fate. He had seen his home go up in flames, he had to leave the land of his fathers, had lost most of his fortune, had to live in a country hostile to his people and to his God, yet not a single word of discontent passed his lips.

The Assyrian king, Salmanassar, recognizing the sterling qualities of the elder Tobias, had granted him more freedom, a number of privileges and some minor office, such as were never granted to other Jews. While the other Jews were kept like prisoners under guard, he could go from place to place, work wherever he liked, stay wherever he liked. God rewarded his efforts with success. His ever increasing wealth, the favor of the king, and his saintly life made Tobias prominent among the captives. Whatever favor and privileges he enjoyed he used to the best advantage. He undertook to visit the Jews in the various parts of Assyria, encouraging them to faithfully observe the law of God, and helped them with money. Of the elder Tobias it can be said that he neglected not a single good work that he could do.

After the death of the king, his son, Sennacherib, assumed the reign. He laid siege to Jerusalem, but was repulsed, and returned home with a small remnant of a vast army. Unable to conquer the city of David, he took revenge on the Jews whom his father had made prisoners. Sennacherib enacted very severe laws against the Jewish captives, revoking all favors and privileges that some Jews had enjoyed during the reign of Salmanassar. An offense hardly noticed when committed by a pagan was made punishable by death if wrought by a Jew, Indeed, the observance of most Jewish customs was forbidden under pain of death.

The elder Tobias had to suffer with the rest. His office was taken from him, and he was deprived of the privilege of freely going about. Still we do not find Tobias any the less zealous for the law of God. It was under pain of death forbidden to bury a Jew. The corpse of a Jew was to be left as food for wild animals. Tobias, however, would hide

269

the corpse in his home, and bury it at night. Through the loss of the royal favor he was no longer able to travel about to console other sufferers. With old age coming upon him he became poor. To aid to his misfortune he lost his eyesight.

At this time the elder Tobias found it necessary to collect a large debt, a debt of ten talents of silver. This meant a fortune at that time. The distance from the abode of Tobias to Rages in Medea was great. It meant a journey of over a week each way. The way, moreover, was dangerous. Wild animals and equally ferocious robbers made traveling very unsafe. In fact, journeys were not undertaken unless a number of men would go together to share the hardships and dangers of the trip. Old Tobias was in a quandary. To whom of all his pagan neighbors could he confide the fact that his son was to collect a large amount of money? Such knowledge would have meant not only the loss of the money but the death of his son. To send his son without any companion was a great risk. How could this youth defeat robbers and wild animals singlehanded?

Yet, there seemed nothing else possible for young Tobias but to go alone, but as he stepped forth from the house, he met another young man equipped for a long journey. He informs Tobias that he, too, is bound for the same city of Rages. Young Tobias re-enters the house with the stranger and who may imagine the joy of the old, blind father on hearing that the young stranger is journeying to the very place to which Tobias himself must go to collect the debt.

With the blessings of the aged parent, Tobias and his companion undertake the journey. On the way they were to stop at the house of a distant relative of Tobias. The two had not traveled very far before Tobias began to realize that his companion was not an ordinary young man. While he did not suspect the truth he had complete confidence in

270

the wisdom and power of his mysterious companion, and obeyed him willingly. Hence, when his companion informed him that he should marry the daughter of the man they were to visit, his word was law to young Tobias. The companion let Tobias stay with these people while he journeyed to Rages to collect the debt. On his return he stopped for Tobias and his bride and accompanied them home.

Upon the return, when the elder Tobias was miraculously cured of blindness, this mysterious companion revealed his identity. Young Tobias had traveled with an archangel of God, and did not know him. When the angel's mission was accomplished he disappeared, asking the astonished people to praise and thank God for His grace and benevolence.

We often hear people say that in our time and country it is almost impossible to raise boys in the proper way. And as the reason for this statement parents will point to the ever spreading bad example round about us.

It depends upon you, boys, to prove that the fears of your parents are without foundation. For this reason I have given you a sketch of the times of young Tobias.

This boy grew up in Nineveh, a godless, pagan city. He grew up among other children, both Jewish and pagan. Since young Tobias was not blind and deaf he could not help seeing and hearing much wickedness. And yet, with all the bad example he had to witness, he did not waver for a moment in his faith. No doubt, a number of his Jewish playmates inclined towards paganism. He could not but see their bad example. Yet he remained steadfast in his faith.

The conditions are similar in our day. The children of lax Catholic or of mixed marriages frequently fall

271

away from the faith. And just as an apostate Catholic is more inimical to the faith than even a Protestant, so a fallen away Jew in those days was more antagonistic to Hebrew customs than even a pagan, and eager to ignore the Jewish laws.

You understand, then, that Tobias saw much wicked example.

In spite of all that, he remained a saintly boy. No doubt, he was exposed to slights and insults, was laughed at and mocked by his own people as well as by young pagans. Nothing, however, could make him forsake the faith of his fathers. His pious parents did all in their power to teach him the requirements of the Mosaic Law, and the virtues he was to practice. The hope of Tobias was a temple of God, and all the wickedness of a pagan people, all the bad example of fallen away Jews, had no bad effect upon him. He remained pure in mind and heart.

Do you think that, if young Tobias had been a boy given to the vices he saw about him, God would have given him the extraordinary grace of having the archangel, Raphael, as a traveling companion? His innocence and piety must have been extraordinary, otherwise he would not have received such singular favor.

Now let us get at the lesson the life of the young Tobias teaches. We are placed in a world in which we cannot help seeing and hearing many things that are wrong and wicked. That we will meet scandals, that we will be sorely tried, goes without saying. We are unable to escape from our surroundings. We will have to stay where we are and make the best of it. All we can do is to let the world go its way while we go ours.

Like young Tobias, so are you surrounded on all sides by wickedness. In factories, offices and shops the very air is often poisoned with foul talk. The time may come when the performance of your religious duties, the saying of prayers, attending Holy Mass and receiving the Holy Sacraments, may appear a burden for you. You will see bad example, not only from those who know not God, but from others of whom you would least expect it. But when you see all this spiritual desolation think of young Tobias. He was not misled by it, neither should you. The bad example round about you is no permit for you to do the same. We can never be forced to sin.

You sometimes hear of so-called reformers, trying to reform the whole world at one swoop. To these people everything is wrong. They pose as self-appointed reformers, but make one big mistake. They start at the wrong end. We can never reform the world with the passage of a law. If we desire to reform the world, so far as it is in our power, we must start at the right end. We must start not with Jones or Smith or Brown, but with ourselves. If each one of us would try to lead a better life the face of the world would soon be changed.

Since most people, however, consider reform somewhat like castor oil, preferring to prescribe it rather than take it, the world will remain what it is. But there is no need to throw up the sponge and follow the way of the world. Think of young Tobias, imitate him in his purity and piety. He met with the same difficulties that you meet with.

To protect you against the example of the sinful world, I cannot give you better advice than that which the rules of the Sodality suggest. Holy Mother Church has the experience of over nineteen hundred years. The fact that she heartily approves of the Sodality and endows it with many spiritual favors shows what value she ascribes to it. Always live up to the rules and regulations of the Sodality, the cardinal points of which are: daily prayers, frequent

Confession and Holy Communion, and a childlike devotion to our Blessed Mother.

Of the dangers besetting youth, it is true, there are many. Many also, are the graces you receive. Endeavor to show that, with the graces at your disposal, it is possible to lead a clean and pure life in a world that teems with wickedness and temptation.

CHAPTER XLV. DANIEL

Daniel, as a boy of fourteen years, was, together with thousands of other Jews, taken captive and brought to Babylon. The boy being of noble birth and of handsome appearance, the king, Nabuchodonosor, selected him to be brought up in the manner of the children of the Babylonian nobility. The youthful Daniel thus received a training that qualified him to attend the royal court and to occupy such position of rank as the king might confer upon him. Daniel, destined to receive greater honors and a higher rank than even this king could give him, showed, as a boy, two certain traits to which I would direct your especial attention, and you will find in the boy Daniel a shining model, worthy of your imitation.

Having been admitted to the royal school, his life had no longer anything in common with the other Jews in this captivity. He enjoyed the liberty and privileges of the native nobility, yet his good fortune and the splendor of the court did not turn his head. Neither did he forget his God. Though only a boy, Daniel did not forget that the Law of Moses was at all times the law of his life. Dishes were set before him made of forbidden meats. He knew he was not allowed to eat them. Did he try to discover some excuse for evading the law? Did he hunt for arguments to dispense himself, perhaps urging the plea that in a pagan land it was impossible to observe the Jewish law to the letter? He did nothing of the kind. He sought and received permission to eat the food of the Jews. Both his teacher and his king, far from being offended at the action of Daniel, thought all

275

the more of him because of his faithfulness to his principles.

In this faithfulness to the Law of Moses, Daniel is for us a grand example of respect for the laws of the Church.

The Law of Moses ended with the death of Christ. The genuine sacrifice having been offered upon the Cross, the symbols that only foreshadowed it had lost the reason for their existence. Since the real sacrifice was to continue to the end of time, the law of the Old Testament had to make way for the law of the New Testament. As the Jews had the Law of Moses, we, of the Church, have the law of the Church. The laws of the New Testament have the same binding power as did the laws of Moses in the Old Testament, since the Author of both is the same--God. Indeed, the laws of the New Testament are still more sacred than the laws of Moses. Those laws were but a shadow of what was to come, and the laws of the New Testament are the fulfillment and perfection of the Mosaic Law. If, then, even the law of Moses had such a solemn and binding force, what should be said of the more perfect law, the law of the New Testament? And yet we find not a few Christians who consider the laws of the New Testament, the laws of the Church, as of little importance. They will observe these laws if the observation is convenient or agreeable, but they will disregard them when inclination prompts them, or when their observance demands sacrifice.

Take, for instance, the law of hearing holy Mass on Sundays and on holy days of obligation. What excuses are discovered to evade this law! There is the excuse of time and distance. This obstacle might easily be overcome by getting up earlier. That, however, is inconvenient. Then there are business considerations that make going to church impossible. Again, it will be either too hot or too

276

cold, the roads are either too dusty or too muddy, and so the lukewarm Catholic will find many excuses to stay away from holy Mass on Sundays. According to the Law of Moses, every Jew was obliged to go to the Temple once a year. Since there was but one Temple, the Temple in Jerusalem, it meant that those who lived far away had a long journey. It took some people a month to make this annual pilgrimage to the Temple. It meant that these people would have to stop their daily work for the entire time this journey would last. The journey meant hardships and expense, and yet the faithful Jews went to the Temple of Jerusalem every year from all parts of the land. When we consider these long and difficult journeys of the Jews to their Temple, it will be hard indeed to explain the laxity of some Catholics.

Another law of the Church frequently broken is the law of fast and abstinence. What idle excuses are invented to escape the obligation of fasting and of abstaining! Protestants may not understand why we abstain from meat on a Friday, or why we fast at certain times of the year. Although they claim their Bible is the rule of life, they seem to overlook some of the things Christ commanded. Penance is one of them. Christ Himself, by word and example, prescribed fasting. But what Protestants do know is that Catholics are bidden to abstain from the use of meat on certain days and to fast at some seasons of the year. And when they see that a Catholic fails to obey the law of his Church, they know that this is either a faithless or cowardly Catholic. Some of our Protestant friends keep a close watch upon us. They may poke fun at us for being overzealous in obeying the laws of our holy Church, but in their heart they will admire us for being loyal to the dictates of our conscience. They may praise some lukewarm Catholic for his indifference to the laws of the Church and call it progress or up-to-dateness, but that will not make them put a great deal of confidence in him, because they feel instinctively that a man who is untrue to God cannot be true to man.

During the Thirty-Year War in Germany, a Franciscan convent was broken into by a mob of Protestant soldiers. The friars were lined up and given the choice of either forswearing their faith and vows and joining the soldiers, or instant death. All but one declared they would rather die than renounce their faith. The one who wavered was the youngest of the friars. He was promised by the officer all kinds of favors if he would yield, and he yielded. The other friars were hanged. The unfortunate young friar took off the holy habit and expected to be treated with much favor. His ready denial of his faith, however, caused the soldiers to distrust the young friar, and quickly coming to the conclusion that he was worthless, the soldiers hung him right next to those saintly men who had willingly died for their faith. A man who denies his faith is mistrusted, and, what is more, he should be mistrusted.

The Jews of the Old Testament had a law of fasting and abstinence. The Jew was not allowed to eat pork. Other meats were considered unclean if the animals were not killed according to the Mosaic regulation. The Jews regarded these laws so sacred that they would die rather than eat forbidden meats.

But we Christians! What a variety of excuses are offered by many of us to render the law of fasting and abstinence null and void! And the people who are so eager to find excuses from fasting ignore the fact that, if really dispensed from fasting, they must perform some other work of penance. There are, of course, legitimate excuses from fasting. But in no case does that mean a general dispensation from all works of penance. Such a dispensation can never be granted. Instead of humbly deploring that they are unable to follow the example of

Christ in fasting, some of these people boast even of the fact that they need not fast; they even ridicule others for being so foolish as to fast.

Another law of the Church persistently misinterpreted in spite of all that can be said in explanation of it, is the law prescribing the reception of Holy Communion at Easter time. The interpretation of this law favored by lax people is that one Communion during the year is all that can be expected from them, and that by obeying this law they are exemplary Catholics, better, perhaps, than those who receive the Sacraments too often! This interpretation, however, is not the one which the Church sanctions. In this law, the Church simply states that the very least a Catholic must do is to receive Holy Communion once a year, during the Easter season. If he fails to do even that, he manifests his intention to be no longer a true member of the Church. The Church was compelled to make this law to meet the laxity of some of her members. If the time had been made every ten or twenty years, there would be some who would limit their receiving the Sacraments to that time. The Church did never imply that this one Holy Communion at Easter time is sufficient for our sanctification. Her intention is that by receiving Holy Communion at Easter time we must show that we are members, and wish to remain members of the Church. If one Confession and Holy Communion a year would be enough, how much would the work of the priest be lessened! There would be no necessity of going to the sick and dying and of hearing their confessions. No longer any need for the priest to spend long hours in the confessional.

Whenever you hear a man talking against going often to Confession, there is usually a "reason." You cannot point out a single saint who had any objection against going to Confession. Some of the saints went to Confession every day, others two and three times a week. None delayed it for more than a week if they could help it. The pioneer priest of Lansing, Michigan, walked all the distance from there to Grand Rapids, about seventy miles, to go to Confession to a brother priest. What excuses will on the Day of Judgment those have for whom a distance of a few blocks to church is too far?

Another law of the Church often treated lightly is the law regarding mixed marriages. Unless you are careful, you boys may be paving the way to such an unhappy union. For that reason, never permit yourself to become too chummy with persons of another faith. I do not mean that you should despise them, or look down upon them, for the law of charity binds you as solemnly toward them as toward those of our own faith. But you must take care not to form friendships that in the end might lead to a mixed marriage. There is in these words no bigotry. Well-meaning Protestants will be as much opposed to mixed marriages as we are. In most such cases, both the Catholic as well as the Protestant party are weak in their faith, and that fact alone is proof that their religious life and the religious training of their children will not amount to much when there is no harmony of faith between the parents.

Many people have a wrong idea about the laws of the Church.

Rigorous as the laws of Moses were, they were for the welfare of the Jewish people. By obeying them to the letter they derived benefits that would never have been within their reach had they ignored them. So, too, the laws of the Church have been enacted for the sake of promoting the temporal and spiritual welfare of the Christian people. Therefore these laws must be revered and obeyed, even though they occasionally demand sacrifice on our part.

We will now consider the other beautiful trait in the boy Daniel, and that was his childlike confidence in

280

God. In the king's presence and in the den of the lions this confidence in the power and mercy of God never forsook him.

We are inclined to depend too much upon ourselves. We glory in our little strength, though even that s not our own but given us by God. We depend upon the health of our body, which God can take from us as easily as He has given it. If we succeed, we take all the credit to ourselves; if we lose, we, say the odds were against us. Yet we have all the reason in the world to put our trust only in the power and mercy of God. He finds ways and means where our ingenuity would be at a loss to know what to do.

Let the life of youthful Daniel be a lesson teaching you always to observe faithfully the laws of the Church. Never seek excuses for evading the laws of the Church when there is a possibility of complying with them. Another good practice for you will be never to make even use of such excuses that in your charity you may consider valid in the case of others. Imitate the saints in this manner.

While they were generous in excusing others, they were most rigorous with themselves. Finally, in obeying the laws of the Church, increase your confidence in the power and mercy of God. God has at all times taken care of his own. We can never lose by pleasing God. The world may not like it, and may invent all kinds of lures or punishments to make us turn away from God. Come what may, like Daniel, we too will remain true to God. He will find a way for us that will increase our consolation on earth, and our greater glory in the world to come.

CHAPTER XLVI. SAMUEL

In our days we notice a sad lack of religious vocations. The few willing ones must often overcome great obstacles before they can realize their fond hopes. Many whom God may have fitted for a religious life shrink back from it, fearing that its duties would prove too burdensome. Like the rich youth whom Christ had asked to follow Him, they have not the heart to make the sacrifice demanded by a religious vocation. And so it happens that misguided people seek happiness in vain, since the world is unable to give what only God has within His power to bestow.

To put before you a model of the religious vocation, let me direct your attention to the boy, Samuel. His pious parents brought him to the temple almost as soon as he was able to walk. There, together with other boys, he was brought up to prepare himself for his sacred calling. Samuel was the son of saintly parents. He had been given to them after years of prayer. The mother, indeed, had made a vow that, if God would give her a boy, he should be dedicated to the service of God. God heard that prayer, and the saintly mother kept her vow. From the very start the little boy showed signs of extraordinary piety. He considered it the greatest honor to be in and of the temple. His virtuous conduct was a model and a source of edification for all the rest. Hence God chose him for great things. Above all, the boy had but one desire--to do the holy Will of God. No task was too hard, no sacrifice too great, when there was the holy will of God. Had God intended nothing more for

Samuel than sweeping the steps of the temple, he would have thanked God for that favor as much as for any other.

The readiness of Samuel to follow the call to a religious life is worthy of our earnest imitation.

A religious vocation is the highest calling to which God can summon anyone. It means the call of God to greater work on earth and greater glory in heaven. It means that God wishes certain souls to occupy higher rank. Kings, emperors and presidents of big republics outrank all others in their respective countries. None equal them there in honors and dignities. But in the kingdom of heaven, the humble lay brother of a religious community will take a higher rank than the mightiest emperor the world ever had.

It is evident, then, that he who has received a calling to the religious life should embrace it gladly and willingly. Alas, such is not always the case. Unfortunately, many vocations to the religious life are thwarted by parental interference, many are ignored by those who are called.

When speaking of vocations in general, I explained to you that both our temporal and our eternal happiness depends upon the choice we take. Indeed, most, if not all, the misfortune and unhappiness in the world is traceable to the fact that these people have not chosen the vocation to which God called them. Bitter disappointments come to those who do not follow their call to the religious life, thinking they are going to have nothing but pleasures in the world. It is exactly as though they tried to get the better of God. Before long they will find out their mistake.

Some years ago, a certain girl entered the convent. The foolish mother then imagined that she could not live without her daughter. She came to the convent frequently and cried and lamented when she saw her daughter dressed in the religious habit. She would talk only of her not being able to live if her daughter would not return. Finally the girl was overwhelmed by the lamentations of her mother, she took off her habit and returned home. Her first words on re-entering her home were: "Mother, I am afraid you will feel sorry for what you made me do." However, the selfish mother was satisfied. She had her girl back home and everything was lovely, so far as she was concerned. But the girl was a changed girl. The mother's preaching began to bear fruit. Before she entered the convent she was known for her quiet and gentle disposition. Upon her return home she soon became frivolous and giddy. While formerly she had loved prayer, her parents soon found it hard to induce her to go even to Mass on Sundays. When at length the mother became troubled and tried to persuade her to drop some of the young men of her acquaintance, she found out that she had nothing to say. The end was that the girl eloped with one of these good-for-nothing men. They were married before a justice. The husband has no religion whatsoever, and she is now a fallen away Catholic. She became the mother of a family, and one thing she teaches her children is to hate the Church and everything the Church stands for. Now the old lady remembers the words of her daughter:

"Mother, I am afraid you will feel sorry for what you have made me do." Had the girl remained in the convent she would have saved her own soul, and would have been the means of saving many more. Now she has brought souls into this world and bends every effort to turn these souls, as well as her own, away from God. She heaps misery upon herself and upon others, whereas she might spread grace and blessings. Such is the result of ignoring, or interfering with, a religious vocation.

I knew a young man who had for some years been studying for the priesthood. All at once, he gave up his studies. When I asked him why he did so, he answered that he did not think he would be able to stand for all that priests must bear silently. "There is not a body of men," he said, "that is more reviled, mistrusted and abused than priests. I might bear some of this from outsiders, but when even Catholics would slander and revile me, I do not think I could bear it."

I tried to explain to him that we are as human as the rest of mankind, and that, if it were not for the plentiful graces conferred upon us in Holy Orders, not one of us would be willing, or able, to undergo all the trials the sacred calling requires of us.

Undoubtedly he lacked one of the most important qualifications, the confidence in God. It may have been just as well that this young man stepped out. Yet, whether he will ever be happy in the world is a great question. A religious vocation is something not to be trifled with.

It is my opinion that boys are all too hasty in deciding their vocations. Because they may not be called to be priests, they take it for granted that they must learn some trade and get married. While it is true that the majority of mankind is intended for the married state, this does not apply to all without exception. A boy may not be called to the priesthood, and yet God may want him to enter the religious life. God may still desire a great sacrifice from him. The religious life includes other vocations besides the priesthood. God may wish some boy to be a lay brother, devoting his life to one of the various callings in a monastery. Then we have orders that devote all their efforts to teaching. They supply teachers for schools, for colleges and universities. Other orders there are that devote all their time to caring for wayward and homeless boys, teaching them various trades, so they may earn an honest living. Other orders take care of orphanages. There are brothers who tend incurable patients. These brothers take only the

285

worst cases, such that ordinary hospitals refuse to handle. The variety of work which the various orders make their object, correspond with the various gifts and talents and inclinations of those zealous for a religious vocation. You see, then, that a boy need not necessarily become a priest to partake of the religious life. Physicians have been known to become brothers at some hospital, and they made themselves very useful indeed. Any trade you know would qualify you to enter a brotherhood that has for its object the bringing up of homeless and wayward boys. An inclination to teach may fit you to become a member of a brotherhood that devotes all its efforts to teaching in schools, colleges and universities. It is true, you may be a physician in the world and do much good, you may be an industrious workingman, or teacher, or professor, but by embracing a religious life and practicing your vocation you do greater good, and at the same time sanctify your life in a more perfect manner.

Two of your school mates are now preparing themselves to become priests. For a crowd of boys as great as this, two is indeed a small number. There should be more religious vocations in a number as large as yours. Possibly God may have called only these two of you to be His priests, but He may desire to see a number of you as lay brothers in some hospital or monastery. The harvest, indeed, is great, but of workers there are few. In times of yore convents were overcrowded. Now the orders go begging for applicants. They are handicapped in their work and in their growth, all for lack of vocations. There is a crying need for them in our country as well as in pagan lands. The Church could open more schools, more hospitals, more orphanages, if she had more religious.

Since we must take it for granted that God wants the work of saving souls carried on the same as in the past, we cannot help but think that vocations must be as

286

plentiful as the work at hand. Hence, when we see convents and monasteries half empty, there is grave reason to fear that many religious vocations are ignored.

Nor is it very hard to detect the chief reason for the neglect of vocations. The world is money-mad. Money means power, it means greatness, it means honor, it means pleasure. Money covers a multitude of sins. The worst scoundrel, if he has plenty of money, is a respected man. The honest man without a bank book is despised.

Money has a charm that few can resist. You, too, will come under the spell if you do not look out. Bear in mind that money is not everything in this world. The holy Will of God is above and beyond every earthly consideration. And if it is the holy Will of God that some of you should enter the religious life, and devote your time and talents to teaching or any other work of charity, be as willing and ready as was the little boy Samuel. Say with him:

"Speak, Lord, Thy servant heareth."

CHAPTER XLVII. ST. SEBASTIAN

To find a youth reaching the years of manhood and still having the heart of a child is not an easy matter. Even more difficult is it to find a soldier with childlike simplicity. Yet both were true in the case of St. Sebastian. He was the son of wealthy and noble parents. For a boy in his station of life, it was the natural thing to join the army. Worldly people saw in this course the opportunity to reap the honors and glories of war. St. Sebastian saw another opportunity in being a soldier. On account of his bravery, his noble birth, and, above all, on account of his amiable qualities, the emperor Diocletian bestowed special favor upon him. His rise in rank was rapid. Honors that come to others only after they have passed the better part of their life in the military service, were his at the very threshold of life. Eventually, the young saint was given one of the most important and coveted honors when the emperor appointed him captain of the imperial body guard.

The time of this emperor's reign was a sad and yet glorious time for holy Church. Her sons and daughters were slain by the hundreds and thousands, for no other reason than that they were Christians. No age and no sex was spared. No Christian family was influential enough to escape the hatred and the fury of the heathen mob. Not a day passed but some Christians had to shed their blood for the faith. The prisons were crowded with Christians destined to suffer torture and death. Many Christians sought a hiding place in the catacombs. Among these oppressed Christians the presence of an imperial officer as their friend must have been a strange sight. When Sebastian had performed his military duties of the day he was found with the Christians. He would go from prison to prison, encouraging the suffering Christians and having a kind word for all. He would seek those that were in hiding, assisting them with advice and with money, clothing and food. Whenever he heard of some who, overcome by adversity, gave indications of denying their faith, he hastened to see them and admonish them. As one of the results we have two saints who in all probability would have fallen away had it not been for the admonition and instruction of Sebastian. Two brothers were accused of being Christians and placed in prison. Their parents and wives, being pagans, came to the prison daily, begging them to make a public retraction and thus save their lives for their sakes. The judge, feeling confident that the combined appeals of wives and parents would win in the end, delayed the execution of sentence. In the meantime, these two brothers had to undergo many trials. How were they to resist steadfastly the tearful appeals of parents, of wives and children? They began to waver in their faith. St. Sebastian heard of the distress of these two brothers, Marcus and Marcelinus, and at once he went to their prison to speak to them. His visit was so successful that he not only made them steadfast in their faith, but he converted their father and mother, and even the soldier who guarded the prisoners. They all became martyrs and saints.

Once he healed the wife of a soldier by making the sign of the cross over her. Seeing her miraculous recovery, both she and her husband asked to be baptized. The saint converted also the military governor of Rome, Chromatius, and many others.

St. Sebastian had devised a wonderful plan for his life. He chose to be a soldier, not for the sake of glory, but to do good. Knowing the sore distress of the Christians, he

289

saw that he could be of more help to them as a soldier than in any other calling. Had he so desired he might have stayed in Milan, his native city. But since the Christians were not much molested there, he asked to be transferred to Rome. He lived in Rome from 283 to 288, when he died the death of a martyr. With many spies about him, it was no easy matter to do for the Christians what the saint was doing for five years. At last he was accused of being a Christian. The emperor acted as though he had never seen Sebastian. He forgot all at once that Sebastian was his most trusted officer. Rank, wealth and influence were unable to save Sebastian. He was condemned to die.

The emperor, in his rage, decided that the saint should die a peculiarly cruel death. A company of soldiers was detailed to make a target of the saint. They were to hit him with their arrows, but were directed not to touch a vital spot, so that his death was to be lingering and most painful. When the soldiers thought that they had done their work they left the saint. That night, a Christian woman found him. Thinking that he was dead, she carried him to her home to prepare the body and bury it in the catacombs with the bodies of other martyrs. To her great surprise the saint gave signs of life. She dressed his wounds and cared for him until he fully recovered. When the saint was again able to walk, he went to see the emperor. Diocletian, being superstitious and having a bad conscience, was seized with terrible fear when he saw the late captain of his bodyguard. He thought he saw a ghost. But the saint did not leave him long in doubt. He told the emperor that he, too, would one day meet his judge, and would have to render an account for all the blood he had on his conscience, and that this judge would be the living God whom the Christians adore.

These words were anything but pleasant to the emperor. When he got over his fright he ordered the soldiers to put the courageous saint to death on the spot.

And so the saint died, having been active in Rome for five years to help and console the oppressed Christians, who were much in need of a hero like him.

After his death the saint appeared to a pious woman, revealing to her where his body might be found, and requesting a Christian burial. His body was thus recovered and brought to the catacombs. Subsequently a church was built in Rome in honor of the saint, and his remains were transferred to that church as their final resting place.

The life of St. Sebastian teaches us two important lessons:

At the present time, people are too prone to leave all spiritual work to the priest, never thinking for a moment that they, too, should do their share of it. People of the world content themselves with the poorest kind of religious knowledge. They leave to the priest the work of making converts. That, they claim, is the business of the priest. When a Catholic is asked the easiest kind of a question regarding his religion he is likely to be at a loss for an answer. He may say he has no time to bother with such affairs. The truth will be often that he knows absolutely nothing about his religion, and he tries to cover up his ignorance by a flippant answer. If anyone of you should see another boy growing careless in his religious duties, will you have the heart to go up to that boy to remind him gently of his religious duties, to encourage him in a kindly way to do better in future? "Why," you may say, "That is none of my business. Let the priest see to this case." In this matter, St. Sebastian teaches us an impressive lesson. He was not a priest, yet he made converts. He was a soldier, not a member of a missionary society. Yet he thought it his duty to do the very thing that people now leave entirely to the priest. From a soldier one would scarcely expect such fervor and conviction as this saint showed in his short but beautiful life.

How many converts have you brought to the Church? If you intimately know a Protestant boy, do you ever try and bring him to church on some solemn occasion, such as a mission, Forty Hours Devotion, or other special services? Do you ever hand him a book to read that offers instruction in religious matters? When others talk about religious matters in a sincere way, are you willing to help them find the truth by giving them the benefit of your information? Do not answer that is the business of the priest! Of course it is his business. No one will deny that. But the priest needs your help. It is your business to help the priest in making converts. In the first place, those of another faith often have an inexplicable fear of the priest. They will avoid the priest if they can. It is your business to remove that fear or prejudice. What the priest wants is that you pave the way for him. He will gladly do the rest. Bring such people to church from time to time. Let them listen to an able sermon. Give them some suitable book, like the "Faith of Our Fathers," and above all, give them the benefit of your own good example. Very few Protestants will have the grit to go to a priest without some Catholic friend coming along with them. They may have doubts about their religion and long for an opportunity of being introduced to a priest. And if that opportunity is denied them, they will live in constant dread and doubt for years, and possibly die in that state. Yes, many of you boys could bring converts to the Church if you had a little of the zeal that St. Sebastian had.

And then there is a certain class of Catholic boys and young men that will hasten out of their way when they see their priest coming along. You know who they are. For a time they were members of the Sodality, and then they began to grow careless. You missed them at the roll call of the conferences, at monthly Communions, at holy Mass on Sundays. They drop their friends of the Sodality and pick up bad company. The priest can do very little with such boys unless you make the start. They will avoid the priest. In such cases it is your duty to speak to them in a kindly way, asking them to come to church with you. Pick out the Sodality Sunday and ask them to receive the Sacraments with you. If they will not listen to you the first time, pray for them all the more, and try again. If they do go to Confession, the grace of God and the words of the priest will do the rest. But don't you see that you must help?

Look at the example of St. Sebastian and get rid of the notion that the priest is the only missionary in his parish. Each one of you should be a little missionary. If every one of you would be a missionary as St. Sebastian was, if every one of you brought only one convert to the rectory, how both the parish and the sodality would grow! These converts then would add their share of converts, and thus form an endless chain of zeal for the salvation of souls. Make it a point to note all those who, for some reason or other, have a dread of approaching the priest. If they are Catholics, remind them gently and kindly of their duties; if they are not Catholics, do all you can to remove their doubts, their fears and prejudices.

The other lesson this saint teaches us is seen in his tender care of the poor and suffering.

Of course we have a St. Vincent de Paul Society to take care of the poor. But the strength and result of any society depends on the quality and number of its members. You are in error by thinking that this society is to be joined only by the few rich of the parish. If you have only a few pennies to spare you may be one of its members. You can help the investigating committee to find poor who are ashamed to beg, and thus help in lessening suffering both temporal and spiritual.

St. Sebastian spent his wealth in alleviating the suffering of the poor and of the prisoners. He realized his risk in visiting the poor and the prisoners, yet that did not prevent him from exercising his works of mercy.

Let us, then, ask this gentle saint that, through his intercession, we may become possessed of his zeal for the salvation of souls, and that each one of us may be a missionary and an angel of mercy.

CHAPTER XLVIII. ST. ALOYSIUS

There are few churches without a statue or picture of St. Aloysius. Many churches are named in his honor. Most Sodalities of boys are under the protection of St. Aloysius. He is without doubt a sublime model for a Catholic boy.

St. Aloysius was born March 9, 1569, at Castiglione, Italy. His father, Ferdinand de Gonzaga, was the reigning duke of the principality of Castiglione. His parents were very pious people. The first words his saintly mother taught him were the holy names of Jesus and Mary. He was able to make the sign of the Cross before he could say the words of that blessing. His conduct from childhood up was so blameless that he was called an angel in the flesh. At the age of eight years, he was brought to the court of the Medici's, where his gentle manners and his piety gained universal admiration. At the age of twelve, he had the grace of meeting another saint, St. Charles Borromeo, by whom he was prepared for his first Holy Communion. What a beautiful sight it must have been for God and the angels to see these two saints, the one teaching and the other eagerly listening to every word regarding Jesus, the Son of the living God, in the Tabernacle. Sometime after his first Holy Communion, his father introduced him to the court of Spain, where he, together with his younger brother, was made a page. At the Spanish court the young saint was noted for his great modesty. Though as a page he was almost constantly in the presence of king and queen, he never raised his eyes to look at the face of the queen. When he left the court he had never seen the queen's face. Even before the saint was introduced at the royal court he had resolved to leave the world and enter a monastery, and the glitter and pomp of the court never caused him to waver in this intention.

Needless to say, his resolution to renounce the crown in favor of his younger brother was a great shock to his father. "You have inflicted a wound," he said, "that will bleed for years to come. But," he continued, "If it is the holy Will of God that you should enter a monastery, by all means do so in the name of God."

St. Aloysius then renounced all rights and claims upon the crown of Castiglione in favor of his younger brother. Immediately after, he appeared before the General of the Society of Jesus, applying for admission.

His father had planned a brilliant worldly career for his saintly boy. He had felt that the honor of his name, the welfare of the crown and his people, would be in able hands after his death. Inside and out of the castle, Aloysius was idolized. In his manners he was unassuming, yet always graceful, cordial yet never free or bold, dignified and yet without airs. In his studies, he outclassed all. He was advanced beyond those of his own age. Yet he was never haughty or inclined to indolence, although one or both of these characteristics often go with a brilliant mind. It is no wonder, then, that his father was so reluctant to lose him. No wonder he broke out in those famous words of a heartbroken father: "You have inflicted a wound that will bleed for years to come."

The members of the Society of Jesus are known for having most brilliant minds among them. But even among that select circle of great minds the brilliancy of Aloysius called forth words of unstinted praise. He finished his university course at the age of seventeen, and passed

296

with highest honors a public examination in philosophy and theology. At the age of nineteen, he passed the examination of his order, to which, as a rule, its members are hardly ever called before they are nearly twice this age. When we recall that the saint finished his university course when only seventeen years of age, we need not be surprised that his teachers and professors foretold a great future for him.

In the year 1591, a pestilence broke out in Rome and carried off many of the people. The youthful Aloysius asked permission to take care of the sick and dying.

In times of such calamities, churches and convents were often turned into hospitals. Pious men of the world formed societies for the care of the sick and the burial of the dead. The sickness being very contagious, most of these willing workers contracted it and died as martyrs of charity.

Aloysius, having weakened his health with works of mortification and with fasting, was not strong enough to withstand the strain of the hard work, and he died as one of these martyrs of charity on June 21, 1591, when he was twenty-three years of age.

The predominant virtue of the saint was his holy purity. When people called him an angel in the flesh it was no idle flattery. According to the testimony of all those that knew the saint intimately, he is never known to have committed even a deliberate venial sin. He preserved his baptismal innocence up to his last breath.

When Aloysius was not quite seven years of age, his teachers overheard him using an expression he had learned from the soldiers of his father. He did so without understanding the meaning of the word. Upon being told that the word was highly improper, Aloysius began to cry most bitterly, asking pardon of all who heard him use the word, and ever after he called that time the time of his conversion. Theologians doubt whether he even committed a venial sin by repeating a word, the meaning of which he did not fully understand. And yet the sorrow of the saint over this one fault was lifelong and most pathetic. And do you wish to know what a life of penance this innocent boy led? At home as well as elsewhere, whenever he could escape from the general meals with others of his rank and station, he would eat so sparingly, and then only foods for which he had the least desire, that people often wondered how he could keep alive. His eyes and ears he kept in perfect control. Whatever might in the least violate his feeling of modesty he wanted not to see or hear. His mortifications when still in the world were far greater than even the mortifications expected of pious souls in convents.

And now, let me ask you, what have we to show in comparison with this saint. Do we keep our eyes and ears in such perfect control that we permit nothing to enter through them into our souls that would in the least injure our feeling of modesty? Is it not a fact that we are eager to see and hear everything under the plea that we are wise enough to know when to quit? And we only imagine that we are wise enough. The fact is that none of us could match our little learning against that of this saint. If he with all his learning was so careful, how much more careful ought we to be!

Christian art pictures St. Aloysius with a crown at his feet, to teach us that he thought little of earthly honors. At his side, we see a skull and a scourge. The skull indicates that he saw clearly the vanity of all earthly things; the scourge indicates his spirit of penance. The saint chastised his body by scourging, by sleeping upon a bare board instead of a soft bed, and by many other acts of penance and self-denial, what can we show in penance and mortification? The Church, it is true, does not require you

298

to fast until you are of age. Still, a fast day now and then would, by no means, mean a hardship to you. The saint did not wait with fasting until he was of age. We might practice many various acts of self-denial without injuring our health. But, alas, our desire for ease, comfort and pleasure gets the better of us. Whenever we are put to extra effort or some little annoyance, do we not try industriously to escape it?

At the present time modesty is difficult to preserve, because we will not hear of penance or of any kind of mortification. We exercise no control over eyes, ears or tongue. We give the enemy of souls full sway to do as he likes, and he makes good use of his opportunities. And then we go and complain that we are so much vexed with temptations. If we had our senses in perfect control, as St. Aloysius had his, if we were lovers of mortification as he was, we would have less ground to complain about temptations. Those who think that penance and mortification belong only within the walls of convents and monasteries make a great mistake. I think we can safely take it for granted that there is more reason for penance and mortification outside of convents than within them. Though God may not have chosen you to live the life of a monk, you are not dispensed from doing penance.

Again, the saint is, to us, a model of humility. He had every qualification to allow of some reasonable pride. The crown and title of duke were to be his; he had wealth at his command; he was liked and admired; his wonderful learning gained respect for his wisdom. Yet we find the saint simple and plain, as though he had been the child of a poor farmer. Neither learning nor rank, neither wealth nor honors, could turn his head. And we, while we have not much to boast of, fairly burst with pride. Others are brighter than we, others outrank us in station and honor, others may be more attractive than we, yet we are always ready to belittle others and to push ourselves to the

299

foreground, fondly imagining that we are so much better than all the rest. Ignorance and pride go usually side by side. Much reason indeed we have to feel ashamed of ourselves when we consider the humility of a St. Aloysius!

Lastly, St. Aloysius shines forth as a model of piety. The environment in which he lived was not always favorable to a pious life. At the court of princes and kings, and at universities, life offers few opportunities for true piety. Still, the saint never neglected the duty of prayer. Little is the praying that we do. We may perform some little good work, perhaps not even with the right intention, and immediately we imagine that we are almost too good for this world! To receive Holy Communion once a month seems unnecessary to many. They actually fear they may become too saintly! To spend a quarter of an hour saying the rosary is too long a time, while we do not worry over hours spent foolishly, perhaps even sinfully. St. Aloysius went to Confession and Holy Communion every Sunday. On Monday, Tuesday and Wednesday he thanked God for the grace he had received, and on Thursday, Friday and Saturday prepared himself for the next Holy Communion.

When we think of our own indifference and compare it with the zeal of this saint, we must come to the conclusion that all our aspirations are for our earthly welfare and that we care little for our soul.

Let us pray to St. Aloysius, the patron of our Sodality, that through his powerful intercession we may be animated with a holy zeal for the glory of God and for the salvation of our soul.

CHAPTER XLIX. THE BOY AND HIS GUARDIAN ANGEL

The pictures you see of the Guardian Angel show him in the act of protecting a small child. By picturing man as a little child, Christian art desires to emphasize our own helplessness and the superior power of the Guardian Angel. When we were children, we had all confidence in the power of this angel. Gradually, as we grew older and stronger, the importance of the Guardian Angel began to grow less and less, till at length we hardly felt a necessity of having an angel with us. A boy of sixteen or over often feels as though he needed no one to take care of him. Because he earns a few dollars he feels that he can well take care of himself.

Such a boy overlooks two important truths:

The first truth is that a Guardian Angel has been given to us not only for the years of childhood, but for our entire life.

The second truth is that if we need the help of a Guardian Angel when we are little, we are a great deal more in need of him as we grow older, because dangers and temptations increase as our ability to sin increases.

Let us consider these two truths separately, drawing from each its wholesome lesson.

From all eternity God had us in mind. He saw the many dangers to which we would be exposed, and He determined upon giving each one of us, throughout our

301

whole life, a companion who would never be wanting in either power or wisdom to guide and protect us. This responsibility He considered so great that He did not entrust it to anyone man or set of men, but to one of His own angels, an unmistakable proof of God's loving forethought.

No sooner does God create a soul, when He places it in charge of one of His angels. That angel remains with that soul until it returns to its Maker. Nor is the Guardian Angel simply like a shadow of a man, without any more influence than a shadow. The angel actually does what his name implies--he guards and protects. In his tender solicitude, he guards and protects us, first of all, out of love of God, and, furthermore, because in our souls he recognizes beings who are to share with him the happiness of heaven. He knows the place that is waiting for us in heaven. He knows that we, though weak and frail, are chosen heirs of the kingdom of God. Without any feeling of envy, he sees that we are called to taste in Holy Communion even now spiritual joys that are denied him. Our frailty and helplessness make him care for us all the more, because the promotion of the honor and glory of God is a source of joy and happiness to him.

And what sublime lessons we should draw from the constant presence of our Guardian Angel! Our home may be ever so humble; it is the home of our angel. Our work may be ever so lowly, he is at our side. We may not be able to boast of a single true friend on earth; our Guardian Angel will stand by us always. The world may be inclined to judge us by the clothes we wear, or by our rank; he sees in us children of God and heirs of heaven. The world may judge us wrongly and condemn us, he, knowing our hearts, will tell us: "Fear not, for I am with you. I am stronger than all the world." What consolation this thought should give us!

302

Again, the constant presence of our Guardian Angel should be a source of strength for us. Being constantly with us, he certainly cannot be pleased when we associate with bad company. You know what it means to bring two people together who are deadly enemies. They consider it an insult to be brought into one another's company. Have you ever thought that by going with bad companions you insult your Guardian Angel? With those bad companions will be found the spirit of darkness, the devil. If you realized how your Guardian Angel must feel to be near the archenemy of God, not one of you would be found with bad company in future. Would you think for a moment of taking your mother or sisters into the company of thieves and cutthroats? No, you would never think of doing that. You would fear that your mother or sisters would be exposed to insults and even harm. It behooves you to show the same consideration for your Guardian Angel.

Some supposed friend may propose to take you to a theatre to which you would not dare take your mother or sisters. If the show is too bad for them to see, it is not the proper place to which to take your Guardian Angel. An evil companion might tempt you to commit a sin you would not dare to even think of with the knowledge of your father or mother. The sin may be so vile that your wicked companion will pick out a hidden place to commit it. But no place will be so well hidden that it will prevent your Guardian Angel from being a witness of it. You have even greater reason of feeling ashamed of yourself in the presence of your Guardian Angel, because he is far more pure and holy than the best parents ever can be. Therefore, he must despise sin still more than you or your parents could ever despise it. Again, it is in your interest to act so that your Guardian Angel may at all times have a good opinion of you. Parents may be deceived into forming a better opinion of you than you deserve; but you cannot deceive the angel who reads your heart like a book.

In performing some good work you may be misjudged. What a consolation to know that your Guardian Angel judges you rightly. Some good work may be extremely difficult for you; it may mean a sacrifice of which the world has neither knowledge or appreciation. What consolation for you to know that your Guardian Angel keeps exact record of all the good you do and the sacrifices it demands. All these consoling lessons are drawn from the constant presence of the Guardian Angel.

The second truth is that since dangers and temptations increase as we grow older, the need of a Guardian Angel also increases in the same measure.

You have found that your temptations are far greater now than at the time you began going to school. At twenty, they will be more vehement than now, and, at thirty, they will be even more intense. The most dangerous and greatest temptations will be experienced in the hour of death. The devil will realize, far better than we, that our end approaches and that, unless he succeeds now, he will see us beyond his reach. Hence, he will spare no efforts to make us fall into sin the very last moment. Hence, too, the need of the Guardian Angel is greater at the end of life than at any other time during our life. If we ever need a Guardian Angel it is at that last moment, to reach out a helping hand to guide us when all the world stands back and lets us enter the other world alone.

You may ask: "How can a pure spirit be of help to a being composed of body and soul? The spirit being invisible, how can it affect the visible?" I might answer this question with another question. The devil, too, is a spirit. How is it possible for him to affect us, how can he tempt us? The fact is, he does. He works by offering suggestions and by bringing us in contact with people of his own kind and stamp. If, then, the power of the devil is such, must not the power of an angel of God be still greater? It cannot be possible that the devil is more powerful than God.

While some saints have been given the grace of seeing their Guardian Angels in visible form, we poor sinners are not generally worthy of such a signal favor. Still he has many ways of influencing us. He speaks to us principally by pious thoughts that enter our minds even unbidden. Though the devil may send us many evil suggestions, our good angel will more than outweigh them by pious suggestions. It is to be regretted that we pay so little attention to the voice of our angel. The blame rests with us, since in support of the influence of our Guardian Angel we receive from God the grace to overcome the evil suggestion.

Besides the good suggestions given by him, our Guardian Angel wards off many dangers to which we are exposed, and for which, as a rule, he gets little thanks. Every one of us can recall instances where we were within an inch of death. We read of miraculous escapes in the daily papers. It is usually called good luck. People say they had a close call. In very few instances will they have the good sense of thanking their Guardian Angel.

Ordinarily, God does not work miracles for us. They are the exception rather than the rule. God is powerful enough to guide our destiny according to the natural order of events to obtain His end. Hence, too, excepting in rare cases, the activity of a Guardian Angel is directed along natural lines. In some way, not at all approaching the miraculous, our Guardian Angel will bring us in contact with noble example; he will suggest to us the happiness of serving God, the beauty of virtue, the punishment of vice, the vanity of worldly things. Thoughts of encouragement will rise up in our hearts to strengthen our good resolutions; warnings will be sounded when we are in

305

danger of sinning. In difficulties we see a sudden light that shows us the way out, though we have struggled in vain to find a solution. All this is the work of a Guardian Angel, who is at all times true to his sacred duty. Two places to which he will especially try to lead us are the Confessional and the Tabernacle.

What else need be said to show that we should have now the same devotion to our Guardian Angel that we had as little children?

When we were little children we were told to pray to the Guardian Angel every day. Let us make it again a custom to pray to him every day, and pray as fervently as we did in the days of childhood.

When we were little children we were told to thank our Guardian Angel for all favors received. At our present age, we receive more favors from him than ever before. We have had the benefit of his protection for years and years, without troubling to thank for it. Let us begin again to thank him daily for the interest he takes in our bodily and spiritual welfare.

When we were little children we were told to obey our Guardian Angel. This duty of obeying his commands has not ceased with childhood. We are as much in need of his guidance as ever. We have as much reason to obey him now as ever. His authority over us does not grow less with our increasing years. Let us give ready attention to every pious thought and suggestion he conveys to us.

By following the rules of conduct laid down to us when we were children, his guardianship over us will be a source of joy and happiness to him and to us a source of consolation. Our Guardian Angel will stand by us no matter what the odds may be. At all times, he is stronger than all the powers of hell combined. Especially at the last moments of our life, will we be able to rely upon his power and wisdom if, through our life, we follow his holy guidance.

CHAPTER L. THE BOY AND HIS DEVOTION TO THE BLESSED VIRGIN

In the early part of the eighteenth century, there lived, in France, a young man who publicly denied his faith and did everything in his power to hurt the Church. Out of hatred for the Church he decided to go and offer his services to the army of the Sultan of Turkey, to make war upon Christians. So he set out for Turkey. On his way he was attacked by robbers. Fearing for his life, he began to pray and promised the blessed Virgin that if the robbers would spare his life, he would return to France and do penance for the rest of his life. The robbers, after searching him for money, gave him his liberty. When out of danger the young man forgot his promise and continued his journey, reached the capital of Turkey and tendered his services to the Sultan. He was soon made an officer in the army.

One night, this young man had a terrible dream. He heard the voice of Satan demanding his soul from God, claiming that it had deserved hell a thousand times. The devil stated that he himself was condemned for a single sin, whereas this wretch had offended often, renouncing even his God by joining the army of the infidels. Since no answer was given by God, the devil urged his demand, asking whether it was fair to save the soul of this man just because he made a vow he never thought of keeping, and he then reproached God most bitterly for permitting the Immaculate Mother to interfere in this, as in countless other cases.

The terrified young man awoke. The dream was so vivid, he imagined he still heard the voice of the devil ringing in his ears. That very morning, he resigned his commission and left for France. There, at Paris, he began to study for the priesthood and was finally ordained a priest. In the course of time, he became famous as Father Bernard. Above all, he was the priest of the poor and of erring souls. He lived a life of most austere penance, brought about many wonderful conversions, and was one of the most loyal promoters of the glories of Mary. His zeal for souls, his tireless work among what others would regard as hopeless cases, and his love for the poor, together with his works of charity and mortification made him the most popular and most prominent priest of his day. The scandal he had given in his younger days was atoned for by his great zeal and penance.

Father Bernard had learned that the power of the Blessed Virgin was more efficacious than all the powers of hell. To her intercession, he owed not only the saving of his life but the saving of his soul, as also the graces he received through his holy vocation for saving the souls of numerous other people. Hence, he was a most ardent promoter of the devotion to the blessed Mother. Had anyone told this man before his conversion that he would ever return to the Church and become a priest, he would have ridiculed the very thought. Yet the apparently impossible did happen. The wolf was turned into a lamb.

The life of Father Bernard is but one of countless examples that show us the great power of our blessed Mother. We might gather enough such examples to fill a big library, and even then we would not exhaust all the facts that could be recorded.

In our conferences we have reviewed the lives of a number of boy saints and learned from them lessons

309

fitted to your age and needs. It would be a grievous wrong, indeed, were we to overlook the Queen of all saints, the ever blessed Virgin Mary.

And so let us try to understand the spirit of the devotion in her honor, and consider two of the principal benefits bestowed upon her zealous children.

The devotion in honor of our blessed Mother is in a class all by itself. It is of a more intimate nature than our devotion to other saints, because she is our Mother, whereas they are only our friends. Hence, the honor, reverence and homage we pay her is second only to that we pray to God. We adore God as our Lord and Maker. We do not adore the blessed Virgin and Mother Mary, but we honor and love her as our Mother. This is the reason why her praises are and should be sounded more than those of all other saints combined. Of her it is prophesied that "all generations shall call her blessed."

Various times and needs call for special devotions. But the most general devotion, the devotion not limited by time or circumstances, is the devotion to our blessed Mother. That devotion was known and practiced in the catacombs of Rome. We can still see her pictures adorning the walls of those historical places. The early Christians looked up to her picture to gather strength for the great struggle they had to undergo for the sake of her Divine Son.

And in what does this devotion consist? First of all it consists in a childlike love for the blessed Virgin. Though a child recognizes the father as the head of the family, it will be much attached to the mother. For, while the child expects all benefits from the father, as the provider of the family, it will expect them more confidently if able to reveal its wants to the mother, depending almost as much upon the mother's intercession as upon the generosity of the father.

This explains why we, as Catholics, have such an unbounded confidence in the ever blessed Virgin. She is our loving Mother. Her motherly love removes our fear or doubt, and we ask favors of her that we feel almost unworthy to ask of the heavenly Father.

The love a child has for its mother does by no means lessen its love for the father. If anything, it tends to increase it. In a like manner, the love we have for our blessed Mother does by no means interfere with or lessen our love for our heavenly Father. The sublime love of God manifested by the blessed Virgin remind her children that they cannot truly love her without loving God even more.

Our love for our blessed Mother will find expression in saying the prayer she likes most--the Rosary. We show our love by wearing her scapular, and by reciting the prayers she wants us to say. She likes us to carry a medal of her, to honor her pictures, to observe her feast days. A devout child of Mary will not let a single day pass without saying some prayer and doing some good work in her honor. What she likes, above all, is for us to offer some good work or an indulgence to be applied to some poor soul in purgatory who, during life, was a devout child of hers. A good child will be so zealous in doing the will of his mother that her slightest wish has the power of a command. In like manner, we need not be told what our blessed Mother wants us to do. We should know by intuition to do what she likes to see us do, and to avoid what she wants us to avoid.

Hence, we should not be content with only saying prayers in her honor. That is only part of the devotion we owe her. The better part of our devotion will consist in imitating her holy life.

311

With not a stain of sin upon her, without original sin and its inclination towards evil to cloud her spotless purity, and with so many graces as to be called "full of grace," the life of the blessed Virgin and Mother is indeed a worthy model for all mankind to follow. The various saints of holy Church each excelled in some of the many virtues. Our blessed Mother is a perfect model of all virtues. Hence, she is worthy to be called "the mirror of justice." In as far as human nature can be perfect she has attained perfection, not in one virtue only but in all of them. As Virgin she is most wise, most holy and most chaste. As Mother she

is the most perfect of mothers. Our blessed Mother is therefore the most perfect model for all mankind. Rich as well as poor, the high and the low, young and old, boys and girls, married and single people--all find in her a most worthy model, according to which they should form and shape their lives. The imitation of her life is, furthermore, not left to us as a matter of choice. We are bound to imitate her for the reason that, being her children, we should resemble her. Children will imitate various traits of father and mother without being aware of it. They will resemble mother or father not in looks only, but they speak, walk and act like them. As a mother takes so much greater pride and satisfaction in her children the more they resemble her in good qualities, so our blessed Mother will take pride and comfort in us when she can see that we earnestly try to resemble her more and more. The more we try to be like her, the more she will be promoted to love us.

For this reason, the benefits those receive who try to make a special effort of pleasing her are manifold. To enumerate them all would be a pleasant but a lengthy task. Let us point out two of the principal benefits. One of them is purity of heart. Since purity of heart was the most beautiful of all her many virtues, our blessed Mother is desirous that her favorite children should imitate her above all in this particular virtue. You, my boys, can never expect to remain pure at heart unless you entertain a childlike love for our blessed Mother, Indeed, our love for the virtue of purity grows in us in proportion as our love for our blessed Mother grows. It is simply impossible to be a devout child of our blessed Mother and at the same time to lead an impure life. Purity of heart and the devotion to our blessed Mother go hand in hand.

Another favor especially granted through the devotion to our blessed Mother is the grace of final perseverance.

It is the experience of the saints and their universal opinion that, as no soul is saved excepting through her glorious intercession, neither will a soul that has loved and served our blessed Mother be found among the numbers of the damned. If you want to know whether you are to be among the elect or the damned, just look at the quality of your devotion to our blessed Mother. If we love her and serve her sincerely and try to imitate her, we need have no fear of the final outcome. Our blessed Mother will take care of us. If, however, we are too indifferent to say even a little prayer in her honor, if we never think of her, then, indeed, we have reason to fear for our final salvation.

Your patron saint, your Guardian Angel, and other saints to whom you feel yourself drawn for some reason, they all expect some act of devotion from you every day. But the devotion to our blessed Mother should excel all these. Let us never consider the work of the day done unless we pay our blessed Mother, as best we can, the honor, reverence and love due to her. When all other tasks might seem burdensome, that one should prove pleasant

313

and sweet. If we serve her faithfully we may depend upon it that she will intercede for us now and in the hour of our death. Amen.

ABOUT THE AUTHOR

FR. REYNOLD KUEHNEL

Reynold, or Reinhold Kuehnel, was born July 1872 in Ludwigsdorf, Germany. He arrived in the US in 1882 with his parents, Ferdinand and Philomena (Weidlich) Kuehnel, and lived in St. Anthony's parish in Detroit. He was educated in Cincinnati and Baltimore and ordained for the Detroit Diocese 1896. Father Kuehnel served in Detroit, New Salem, and Pewamo Michigan; and in 1917 was assistant pastor at Sacred Heart Cathedral in Dallas TX. He suffered from nephritis, and had to take time off from his duties to treat his illness. He was a fairly famous priest as priests go since he published four books of advice for Catholics as well as articles in various periodicals for clerics. These are still owned by libraries across the globe! At some point, he moved to Los Angeles where he died on October 25, 1928 at Queen of Angels Hospital and was buried from Sacred Heart Church, in Calvary Cemetery.